HÖLDERLIN AND THE DYNAMICS OF TRANSLATION

THE EUROPEAN HUMANITIES RESEARCH CENTRE

UNIVERSITY OF OXFORD

The European Humanities Research Centre of the University of Oxford organizes a range of academic activities, including conferences and workshops, and publishes scholarly works under its own imprint, LEGENDA, as well as *Oxford German Studies*. Within Oxford, the EHRC bridges, at the research level, the main humanities faculties: Modern Languages, English, Modern History, Literae Humaniores, Music and Theology. The Centre stimulates interdisciplinary research collaboration throughout these subject areas and provides an Oxford base for advanced researchers in the humanities.

The Centre's publications programme focuses on making available the results of advanced research in medieval and modern languages and related interdisciplinary areas. An Editorial Board, whose members are drawn from across the British university system, covers the principal European languages. Titles include works on French, German, Italian, Portuguese, Russian and Spanish literature. In addition, the EHRC publishes *Research Monographs in French Studies* in association with the Society for French Studies, and *Studies in Comparative Literature* in association with the British Comparative Literature Association. The Centre has also launched a Special Lecture Series under the LEGENDA imprint.

Enquiries about the Centre's publishing programme should be addressed to:
Professor Malcolm Bowie, Honorary Director (Publications)

Further information:
Kareni Bannister, Senior Publications Officer
European Humanities Research Centre
47 Wellington Square
Oxford OX1 2JF
E-mail: ehrc@modern-languages.ox.ac.uk
www.ehrc.ox.ac.uk

LEGENDA

EUROPEAN HUMANITIES RESEARCH CENTRE
STUDIES IN COMPARATIVE LITERATURE 2

Hölderlin and the Dynamics of Translation

❖

CHARLIE LOUTH

LEGENDA

European Humanities Research Centre
British Comparative Literature Association
1998

Published by the European Humanities Research Centre
of the University of Oxford
47 Wellington Square
Oxford OX1 2JF

In association with the British Comparative Literature Association

LEGENDA is the publications imprint of the
European Humanities Research Centre

ISBN 1 900755 11 4

First published 1998

British Library Cataloguing in Publication Data
A CIP catalogue record for this book is available from the British Library

LEGENDA series designed by Cox Design Partnership, Witney, Oxon
Printed in Great Britain by
Information Press
Eynsham
Oxford OX18 1JJ

CONTENTS

ACKNOWLEDGEMENTS

I should like to thank Roger Paulin for his supervision of the original dissertation; and, especially, David Constantine for his generous help and encouragement at every point; also Nicholas Boyle and Elinor Shaffer for their useful comments and suggestions. Bridget Thomson and Philip Ward read chapters too, and helped me improve them. I am also grateful to David Lowe, of the University Library, Cambridge, and the staff of the Hölderlin-Archiv, Stuttgart, particularly Frau Luitgard Nuss and Frau Marianne Schütz, all of whom have been very kind.

Money from the Jebb Fund and from Gonville and Caius College, Cambridge, allowed me to learn Greek in Berlin. The British Academy and the German Academic Exchange Service (DAAD) generously gave me funding after that. *German Life and Letters* and the Arts Fund of the University of Bristol were kind enough to contribute towards the costs of publication.

PREFACE

References to Hölderlin are usually to the *Große Stuttgarter Ausgabe*, the only complete critical edition. They are given by volume and page number, divided by a slash, thus: v/275. The seventh volume is in four parts and this is indicated, for example, vii,1/58. If prefixed by *FA*, references are to the *Frankfurter Hölderlin-Ausgabe*, thus: *FA*, xvi/431. Where a poem's title is given, it is referred to by line-numbers only, unless there is a reason for preferring one edition over the other. I only do this when the text is undisputed, but it should be noted that the volumes of the Frankfurt edition which are to contain the hymns and late fragments have not yet appeared.

Likewise, the translations are referred to simply by titles and line-numbers. There are a few disagreements as to lineation between the editions, but where they affect a reference this is always noted. The Sophocles plays are referred to as *Antigonä* and *Oedipus*, but Pindar's Olympian and Pythian odes are shortened to O and P. P3 165 signifies Pythian 3, line 165. Line-numbers always refer to Hölderlin's translations, and not to the originals.

Quotations from the Greek are taken from the texts reproduced alongside Hölderlin's translations in the *Frankfurter Ausgabe*. They are the ones Hölderlin used, at least in part, and often differ greatly from modern recensions, especially as regards punctuation.

Whenever possible, references to Hölderlin are included in the body of the text.

The following abbreviations are used in the notes and Bibliography:

FA *Frankfurter Hölderlin-Ausgabe*
StA *Große Stuttgarter Ausgabe*
HJb *Hölderlin-Jahrbuch*
LpH *Le pauvre Holterling: Blätter zur Frankfurter Ausgabe*
MLR *Modern Language Review*

Where a book is part of a series, this is recorded in the Bibliography but not in the notes. Publishers are likewise listed only in the Bibliography.

I have provided translations of quotations. I imagine them not so much as alternatives, but as aids for people whose German is out of use; in spite of this, I have tried to translate the verse into verse, partly because the typography of verse makes comparison of original and translation easier, but mainly because prose seemed unsatisfactory. Of the verse passages, only Voss's hexameter versions of Homer have been given as prose. The translations of Hölderlin's translations particularly are meant only as a guide and must not be allowed to replace the original. There seemed no point in doing them unless very closely, but the oddness in English is not properly equivalent to the oddness of the German. In some cases, where meaning is quite irrelevant, no translations are given; and words or passages quoted more than once are not normally retranslated. Material in footnotes is also left in the original, as are most titles, including titles of Hölderlin's poems. Readers with little or no German can find these in Michael Hamburger's bilingual edition of Hölderlin, which contains nearly all the poems and fragments (see Bibliography).

INTRODUCTION

This is a study of the interactions between Hölderlin's translations and his other writings, particularly the poetry, his thinking about it and his manner of composing it. The translations I concentrate on, and from which the term *translation* draws its specific content, are those of Pindar and Sophocles. This is not new: some of the earliest and most enduring Hölderlin criticism, by Hellingrath and Beissner, treats of them, and they have received much attention since, especially the Sophocles. There is thus no need of assertions on their behalf, indeed they belong to the very small number of translations, like the King James Bible, Voss's Homer or Pound's *Cathay*, which stand in their own right (the Sophocles translations have themselves been translated). I examine their form closely—it is always the ground from which more general reflections take off and to which they return—but what interests me above all are the links running from the translations to other aspects of Hölderlin's work, their appositeness to the larger poetic project. By *dynamics* I mean to suggest these two separate but related things: the particular tensions and movements at work in the texts of the translations, the nature of the exchange between Greek and German as far as it can be discerned; and the way these features of the translations mesh with Hölderlin's concerns as a poet, the part the translations play in the whole economy of his work.

The German words for translation (*übersetzen, übertragen*) appear to bear their literal sense closer to the surface than the English word: they all mean transference, a carrying over, like *trans-latio* and μετα-φορά, which themselves signify in their figurative meaning not translation, but metaphor. Metaphor and translation thus share in their etymology a sense of transition, and Hölderlin often uses the words 'Metapher' [metaphor] and 'Übergang' [transition] indiscriminately (e.g. iv/245); a similar literalness seems to have applied to his understanding of translation. Translation is akin to metaphor in that it is about presenting things in a more tangible form, rendering the foreign into a language in which it becomes more knowable. Both bring together what is disparate. What the poet Empedokles, in Hölderlin's play, has to say about his mediation between 'die Sterblichen und die Götter' [mortals and gods] is equally germane to translation:

> Denn ich
> Geselle das Fremde,
> Das Unbekannte nennet mein Wort,
> Und die Liebe der Lebenden trag'
> Ich auf und nieder; was Einem gebricht,
> Ich bring es vom andern, und binde
> Beseelend, und wandle
> Verjüngend die zögernde Welt
>
> (iv/95)

> [For I
> Conjoin what is foreign,
> My words name the unknown,
> And I bear the love of the living
> Up and down; what one lacks
> I bring from another, and bind
> And inspire, and alter,
> Renew, the hesitant world.]

A translation brings what is held in the foreign tongue ('das Fremde') into our ken, gives it life in the vernacular; what was, to the receiving language, unknown, acquires a name: 'Das Unbekannte nennet mein Wort'. The two spheres are joined and can complement each other ('ich [...] binde/Beseelend'), and the original, being changed, is renewed ('wandle/Verjüngend'). The 'zögernde Welt' of the source text ('zögernd' because only half-perceived across the frontier of language) is brought out and becomes distinct as, passing into a new idiom, it assumes a new form. Of course, the passage has nothing explicitly to do with translation, but the movements and relations it describes do belong to it, as will, I hope, become clear.

To speak of a correspondence between Empedokles' words and the nature of translation is to draw an analogy. Analogy runs through this book, and with it a certain anxiety as to its validity or aptness. In science, analogy is a tool, it is heuristic: it points you in a direction, towards a possibility, which may then be confirmed by other means. Romantic scientists discovered ultra-violet light by analogy with infra-red; analogy was used to find the unknown by guessing that a perceived similarity in structure would hold consistently. I am not doing that. In literary criticism analogies can be generated boundlessly, and as there is no certain means of testing them they can neither be proven nor disproven. Mallarmé wrote of 'le démon de l'analogie'.[1] The likenesses I identify in Hölderlin, between the concerns of his poetological writings and the structure of the Pindar translation, for example, or between the technique of translation and his manner of composition, are, to me at least, obvious. The question is not so much their rightness, as whether the drawing of these links and analogies helps in understanding the inner logic of Hölderlin's work, which, as I see it, exists. I am less interested in interpreting Hölderlin, in analysing him, than in exploring the various interrelationships in the writings and following through some of the patterns, though this inevitably involves interpretation as well. Perhaps this course allows some acquaintance with what Martin Walser calls Hölderlin's 'prozessuales Denken' [processual thinking][2] and with the movements and tensions of his poems.

Analogical thinking was dear to Hölderlin himself, and to the Romantic writers generally; it was their characteristic mode of thought.[3] In dealing in analogies I thus run the risk of looking at Hölderlin through his own spectacles, and in the end it is impossible to distinguish between the perception of (existing?) analogies within the work and the constructing of them from without. It is probably wrong-headed to wish to do so; as Abrams says, 'in the criticism of poetry, metaphor and analogy, though less conspicuous, are hardly less functional than in poetry itself' (p. 31), and perhaps it is as well to admit it from the start. It is the discovery of the analogy that creates it, and the only further question, whether Hölderlin himself was aware of the correspondences between the parts of his work, is not answerable, though it is interesting. 'Alle Analogien sind auch Approximazionen' [all analogies are also approximations], Friedrich Schlegel said, encapsulating the shortcomings and the capacities of analogy.[4]

Though Benjamin implies that it is not, a translation is itself an

---

[1] Stéphane Mallarmé, *Oeuvres*, ed. Yves-Alain Favre (Paris, 1985), 123.

[2] Martin Walser, *Hölderlin zu entsprechen* (Biberach an der Riss, 1970), 20.

[3] Cf. M. H. Abrams, *The Mirror and the Lamp: Romantic Theory and the Critical Tradition* (Oxford, 1953; repr. 1979), esp. ch. 3: 'Romantic Analogues of Art and Mind' (47–69).

[4] Friedrich Schlegel, *Kritische Ausgabe*, ed. Hans Eichner and others, 35 vols. (Paderborn, 1958–), xviii, 311. In future notes this edition will be referred to as *KA*.

analogy of its original, and the problems of analogy and of translation are thus intrinsically related.[5] Benjamin's thought that the connexion between original and translation can somehow go beyond analogy, that the relationship is in fact in a special class of its own, nevertheless finds occasional corroboration in what follows. The particularity of translation is something that became apparent, as perhaps never before, towards the end of the eighteenth century in Germany, especially among the Romantics, who invested translation with enormous importance. As is well known, German literature at this time drew heavily on the resources of translation, and it was much discussed. The Greeks, being at the source, hardly translated. The Germans, in a period of careful appropriation and self-definition, did so in quantity and quality. Novalis, in a letter quoted below, compares them to the Romans in this respect. Hölderlin's translations, and his whole work, belong in that context, which is one of an 'age of translation'. My first chapter gives an account of it. It is a partial account, intended to point out a way towards Hölderlin rather than map out the whole period. It thus concentrates on the areas of classical and biblical translation, and, particularly, on how they came to overlap. And although some examples of practice are given it focuses more on ideas about translation, both for their intrinsic interest, and because, in what is only a cross-section, theoretical remarks may give a clearer, conciser picture of the development I want to bring to bear on Hölderlin's work as translator and poet. Nearly all the theorists were themselves translators of one sort or another. Against this backdrop, in the chapters that come after, I try to trace the dynamics of translation in Hölderlin.

---

[5] Walter Benjamin, 'Die Aufgabe des Übersetzers', in: *Gesammelte Schriften*, ed. Rolf Tiedemann and Hermann Schweppenhäuser, 7 vols. (Frankfurt a. M., 1972–89), iv, 9–21 (p. 12).

CHAPTER 1

A Context: Translation in Eighteenth-Century Germany

L'art de traduire est poussé plus loin en allemand que dans aucun dialecte européen.
(Mme de Staël)

Die Deutschen sind ja Allerweltsübersetzer.
(A. W. Schlegel)

The translator between languages is pulled at from both sides, and all translations in some sense partake of this tension. On the one hand there are the words of the text to be translated, and on the other the patterns of the translator's mother-tongue. And whatever the type of translation, it must always represent some form of a resolution, an uncomfortable one perhaps, of these demands. This may take the form of a conscious decision to favour either the original words or one's own language, but the two modes will coexist in one translation; and then there are endless permutations of what can only be usefully spoken of at all as *directions*, or tendencies. The translator who wanted to fasten attention on the original to the exclusion of all else would be reduced to copying out the foreign words; and to abandon contact with it altogether would no longer be to translate. To August Wilhelm Schlegel, Wilhelm von Humboldt put it like this: 'jeder Uebersetzer muss immer an einer der beiden Klippen scheitern, sich entweder auf Kosten des Geschmacks und der Sprache seiner Nation zu genau an sein Original, oder auf Kosten seines Originals zu sehr an die Eigenthümlichkeit seiner Nation zu halten' [every translator will always come to grief on one of these two rocks: either, to the detriment of his national taste and language, sticking too closely to the original, or, to the detriment of the original, keeping too close to the peculiarity of his nation].[1]

Goethe, in his 'Noten und Abhandlungen zu besserem Verständnis des westöstlichen Divans', talks of different epochs of translation. The epochs are stages in our gradual understanding of and opening to the foreign. The first stage 'macht uns in unserm eigenen Sinne mit dem Auslande bekannt' [makes us familiar with the foreign country according to our own lights].[2] Luther's Bible is the paradigm of this type. The third and last stage is 'der höchste und letzte [...] wo man die Übersetzung dem Original identisch machen möchte, so daß eins nicht anstatt des andern, sondern an der Stelle des andern gelten solle' [the highest and last, where one would like to make the translation identical to the original, so that one is not instead of the other, but in place of the other]; and Voss's translations are the prime example.[3] Thus Goethe traces a development away from the kind of translation which only receives of the foreign text what it can hold without doing violence to the receiving language, and towards a kind which allows the source language to affect the nature of the language it is conveyed into. The proper medium of the former is prose, irrespective of the form of the original; the proper medium of the latter is the same form as the original, or a close approximation to it. These two modes, which really override the three-part presentation of the 'Noten und Abhandlungen', were described by Goethe six years before, in an essay devoted to Wieland:

Es gibt zwei Übersetzungsmaximen: die eine verlangt, daß der Autor einer fremden Nation zu uns herüber gebracht werde, dergestalt, daß wir ihn als den Unsrigen ansehen können; die andere hingegen macht an uns die Forderung, daß wir uns zu dem Fremden hinüber begeben und uns in seine Zustände, seine Sprachweise, seine Eigenheiten finden sollen.[4]

[There are two maxims of translation: the first requires the author of a foreign nation to be brought across to us in such a way that we can consider him one of us; the second on the other hand requires of us that we betake ourselves

---

[1] Letter of 23 July 1796, in Anton Klette, *Verzeichniss der von A. W. v. Schlegel nachgelassenen Briefsammlung* (Bonn, 1868), pp. v–vi (vi).

[2] J. W. Goethe, 'Übersetzungen', in: *Werke*, ed. Erich Trunz, 14 vols. (Munich, 1988), ii 255–8 (255).   [3] Goethe, ii 256.

[4] From 'Zu brüderlichem Andenken Wielands' as excerpted in: Hans Joachim Störig (ed.), *Das Problem des Übersetzens* (Darmstadt, 1969), 35. Further references to this anthology are incorporated in the text.

across to the foreign author and reconcile ourselves to his conditions, his idiom and his peculiarities.]

Translation is here viewed as a journey, either one made by the original author or one made by us as readers. If, with Goethe in his distinction of epochs rather than types, we accept a tendency of ever closer encounter with the texture of foreign works culminating in Hölderlin's word-for-word translation of Pindar in 1800, then the first 'Maxime' corresponds to most translation in Germany until the fading of the Enlightenment. It requires the foreign text to don the garb of the country it is visiting, or that 'man solle einen Autor so übersezen, wie er selbst würde deutsch geschrieben haben' [one should translate an author into the language he would have used had he been German].[5]

Throughout the period, defining their own understanding of translation, all the writers I shall mention from Breitinger onwards refer to this method very denigratingly as the French method. A specifically German mode was in large part arrived at via opposition to what they saw as the domination and assimilation foisted on foreign texts by translators in France. The debate on translation is thus bound up with the larger one on a national literature and the question of models.

This ('French') type of translation persisted in Germany, and persists today, but Voss's version of the *Iliad* and revised version of the *Odyssey* published in 1793 are the central landmark of a new age of translation that was more willing to cross over into foreign territory and adapt to what it found there. In 1813, Schleiermacher went so far as to propose a specific language of translation, 'ein eignes Sprachgebiet' (Störig, p. 70).

What follows is an account of this modulation, from Luther's 'Sendbrief vom Dolmetschen' (1530) to Schleiermacher's 'Ueber die verschiedenen Methoden des Uebersezens' (1813), and from Luther's *Das Newe Testament Deutszsch* (1522) to Hölderlin's *Die Trauerspiele des Sophokles* (1804). The shift is accompanied by a progressive widening in the awareness of the meaning and potential of translation that becomes an explosion with the German Romantics. Two traits then, both vital for a grasping of Hölderlin's position at the end of the

---

[5] Friedrich Schleiermacher, 'Ueber die verschiedenen Methoden des Uebersezens', in: Störig, 38–70 (48). Schleiermacher shows the vanity of this intention.

eighteenth century: first, a shift of emphasis towards the ultimate logic of a word-for-word rendition; and second, an expansion of the terms in which translation can be understood. This latter aspect involves both the metaphorical force of translation freed from the specificity of a literary act and the part translation has to play in a German national literature and even in the German nation itself.

Luther

All translation in German stands under the example of Luther. The importance of his Bible translation is huge because it is a turning-point in the development of the German language itself. Readers of German can still understand Luther's language today, whereas the German written immediately before, or even contemporaneously with Luther but not influenced by him, is much more alien. As Franz Rosenzweig points out, the language's development once it had been given such authoritative shaping slowed down dramatically.[6] One could compare this process to Dante's influence on Italian, or Mohammed's on Arabic; the *Divine Comedy* and the Koran were similarly epoch-forming works. What is decisive in this case is that the book which established written German is a translation. There is thus at the beginning of modern German an intimate link between the evolution of the language (and of the identity of the nation—Luther's Bible was widely disseminated and could be readily understood in the several dialectal regions) and translation.[7]

Luther's two achievements were to write in direct, intelligible German and to have recourse to the original texts, not just to the Vulgate. His 'Sendbrief vom Dolmetschen' recounts his negotiation between these two points. His main desire is to communicate, and one of his problems is simply how to create a written vernacular.[8] Radically, Luther attempted to translate the Bible into the language people actually spoke:

ich habe deutsch / nicht lateinisch noch kriegisch reden wöllen / da ich teutsch zu reden ym dolmetzschen furgenommen hatte / man mus nicht die buchstaben inn der lateinischen sprachen fragen / wie man sol Deutsch

---

[6] Franz Rosenzweig, 'Die Schrift und Luther', in: Störig, 194–222 (199).

[7] Cf. Antoine Berman, *L'Epreuve de l'étranger: Culture et traduction dans l'Allemagne romantique* (Paris, 1984), 49.

[8] Martin Luther, 'Sendbrief vom Dolmetschen', in: Arnold E. Berger (ed.), *Drei Schriften* (Hanover, 1948), 81–96 (86).

reden / wie diese esel thun / sondern / man mus die mutter jhm hause / die kinder auff der gassen / den gemeinen man auff dem marckt drumb fragen / vnd den selbigen auff das maul sehen / wie sie reden / vnd darnach dolmetzschen / so verstehen sie es den / vnd mercken / das man Deutsch mit jn redet. (pp. 86–7)

[when I decided to translate into German I wanted to speak German, not Latin or Greek. One mustn't ask the letters of the Latin languages how to speak German, as those idiots do, but the mother in her home, the children on the streets, the common man in the market-place, and listen to what these people really say and translate in that way: then they'll understand and notice you're speaking plain German with them.]

The great success of his Bible proves how well Luther did this, what a good ear he had. But although this can be seen as the dominant tendency of his practice as a translator, the opposite pole, that of attention to the letter of the original and the adaptation of the translator's tongue to it, also exerts a strong pull, as it will particularly in the translation of a religious book, where the exact wording commands the utmost respect:

Doch hab ich widerumb nicht allzu frey die buchstaben lassen faren / Sondern mit grossen sorgen sampt meinen gehülffen drauff gesehen / das wo etwa an einem ort gelegenn ist / hab ichs nach den buchstaben behalten / vnd bin nicht so frey dauon gangen / als Johannes .6. da Christus spricht / Disen hat Got der vatter versiegelt / da were wol besser deutsch gewest / Disen hat Gott der vater gezeichent / odder disen meinet Gott der vater. Aber ich habe ehe wöllen der deutschen sprache abbrechen / denn von dem wort weichen. (pp. 89–90)

[But then again I haven't been all that free with the letter of the original. Together with my assistants I have taken great care to make sure that in important passages I have kept to the letters themselves and have used very little freedom; as for example in John 6[:27] where Christ says: 'Him hath God the Father sealed', where it would probably have been better German to say 'Him hath God the Father set his mark on' or 'He is the one God the Father has singled out'. But I preferred to infringe the German language rather than diverge from the Word.]

This meant that the German language was extended as well as consolidated by Luther's translation: there is a double movement at work, as there must be in all translations, and in the 'Sendbrief' Luther does not attempt to effect a resolution; that resolution is the Bible translation itself.

Opitz and Schottel

Luther's is an overpowering example of great practice. There are no other translations into German of remotely comparable importance until the great age of translation at the end of the eighteenth century, starting with Voss's first *Odyssey* in 1781. But translation continued to be discussed. And certainly by the time of the Enlightenment it was also practised in profusion; an index of the acceleration in the eighteenth century is the large number of new versions of the Bible, either reworkings of Luther or fresh attempts according to new principles, though no Bible translator after Luther could claim complete independence from him. Luther's piety before the actual words of the original was not representative of translation generally— it was largely determined by the fact that he was rendering a religious text. The general tone was more or less set by the pronouncements of the classical writers, who favoured transfer of sense rather than literalness (Cicero, Horace) and recommended translation as an exercise to enrich a writer's range and flexibility (Pliny, Quintilian). Opitz's comment in his *Buch von der Deutschen Poeterey* (1624), which incorporates a translation of the relevant bit of Pliny, can stand for a sentiment that recurs especially in the works on poetics of the early *Aufklärung*:

Eine guete art der vbung aber ist / das wir vns zueweilen auß den Griechischen vnd Lateinischen Poeten etwas zue vbersetzen vornemen: dadurch denn die eigenschafft vnd glantz der wörter / die menge der figuren / vnd das vermögen auch dergleichen zue erfinden zue wege gebracht wird.[9]

[A good exercise is to translate something from the Greek and Latin poets from time to time; this will increase the qualities and the splendour of your words and the number of figures at your disposal, as well as the ability to invent your own.]

There are many comments like these: not on the problems of translation, not trying to get to grips with its nature, but simply advising it as a means to the end of improving one's style. They are taken over wholesale from the classical rhetoricians, and not yet applied to the particular situation in Germany. Opitz translated extensively himself, including Sophocles' *Antigone*, which version was

---

[9] Martin Opitz, *Buch von der Deutschen Poeterey*, ed. Richard Alewyn (Tübingen, 1966), 54.

more literal than any other translation anywhere at the time.[10] But this in itself shows how much the idea of what a translation should be altered during the latter half of the eighteenth century: Opitz's *Antigone* set beside the translations of Voss or Hölderlin's *Antigonä* appears more distant from them than they are from their originals; it is entirely the product of Opitz's rationalizing, classicizing outlook.[11] Justus Georg Schottel, writing in 1663, probably represents the common opinion on literary translation (as against biblical) in his contempt and lack of understanding for the translator who

gibt von Wort zu Wort die frömden Wörter mit Teutschen Wörteren / und setzet die also aneinander / und das sol dan einen Teutschen Verstand haben / und in Teutscher Sprache was wollautendes seyn / da doch armseliger weise die Teutschen Wörter also verfrömdet / und die frömde sonst gute Meinung verteutschet / das ist durch gemachtes Teutsch verdorben und verformet ist.[12]

[word for word, renders the foreign words with German words and keeps the same word-order. And that is then supposed to have a German sense, to sound good in German, when the German words are so pitifully estranged and the perfectly good foreign meaning Germanized, that is, spoilt and deformed by contrived German.]

The only reason Schottel can think of for a translator's adopting such a practice is deficient knowledge and skill 'im Teutschen' [in German]. There is as yet no conception of the benefits that might be had from forcing the language down paths it has ignored. Attentiveness to the letter of the original is restricted to attentiveness to the Word; otherwise what appears to us now as unaccountable variance from the text is simply not perceived. Whole aspects of biblical translation do not impinge on the literary domain.

The German Enlightenment

One of the earliest discussions of translation in the German Enlightenment is also the only one in the form of a free-standing essay on the subject. Georg Venzky's 'Das Bild eines geschickten

---

[10] According to Richard Alewyn, *Vorbarocker Klassizismus und griechische Tragödie: Analyse der 'Antigone'-Übersetzung des Martin Opitz* (Darmstadt, 1962), 20. Opitz was aiming at this fidelity.   [11] Cf. Alewyn, 21.
[12] Justus Georg Schottel, 'Wie man recht verteutschen soll', in: Ausführliche Arbeit von der Teutschen HaubtSprache (Braunschweig, 1663), 1216–68 (1221).

Uebersetzers' appeared in 1734 in a journal directed by Gottsched.[13] In part, Venzky is just giving Gottsched's own precepts a systematic form, and Venzky's pedagogical manner stems entirely from him. Venzky's article is interesting chiefly because it gives a clear idea of what a translation was to the Enlightenment and also of how slipshod most of the translations published were: translations should, according to Venzky, be printed with the original *en face*, which seems to have been intended not as a control to exert a certain discipline but as an excuse for different kinds of divergences from the text. The five types of translation Venzky distinguishes are: something approaching a word-for-word version, 'doch so, daß beyder Sprachen besondere Art zu reden beobachtet wird' [but such that the idiom of each language is observed]—'die natürlichsten' [the most natural kind]; 'die freyen' [free translations], which mainly means the translation of verse into prose or of prose into verse; 'vermehrte' [expanded] and 'verstümmelte' [mutilated] translations, which have additions or omissions; and finally 'die vollständigsten Uebersetzungen' [the most complete translations of all], which are annotated (p. 65). 'Einer jeden Gattung gebühret ihr Lob, und ist nach ihrer Art nützlich und angenehm' [Every genre is worthy of praise and is useful and pleasant in its own way] (p. 65). Despite this apparent *bonhomie*, Venzky really prefers translations which explain; interlinear versions are for him 'die geringsten und schlechtesten' [the least and worst] (p. 69) and, following Gottsched, transmission of the sense is so important that form must be neglected (which for the most part means a translation will be in prose).

In one respect Venzky exceeds these Enlightenment notions. At the end of his list of the qualities needed in translators (which even includes the stipulation that they should be competent in both languages involved—Lessing's unsparing critiques in the *Literaturbriefe* show how often they were not) he puts '*die Gnadengaben des heil. Geistes*, die brennende *Liebe Christi*, und ein *göttliches Licht*' [*the grace bestowed by the Holy Spirit*, the burning *love of Christ*, and a *divine light*] (p. 96). This may just be a piece of religious piety, but it joins for the first time the strands of literary and biblical translation. Jerome, the translator of the Vulgate, is said to have transcended the conflict

---

[13] *Beyträge zur Critischen Historie der Deutschen Sprache, Poesie und Beredsamkeit, herausgegeben von einigen Mitgliedern der Deutschen Gesellschaft in Leipzig* (Leipzig, 1732–42), pt. 9 (1734), 59–114. Further references as page-numbers in text.

between his general preference for *sensum de sensu* translation and his consciousness that the exact word-order was part of the mystery of God by relying on divine inspiration.[14]

In general, ideas about the nature of translation among the thinkers of the German Enlightenment were severely bound by their understanding of language itself. Apart from the essay by Venzky, all extended pronouncements on translation were parts of much larger studies of poetics or rhetoric founded on a theory of language propounded by Leibniz and his popularizer Wolff and first applied to a systematic categorization of literature by Gottsched in his *Versuch einer Critischen Dichtkunst* of 1730. Gottsched's own ideas remain firmly within that framework, but the insights of Breitinger and Bodmer are held back too, rendered hesitant, by the prevailing understanding of language. Even Lessing's scattered remarks still rest on essentially the same philosophy of language as Gottsched's, though his differences with Gottsched are even greater than those of Breitinger or Bodmer. The turning-point in thinking about translation comes with the new attitude towards language brought about by the writings of Hamann and Herder.[15]

According to Leibniz language is merely an instrument of reason; thoughts govern words, and a new thought (or feeling transmuted into a thought) either forms a new word or expresses itself through a new assembly of existing words. Words are not an essential part of the thought, they are simply its expression, its dress, and always separable from what is seen as the real 'meaning'. 'Die Wörter an sich selbst sind willkührliche Zeichen unserer Begriffe.'[16] (A rigorous word-for-word translation such as Hölderlin practised on Pindar would be unthinkable because he would only be translating the outward show, the dress, and missing the substance.) The word as such then has very little importance, it is merely the way to the content; and parallel to this, Gottsched's discussions of translation are dominated by an anxiety not as to how a translation has been made, but as to who has been translated (suitable authors are those who conform to his critical norms, for the most part French).[17] At the extreme this results in the

---

[14] Anneliese Senger, *Deutsche Übersetzungstheorie im 18. Jahrhundert (1734–1746)* (Bonn, 1971), 16.   [15] Cf. Senger, 87.

[16] J. C. Gottsched, *Ausführliche Redekunst*, 4th edn. (Leipzig, 1750), 264.

[17] Cf. Thomas Huber, *Studien zur Theorie des Übersetzens im Zeitalter der deutschen Aufklärung 1730–1770* (Meisenheim am Glan, 1968), 14.

notion that, what with progress, the translator can do a better version of the subject-matter than the original author himself, whose understanding is necessarily constrained by his place in history.[18]

The Leibnizian view of language has interesting but restrictive consequences for translation. The first is the concentration on the message of the text to be translated, as something separate from the form:

Bemühe man sich nicht so wohl alle Worte, als vielmehr den rechten Sinn, und die völlige Meynung eines jeden Satzes, den man übersetzt, wohl auszudrücken. Denn ob gleich die Wörter den Verstand bey sich führen, und ich die Gedanken des Scribenten daraus nehmen mus: So lassen sie sich doch in einer andern Sprache so genau nicht geben, daß man ihnen Fuß vor Fuß folgen könnte.[19]

[Attempt to express not so much every word as the proper sense and full meaning of each and every sentence translated. For although the words do bear the meaning in them and I am obliged to extract the thoughts of an author from them, they cannot be rendered in another language so precisely as to make following in their footsteps a possibility.]

Gottsched is aware that the words of the original must be the translator's focus, but sees his task as being to look beyond the words. In a metaphor Enlightenment thinkers used themselves, the translator must unclothe the meaning and then fit it again in native dress. This is a fair summary of the Enlightenment conception of translation even in the ramifications of Bodmer and Breitinger. Gottsched eschewed the exact reproduction of form, because it could, as he saw it, only hinder the clear transmission of content.

New attention to form is initiated by Breitinger. He is only applying the contemporary understanding of language when he states that different languages are merely 'so viele verschiedene Sammlungen vollkommen gleich viel geltender Wörter und Redensarten, welche miteinander können verwechselt werden' [so many collections of completely equivalent words and expressions which can be exchanged with one other].[20] He goes so far as to suggest that true synonyms only exist in different languages.[21]

---

[18]   See Senger, 58–9. This idea *could* be seen as a distant engenderer of Hölderlin's intention to correct the 'Kunstfehler' (vi/434) in Sophocles.   [19]   Gottsched, 394.
[20]   Johann Jakob Breitinger, *Critische Dichtkunst*, 2 vols. (Zürich, 1740; repr. Stuttgart, 1966), ii. 138.
[21]   Compare the directly opposed view of Wilhelm von Humboldt: 'Wie könnte

Translation is thus a matter of exchanging counters, and relatively uncomplicated:

> Von einem Uebersetzer wird erfodert, daß er eben dieselben Begriffe und Gedancken, die er in einem trefflichen Muster vor sich findet, in eben solcher Ordnung, Verbindung, Zusammenhange, und mit gleich so starckem Nachdrucke, mit andern gleichgültigen bey einem Volck angenommenen, gebräuchlichen und bekannten Zeichen ausdrücke, so daß die Vorstellung der Gedancken unter beyderley Zeichen einen gleichen Eindruck auf das Gemüthe des Lesers mache. [...] Darum muß ein Uebersetzer sich selber das harte Gesetze vorschreiben, daß er niemahls die Freyheit nehmen wolle, von der Grundschrift, weder in Ansehung der Gedancken, noch in der Form und Art derselben, abzuweichen. (ii 139)

> [A translator is required to express exactly the concepts and thoughts he finds in an excellent model in exactly the same order, relation, and context, and with just the same emphasis, with the help of other equivalent signs which are accepted, customary, and familiar among a nation; so that the presentation of the thoughts in both sign-systems makes an equal impression on the mind of the reader. For this reason a translator must set himself the strict rule of never taking the liberty of diverging from the original, neither as regards the thoughts nor in the form and style.]

As well as the emphasis on 'Form und Art', Breitinger here introduces the idea of equivalence into the discussion: the aim should be to engineer a similar effect on the reader of the translation as a reader of the original in his or her own language would receive. In fact the two strands are wound together, as the concern for form is a move away from the exclusive attention to rational content and towards the impression a work makes, as a whole, 'auf das Gemüthe'. Nevertheless the 'thoughts' and the 'form and style' are still seen as separable and separate, in line with the dominant view of language, and the differences between Breitinger and Gottsched are slighter than they at first appear.

The two approaches sketched out by Gottsched and Breitinger are polarized into opposing undertakings by Bodmer, who is thus the first clearly to define the two main intentions in translation which Goethe later takes for granted and Schleiermacher gives exacter analysis to. He

---

[...] je ein Wort, dessen Bedeutung nicht unmittelbar durch die Sinne gegeben ist, vollkommen einem Worte einer andern Sprache gleich seyn?' from the 'Einleitung' to his translation of *Agamemnon*, in: *Wilhelm von Humboldts Gesammelte Schriften*, ed. Albert Leitzmann, 17 vols. (Berlin, 1903–36), viii, 119–46 (130). In fact Humboldt doubts whether even words denoting a concrete object are truly equivalent.

realizes that the translator is presented with two fundamental options whose premisses are quite different:

ist die Absicht, die in der Urschrift enthaltene Materie in einer andern Sprache der Welt einfältig mitzutheilen, so liegt dem Uebersetzer ja ob, alles auf das kläreste und deutlichste nach dem Genius seiner Sprache vorzutragen: Will man aber eine genaue Uebersetzung haben, die nicht nur die Gedancken der Urschrift vorlege, sondern auch alle die Arten und Weisen, die der Urheber gebraucht, seine Gedancken an den Tag zu geben, beybehalte, so muß auch solches gantz genau bewerckstelliget werden, und darf man sich nicht förchten, man werde unerhörter Seltsamkeiten oder wohl gar der Original-Fehler beschuldiget werden.[22]

[if the intention is to convey simply the material contained in the original in another language of the world, it behoves the translator to articulate everything as clearly as possible according to the spirit of his language. But if one is aiming at a close translation, which does not just present the thoughts of the original but also preserves all the ways and means the author uses to realize his thoughts, it must be carried out with great exactitude and one must not be afraid of being accused of eccentricities or even mistakes.]

Bodmer sees the dangers in what he calls 'eine genaue Uebersetzung', but his intensification of Breitinger's ideas about form also allows him to see the quite new advantages which can be won from attentive translation:

Wer die Mühe nimmt eine Schrift, besonders eine poetische, buchstäblich in seine Muttersprache zu übersetzen, der wird [...] finden, daß die meisten Redensarten, die uns fremd und ungewohnt vorkommen, wo sie recht untersucht werden, nicht nur nichts unanständiges an sich haben, sondern öfters die Sachen unter sehr bequemen Bildern vorstellen, und darum die Aufmerksamkeit des Lesers auf eine besondere Weise rege machen. (pp. 523–4)

[Whoever takes the trouble to translate a work, especially a poetic work, literally into his mother tongue will [...] find that most of the expressions which seem at first sight strange and unaccustomed turn out on closer inspection not only to have nothing improper about them but often to present things in very apt images and therefore arouse the attention of the reader in a special way.]

This is a particular development of the enrichment topos. Bodmer sees literal translation of a text, especially poetry, as a means of

---

[22] Johann Jakob Bodmer, *Der Mahler der Sitten* (Zürich, 1746; repr. Hildesheim, 1972), 521.

introducing into German new images which will have a particular effect on the reader. Poetry itself could be seen to incite a particular attention through its divergences from and contradictions with common usage, and if Bodmer is not actually suggesting that a similar effective discrepancy might be arrived at through deliberate cleaving to the text when translating, he *is* going in that direction. This idea, that a poetic diction might be generated by mechanical means, seems to have been entertained by Hölderlin when he set about his translation of Pindar. Bodmer intimates it here, but he does not actually specify a word-for-word rendition, and he is mainly concentrating on the literal translation of idioms. This does not appear to be purely theoretical. Bodmer translated himself, and his version of Homer (published 1778) contains some direct transpositions of Greek adjectival phrases.[23] He also refers to certain translators who have tried to convey the 'Weisen, wie ein Urheber die Sachen vorgetragen' [ways in which an author has presented his subject]; but these have, he says, all been treated with derision.[24] Bodmer points towards the possibilities word-for-word translation might hold, but the logical extreme of a true *verbum de verbo* transposition is never seriously considered, mainly because the actual texture and fabric of a work, its words, are never quite taken seriously enough under the regime of the Leibnizian view of language.

Johann Jacob Junckherrott's New Testament

We have seen that a text's actual words are attended to when the text is a holy one, because they are a revelation of divine sense; particular words are in a particular order because by those means are the workings of God best expressed. In a translation from the Bible the dual exaction any translator is subject to becomes especially acute: on the one hand the religious status of the text demands the strictest adherence to its words—any loss or distortion is absolute, divine revelation will have been dimmed; but on the other hand, and the pressure is just as great, the duty of the translator, as a disciple of the disciples, is to promulgate the Word of God, to make it as accessible as can be, to open the foreign words out into the vernacular so that they can have more effect on more people. Luther had on the whole chosen the evangelist course. Johann Jacob Junckherrott, who

---

[23] See Senger, 66–7.   [24] Bodmer, 522.

published his translation of the New Testament in 1732, went in the other direction.

Not much is known about him, but Junckherrott was an eccentric, described as 'ein seltsamer verrückter Kopf' [an odd, crazy chap], who earned his living by gambling professionally. He was so good, or lucky, that he was able to give 10,000 thalers to the poor. The translation of the New Testament he had printed at his own expense just before his death was suppressed on account of its 'abenteuerliche Deutsche Sprache' [extravagant German].[25]

His *Neues Testament* was touched by the same eccentricity, but it is an eccentricity that betokens a deep seriousness, and it was quite outside the conventions of his day. Junckherrott undertook what was at bottom a word-for-word translation, augmented and complicated by his (esoteric) understanding of his duties. All his work went towards the preservation and carrying over of every last scrap of meaning in the original text: his aim was 'sonder leermachung des Creutzes Christi [...] solches in die übliche Teutsche Sprach und Red-Art zu dollmetschen' [to translate into ordinary German language and idiom without emptying the cross of Christ].[26] He is highly conscious of the sacramental nature of the actual words; they contain 'das Licht, darinnen wir mögen sehen das Licht' [the light in which we may see the light], and it is in this light, 'dahin aufpassend auff den Winck der Zeigung des Lichts' [paying attention to the manifestation of the light] that he translates, radically differently from anyone else: 'nicht daß man wolte suchen den Sinn der in andern Ubersetzungen etwa buchstäblich heraus kommt, sondern welcher nur irgend einem hierinnen möchte einleuchten' [not in search of the meaning which occasionally emerges literally from other translations, but of that which may only illuminate us here].

As set out in 'Einige Gedancken des Ubersetzers, betreffend die Dollmetschung Neues Testaments' [A Few of the Translator's Thoughts on Rendering the New Testament],[27] ten rules of which the following is the gist, this means: retention of the word-order, and

[25] Both quotations (from Jöcher's *Allgemeines Gelehrten-Lexicon*) in Senger, 81. I am grateful to Senger for putting me on to Junckherrott in her book. His translation: *Das Neue Testament des HERREN Unserer JESU Christi, eigentlich aus dem Griechischen Grund-Text gedollmetschet und in das Teutsche übersetzt, durch weyland Johann Jacob Junckherrott* (Offenbach, 1732).

[26] From the 'Beygefügter Vorbericht, dem geneigten Leser', which has no page-numbers. The next three quotations come from here.   [27] Also unnumbered.

respect for the etymological links between words in the Greek, which must be kept apparent in German; composite words must not be translated by simplex forms, and exactly the same spectrum of vocabulary should be used in German as in Greek; pronouns must not be translated into possessive adjectives—πατὴρ ἡμῶν ('our Father') is not 'unser Vatter' nor even 'Vatter unser', but 'Vatter unserer' [father of ours]—and punctuation should not be used as this restricts the workings of the Holy Spirit; where personal pronouns occur, they must be translated in addition to the indication of person given by the suffix of their verb (so John 4:38: ἐγὼ ἀπέστειλα ὑμᾶς θερίζειν ('I sent you to reap') translates as: 'Ich hab geschickt ich euch da abhin zu erndten' [I have sent I you over there to reap]), and ἀλλά and καί ('but' and 'and') should be translated for the most part by 'aber' and 'auch' and not 'sondern' and 'und' because these last sever more than they conjoin. The ultimate reasoning behind all these principles is that divergence from them will go against the Holy Spirit and 'den Sinn des Geistes allhier verdrehen' [pervert the meaning of the spirit]; the Bible has been given the exact form it has because the Holy Spirit saw that to be the best form, and no translator has the right to controvert it.

It is obvious that such a technique is not going to produce 'die übliche Teutsche Sprach und Red-Art'. Junckherrott's transliteration of the Greek is further distanced from normal German and conventional sense by his practice of translating according to the root meaning of each of a word's different elements. This is Junckherrott's fourth rule:

Soll eine warhaffte Dollmetschung da heraus kommen, so muß die Signification des Simplicis oder Radicis beybehalten, die da hinzu gesetzte Particula mithin auch exprimiret werden, und nicht, wann ἀλλάσσω, (allásso) ich ändere, gedollmetschet wird, καταλλάσσω (katallássoo) ich versöhne, sondern vielmehr, ich verändere mich da gegenhin, (der Geändertwerdung nach da gegenhin) gedollmetschet werden, als welches den Grund der Versöhnung ausdrucket, dann wann ich mich verändere da gegenhin, werde ich als ein anderer da gegenhin angenommen.

[If a real translation is to be arrived at, the meaning of the simplex or root must be retained and the additional particles must also be expressed. Thus, if ἀλλάσσω is given as 'I change', καταλλάσσω should not be 'I reconcile' but rather 'I change myself there towards' (according to the becoming changed towards); this expresses the essence of reconciliation: when I change myself towards something I will be received as another.]

Junckherrott's translation of ἀποκάλυψις Ἰωάννου ('The Revelation of John') is 'Abhindeckung Johannis da von der gedecktwerdung da abhin' [Uncovering of John away from being covered]. In his concern that no fraction of meaning should go missing Junckherrott slips into pedantry: ἀποκάλυψις does literally mean an 'uncovering', but Junckherrott insists on the fact that what can be uncovered must have been covered ('gedecktwerdung') in the first place.[28] Though his position is as extreme as Hölderlin's in the Pindar translations, his *Neues Testament* does not represent such an exact interaction of two languages because the process is interfered with by his intellect: in the main he translates according to preconceived principles; Hölderlin's Pindar translation is an experiment, an exploration. (This difference is mirrored in Hölderlin's never trying to find a publisher for the Pindar, whereas Junckherrott published *Das Neue Testament* himself.) Junckherrott's translation could be thought of as a description of the Greek, Hölderlin's as an encounter with it.

The result of Junckherrott's method verges on the unreadable, but it is not quite that:

Amen amen ich rede da euch daß werdet weinen ihr da auch daß ihr werdet klagen wehe ihr da die aber welt wird werden freudig da ihr aber werdet gemacht werden traurig ihr da aber die traurigkeit euerer in erfreuetwerdung wird werden da. (John 16:20)

[Amen amen I say there unto you that shall weep you there also that you shall lament you there the but world shall become joyful there but you shall be made sorrowful you there but the sorrow of yours into being-joyful shall be turned there.]

Every word of the original Greek is accounted for, the verbs are translated in their proper tenses, and the word-order is preserved to the point of putting 'die aber welt' for ὁ δὲ κόσμος, where the position of δέ is as correct in Greek grammar as that of 'aber' is false in German. German has to bend to the structures imposed by the Greek throughout. The only word with no direct equivalent in the original is the second 'aber' (in 'ihr aber werdet gemacht werden traurig ihr'), and here Junckherrott *is* employing the proper German means of emphasis to convey ὑμεῖς λυπηθήσεσθε. Putting 'ihr' for the personal pronoun ὑμεῖς and another 'ihr' for the verb-ending

---

[28]   There is a trace of this in the formation of ἀποκάλυψις, but it is very faint. Κάλυψις on its own (which does not occur in the N.T.) means the act of covering or the cover itself, but not the state of being covered.

-εσθε, as according to his rules Junckherrott does, presumably doesn't indicate to his satisfaction the stress ὑμεῖς has by virtue of its position at the head of its phrase, and so he adds the German 'aber'. The exception to this is Junckherrott's 'da'. This is an idiosyncrasy he seems to deploy as a kind of punctuation; there is no apparent source in the New Testament Greek, but it is reminiscent of the abundance of 'meaningless' particles in Ancient Greek (δέ, γε etc.). It marks the whole translation and to a lesser extent, but strikingly, his own preface and notes. It is interesting to see how Junckherrott's own prose-style is affected by the language of his translation; there is a similar interaction between Hölderlin's versions of Sophocles and the appended notes.

Junckherrott's translation was serious and considered, though eccentric, and it is a fascinating, extravagant precursor of the kind of translation Voss practised and engendered, and especially of Hölderlin's Pindar. Junckherrott was a Pietist, and it must not be forgotten that Hölderlin's roots were also deep in Pietism.[29] Another possible common source is the interlinear translation of Latin and Greek done in schools.[30] What is certain is that literary translation that followed the letter of the original in a fashion comparable to Junckherrott's could only occur once the texts of human authors had come to be regarded in the same light as those of putatively divine origins. This was to come about under the influence of Hamann and Herder.

Hamann and Herder

It is significant that both Hamann and Herder were theologians. Hamann's attack on rationalist exegetes of the Bible in his *Aesthetica in nuce* marked a change in the understanding of language which had direct consequences for translation. The Scriptures, Hamann thought, are a poetry in which divine presence is immanent, they are an act of revelation and cannot be elucidated by reason and reduced to an idea. Only in that one commensurate form do we have anything of God at all, and meaning is generated through our interaction with the text,

---

[29] On Hölderlin's contact with Pietism, see Gerhard Schäfer, 'Der spekulative württembergische Pietismus als Hintergrund für Hölderlins Dichten und Denken', in Valérie Lawitschka (ed.), *Turm-Vorträge 1989/90/91: Hölderlin: Christentum und Antike* (Tübingen, 1991), 46–78, and Howard Gaskill, 'Hölderlin's Contact with Pietism', *MLR* 69 (1974), 805–20.   [30] Cf. Senger, 86.

in our labour of understanding; it cannot be extracted from its own fabric. Like a tree, or the appearance of Christ on earth, a text does not denote a separably graspable sphere, but is its only possible embodiment and palpable location. 'Translation', the act of realization, has taken place—into the text—and further exegesis such as Hamann criticizes is thus a retreat, and not an approach. Similarly the act of speech is for Hamann always a translation 'aus einer Engelsprache in eine Menschensprache' [from an angel-language into a human language], and the only form in which this 'Engelsprache' can be perceived.[31] This means that any literary translation is of necessity a translation of a translation, and correspondingly Hamann uses Cervantes's disparaging image of the underside of a carpet to describe translations: all the threads are there but the pattern is disfigured and unclear (p. 321). The secondary status of all translation is underlined. But since implicitly not only the Bible, but all literature is now understood as a unique bodying forth, and not just as the attire of some rationally accessible 'content', a whole new respect for and engagement with its texture is demanded of the reader, and so of the translator.

Hamann's meditations on the nature of genius are of a piece with this new stand. Via Herder and then the *Sturm und Drang* movement they evolved into an alignment of the author with the creator-god: both operate without rules and originate their own world; the author is a creative genius, and his works cannot be given rational definition. With this, a particularly radical aspect of secularization, an original can take up the same position as the holy text, and a new period of translation is potentially opened.[32]

Herder, in his scattered remarks, went a step further and made the claim that the translator himself should be 'ein schöpferisches Genie' [a creative genius].[33] Only if this were the case could every artery and

---

[31] Johann Georg Hamann, *Aesthetica in nuce*, in: *Entkleidung und Verklärung: Eine Auswahl aus Schriften und Briefen des 'Magus im Norden'*, ed. Martin Seils (Berlin, 1963), 315–54 (320). Cf. this corollary: 'Le poète est une espèce singulière de traducteur qui traduit le discours ordinaire, modifié par une émotion, en "langage des dieux"'—Paul Valéry, 'Variations sur les *Bucoliques*', in: *Oeuvres*, ed. Jean Hytier, 2 vols. (Paris, 1957), I, 207–22 (212).

[32] In 1776 Wieland can write to Bürger that Homer's works 'uns Wort Gottes sind' (in a letter quoted by Günter Häntzschel, *Johann Heinrich Voß: Seine Homer-Übersetzung als sprachschöpferische Leistung* (Munich, 1977), 31.)

[33] Johann Gottfried Herder, *Sämmtliche Werke*, ed. Bernhard Suphan, 33 vols. (Berlin, 1877–1913), i 178.

nuance of the original be reproduced, a goal Herder thinks attainable, in theory at least. In practice he is aware of the gap, and despairs of the existence of a translator accomplished enough to answer the need German literature had for adequate translations, especially from the Greek. The translator is seen above all in the role of mediator; a Winckelmann 'in Absicht der Dichter' [for poets][34] is what is required:

Wo ist ein Uebersezzer, der zugleich Philosoph, Dichter und Philolog ist: er soll der Morgenstern einer neuen Epoche in unsrer Litteratur seyn! (i 274)

[Where is a translator who is at once a philosopher, a poet and a philologist? He shall be the morning-star of a new epoch in our literature.]

Wo ist ein Schutzengel der Griechischen Litteratur in Deutschland, der an der Spizze von allen, zeige, wie die Griechen von Deutschen zu studiren sind? (i 286)

[Where is a guardian angel of Greek letters in Germany, to show us all how the Germans should study the Greeks?]

Thought about translation in Herder is part of that wider debate, on how best to deal with the Greek achievement and release its benefits in Germany; and also on the related point of the improvement or enrichment of the German language, which Herder saw to be at a stage in its development when it needed the stimulus and nurture of more 'poetic' tongues, of which the paradigm was Greek:

Eine Sprache vor allen Uebersetzungen, ist wie eine Jungfrau, die sich noch mit keinem fremden Manne vermischet, um aus zweierlei Blut Frucht zu gebären: zu der Zeit ist sie noch rein, und im Stande der Unschuld, ein treues Bild von dem Charakter ihres Volks. Sie sey voll Armuth, Eigensinn und Unregelmäßigkeit: wie sie ist, ist sie Original- und Nationalsprache.[35]

[A language before all translations is like a virgin who has not yet mingled her blood with that of a foreign man to bear fruit from the union: for the moment it is still pure and in a state of innocence, a faithful image of the character of the people. However impoverished, stubborn or capricious it may be it is what it is: an original, national language.]

The image Herder uses here reveals his mixed feelings about

---

[34] Herder, i 294.
[35] Herder, ii 106. In Herder's scheme, German was an aged, prosaic language, but this is not essentially different from Breitinger saying that German is 'noch nicht recht angebauet' in his *Critische Dichtkunst* (143).

translation, and he goes on openly to voice his mistrust of it; but essentially he remains true to the logic of his simile: exact encounter with the foreign he felt to be vital for the furtherance of Germany as a nation at that point in her history, and this could be effected best, though not solely, by translation. Translation thus took on a cultural significance far beyond the limits of previous conceptions, one that ultimately referred back to Luther.

But Herder also changed thinking about translation with the terms he used to describe it: a translation becomes a journey abroad, just as reading itself was for Herder an excursion into the world of the book and a coming home, as in his well-known accounts of reading Homer and Ossian.[36] The successful translator then, must come back at exactly the right moment:

Wenn sich ein munterer Jüngling für sein Vaterland wagt: so wünsche ich ihm einen alten Verständigen zur Seite: nur daß dieser nicht vorgehe: und hat sich je jener zu weit verirrt, so führe ihn ein Genius, wie ein unsichtbarer Menschenfreund, wieder zu den Seinen.[37]

[If a cheery lad ventures forth for his country let him have an old hand at his side, just so long as he doesn't go in front. And if he strays too far let a guardian spirit, like an anonymous well-wisher, lead him back to his own.]

The distance travelled becomes a metaphor for the degree to which conventions are abandoned and the language rendered strange in translation. Translation subjects the language to new experience, and this should be formative but not destructive. There are strong parallels between thoughts like these and late eighteenth-century notions of *Bildung*, of which the journey into the world of experience, or more concretely, the Grand Tour young men of means aspired to, was an essential part.[38] Translation represents the same process in microcosm, but even more importantly it effects it at the point which is the heart of a nation, its language. Herder comes to the conclusion that an 'anpassende Uebersetzung', the more demanding mode of close translation, has the greater part to play because 'sie eifert für beide Sprachen' [it strives for both languages], transferring the fruit from the foreign language and providing the right conditions for its seeds to take and prosper in home ground (ii 108).

[36]   Herder, i 176–7 and iii 168–9.
[37]   Herder, ii 108. This reminds one of Hölderlin's letter to Neuffer of July 1794, where he compares translation to foreign service (vi/125). See pp. 58–9 below.
[38]   See Berman, *L'Epreuve de l'étranger,* 72–86.

Adelung versus Voss

Herder's sense of the need for 'fremde Kolonien' [foreign colonies] to make up for 'die Mängel des Staats' [the insufficiencies of the state] (i 159)—that is, the shortcomings of German—was by no means universal. Very influential voices argued the direct opposite, that the language had reached a degree of perfection previously unattained, and that this state should be fixed and cherished. Johann Christoph Adelung set about classifying it, laying it down as a standard, in his *Wörterbuch*, the first volume of which came out in 1774. Developments in the language after that date he criticized fiercely in the various treatises on grammar and style he published, as well as in the later edition of his dictionary.

Adelung took the language used in the court of Upper Saxony between 1740 and 1760, and by writers from there such as Christian Fürchtegott Gellert, to be exemplary in every way, and he sought to impose it on the German nation as a whole. Any divergences from this standard, even in writers like Goethe, were harmful. It is difficult to see how the compiler of a dictionary can thus deny language its changing nature, but Adelung did. He provided a norm that was at first accepted widely, as the reception of Voss's Homer makes clear. His attitude towards translation, or to any kind of imitation or influence, was one of total rejection, even where the ancients were concerned: 'weder Eigenheiten ihrer Sprache und Vorstellungsart, noch Sylbenmaße, noch irgend etwas' [neither peculiarities of their language and way of seeing things, nor their metrics, nor anything whatsoever] were to be borrowed.[39]

That Adelung's prescriptions were largely adhered to, so that the standardization he projected partly set in, makes the extension and enrichment of the language translation accomplished in the last decades of the eighteenth century all the more vital. Until now, this account has mostly been confined to writings *about* translation, which may want justifying; but apart from Luther there is before Voss no translator who had a decisive influence on translation as such, and so ideas about translation in between either reflect pretty accurately what was going on or are themselves ahead of any practice. In general one can say that until Voss practice lagged behind theory. But with Voss it leapt ahead. The dominant mode of translation before and even after

[39] Quoted in Häntzschel, 163. On Adelung generally see Häntzschel, 150–3.

Voss was the adapting mode, the type Goethe ascribes to Wieland in his notes to the *West-östlicher Divan*, and which nearly all German observers from Breitinger to Schleiermacher singled out as being peculiarly French (and thus reprehensible).[40] Much of this was of poor quality, but there was masses of it: from French, English, Italian, Latin and, to a much lesser extent, Greek. Voss's *Odyssey* though was the first translation since Luther's Bible to reach the status of a classic.

This, in its first version, came out in 1781. A second, much revised, was published in 1793 together with the *Iliad*. Compared to the second version, the first is conventional in its nearer accordance with the contemporary notion of what could be done in German, and models itself less on the Greek. But all three translations (the two of the *Odyssey*, and that of the *Iliad*) were radical and written right against the taste of the day. Even Klopstock, who had been instrumental in introducing Greek forms and revolutionizing diction in his poems, largely also under the influence of Greek, was sharply critical of Voss's innovations. Coleridge reports that in 1799 Klopstock told Wordsworth 'that Voss in his translation of the Iliad had done violence to the idiom of the Germans, and had sacrificed it to the Greeks, not remembering sufficiently that each language has its particular spirit and genius'.[41] This shows how very unconventional the translation was, given that it was the heightening and continuation of a process Klopstock had initiated.[42] This reaction was at first universal.

Voss's method was to adopt a very close equivalent to Homer's hexameters (essentially identical, allowing for the different nature of metrics in German and Greek) and to retain too, as far as possible, the syntax, the word-order and the forms of individual words.[43] Doing this, he found that German was capable of a reflection of the Greek not previously imagined possible, and the whole idea of the shape of German was changed. Voss found for it a flexibility and plasticity it had not hitherto possessed, or which had been deadened by the

---

[40] E.g. Herder, i 290: 'Die Franzosen, zu stolz auf ihren Nationalgeschmack, nähern demselben alles, statt sich dem Geschmack einer andern Zeit zu bequemen'.

[41] S. T. Coleridge, *Biographia Literaria*, ed. J. Shawcross, 2 vols. (Oxford, 1979), ii 176.

[42] Coleridge also reports: 'He seemed to think that no language could ever be so far formed as that it might not be enriched by idioms borrowed from another tongue.' If this is not a contradiction, the line is obviously very fine. Wordsworth thought the practice 'very dangerous' (*Biographia Literaria*, ii 178).   [43] Häntzschel, 130.

normalization and rationalization the *Aufklärung* had subjected it to.[44]
This might be seen as the realization of Herder's theory that German
had reached a prosaic age and could be refreshed by contact (through
translation) with languages at a youthful, poetic stage, such as Greek
or Hebrew. The new resources of expression Voss opened or retrieved
were not solely due to the direct influence of Greek: he also revived
old and dialect words in the manner of Luther, who was a model in
this respect.[45] Voss sought to reanimate and enlarge the language as
Luther had done, making it more concrete and versatile; and in the
end, in defiance of Adelung, his translations did just that. For a second
time in Germany a vital stage in the development of the language is
intimately bound up with translation: Voss's Homer released energies
which are at the heart of German Classicism. I quote here the
opening of the *Odyssey* in Voss's two versions. This gives an idea both
of Voss's style in general and of the shift in taste which was already
beginning during the 1780s. Voss's first version (1781) runs:

> Sage mir, Muse, die Taten des vielgewanderten Mannes,
> Welcher so weit geirrt nach der heiligen Troja Zerstörung,
> Vieler Menschen Städte gesehn und Sitte gelernt hat
> Und auf dem Meere so viel unnennbare Leiden erduldet,
> Seine Seele zu retten und seiner Freunde Zurückkunft.
> Aber die Freunde rettet' er nicht, wie eifrig er strebte;
> Denn sie bereiteten selbst durch Missetat ihr Verderben:
> Toren! welche die Rinder des hohen Sonnenbeherrschers
> Schlachteten; siehe, der Gott nahm ihnen den Tag der Zurückkunft.
> Sage hievon auch uns ein weniges, Tochter Kronions.[46]

[Tell me, Muse, the deeds of the much-travelled man, who wandered so far
after the destruction of the holy city of Troy, saw the towns of many people
and learnt their customs and at sea put up with so many unnamable
sufferings, to save his soul and the return home of his friends. But he couldn't
save his friends, however hard he strove; for they brought about their own
perdition through misdoing: the fools! they slaughtered the oxen of the great
sun-ruler; and look, the god deprived them of the day of their return. Tell
us something of this too, daughter of Zeus.]

---

[44] Häntzschel, 131.
[45] Häntzschel, 141. Doubly a model, since Luther was also a source for such
words.
[46] Homer: *Ilias/Odyssee in der Übertragung von Johann Heinrich Voß* (Munich, 1967),
441. (This edition reprints the 1781 *Odyssey*.)

His revised version (1793) is often similar, but goes further still. Even the lack of capitalization is part of the attempt to come right up to the Greek:

> Sage mir, Muse, vom manne, dem vielgewandten, der vielfach
> Umgeirrt, nachdem er die heilige Troja zerstöret;
> Vieler menschen städte gesehn, und sitte gelernt hat,
> Auch im meere so viel herzkränkende leiden erduldet,
> Strebend für seine seele zugleich und der freunde zurükkunft.
> Aber nicht die freund' errettet' er, eifrig bemüht zwar;
> Denn sie bereiteten selbst durch missethat ihr verderben:
> Thörichte, welche die rinder dem leuchtenden sohn Hyperions
> Schlachteten; jener darauf nahm ihnen den tag der zurükkunft.
> Hievon sag' auch uns ein weniges, tochter Kronions.[47]

[Tell me, Muse, of the man, the many-sided one, who wandered around much after he had destroyed the holy city of Troy; saw the towns of many people, and learnt their customs, also on the seas put up with so many heart-inflicting sufferings, striving for his soul and his friends' return home at the same time. But his friends he couldn't save, though he tried hard to; for they brought about their own perdition through misdoing: the idiots, they slaughtered the oxen of the shining son of Hyperion; whereupon he deprived them of the day of their return. Of this tell us something too, daughter of Zeus.]

All the changes, such as those in line 4, bring the German more in line with the Greek, even when this makes for unusual German like 'im meere', a literal translation of $\dot{\epsilon}\nu \ \pi\acute{o}\nu\tau\omega$, or the word-order and syntax of line 6.

Voss did effect a kind of revolution in taste, in that what was at first almost universally misunderstood came to be accepted as a classic. After about 1798 his translations are hardly mentioned except in admiration and with a sense of the great benefit they have worked. Goethe spoke of the 'Versatilität' [versatility], the 'rhetorische, rhythmische, metrische Vorteile' [rhetorical, rhythmical, metrical advantages] the German language owed to 'der nie genug zu schätzende Voß' [Voss, whose importance can never be stressed too much].[48] In the grammars and dictionaries of the nineteenth century, Voss becomes a point of reference.[49] For a discussion of translation in the eighteenth century, particularly with Hölderlin in mind, there is no more important landmark.

---

[47] *Homers Werke von Johann Heinrich Voss*, 2nd edn., 4 vols. (Königsberg, 1802), 5–6.   [48] Goethe, ii 256.   [49] Häntzschel, 260–1.

Perhaps the most telling aspect of Voss's practice of concentrating intently on the form of the original, sometimes down to the last detail of punctuation and caesura, was that the precise imitation of metre forced Voss's language to take on shapes and rhythms which were also closer to Homer's narrative than any other translations.[50] If metre was perhaps Voss's overriding concern, he was in practice always making carefully judged compromises: his translation was more demanding in every respect than Bodmer's or Bürger's or Stolberg's, but no one consideration was allowed to crowd the others. Still, it is easy to see how Voss gave rise to translations where one principle did prevail to the detriment of other aspects: word-order in Hölderlin's Pindar, or metre in Humboldt's *Agamemnon*.

Counter-Examples

From now on Voss is at the back of people's minds when they think about translation, write on or practise it. In sympathy with his technique or not, they cannot ignore the fact that it expands notions of the aims translation might set itself. 'Transparent' translation becomes viable: the relationship between a biblical text and its version begins to operate in the domain of literary translation. Even if Voss's principles are not adhered to, the status of the letter of the original, of its rhythm and precise design, is hugely enhanced. After Voss there are very few translations of verse which do not attempt to render the original's metrical form.

This is a peculiarly German phenomenon, as those who cared were well aware. The entry on translation ('traduction') in the *Encyclopédie* distinguishes between 'version' and 'traduction', where the first is literal and applies mainly to biblical translation and the second is the free literary style. Being given different names, the two are kept firmly apart and 'version' is allowed no influence on 'traduction'.[51] In England there was at the time no close translation in the manner of Voss either. A good indication of the wide divergence is that the English translation of comparable reputation to Voss's was Pope's Homer. Alexander Tytler's *Essay on the Principles of Translation* (1791), which was translated into German in 1793[52]—the year Voss's *Iliad* and

---

[50] Häntzschel, 80–1.
[51] *Encyclopédie, ou Dictionnaire raisonné des sciences, des arts et des métiers, par une société de gens de lettres*, 17 vols. (Paris, 1751–65), xvi 510–12.
[52] Roger Paulin, 'Die romantische Übersetzung: Theorie und Praxis', in:

Odyssey were published—offers a point from which the German situation can be put in a certain perspective. For Tytler, Pope is the model translator. He is applauded for having 'improved both upon the thought and expression of his original' and for his 'judicious correction of defects'.[53] The very concrete details (Achilles spluttering wine down his guardian Phoenix's front at *Iliad* ix 490 f. for example) which for Voss constitute a good part of the genius of Homer, and which he took pains to bring across, are deliberately glossed over by Pope. Pope's Homer is in heroic couplets, and this is itself a reason for the entirely different Homer he gives us. Voss's hexameter made it easier for him to amalgamate the character of Homer's style, or better, it obliged him to. Tytler, when speaking of translating verse, demonstrates that prose is unsatisfactory, but makes no stipulation as to whether the specific metre of the original be followed (p. 198). He furnishes three 'General Rules' of translation which throw light on the German situation in so far as they give it a context and clarify what is peculiar to the tradition. They are also a good summary of general apprehensions about translation current at the time, to a great extent in Germany too, which like the Rules flow from a theory of equivalence of effect:

the merit of the original work is so completely transfused into another language, as to be as distinctly apprehended, and as strongly felt, by a native of the country to which that language belongs, as it is by those who speak the language of the original work (p. 14).

Tytler's General Rules deriving from this are:

I. THAT the Translation should give a complete transcript of the ideas of the original work.
II. THAT the style and manner of writing should be of the same character with that of the original.
III. THAT the Translation should have all the ease of original composition. (p. 15)

To these he adds that 'the Genius of the Translator should be akin to that of the Original Author' (p. 361), meaning not that the translator should be capable of having written the work himself, but that he should have a congenial and empathetic understanding of it. These

Nicholas Saul (ed.), *Die deutsche literarische Romantik und die Wissenschaften* (Munich, 1991), 250–64 (254).
[53] Alexander Fraser Tytler (Lord Woodhouselee), *Essay on the Principles of Translation*, 2nd edn. (London, 1797), 90, 98.

guidelines do not rule out the option of adding to the original material; pay no real attention to the question of form (Rule II is very vague and is really concerned with 'tone' rather than form[54]); and with the precept that a translation should have the ease of an original composition reveal fully their distance from considerations crucial in Germany. Tytler's *Essay* deals solely with the specific problems of literary translation, an activity that needs no justifying. He never asks the question: Why translate? The possibility of translation is not in doubt, nor does he consider the effects it might have on the language; it is simply an interesting literary task, with no implication beyond that. But if a translation is to dynamize and replenish the language, it will very rarely be characterized by ease, because it will be stretching and puncturing the limits which convention has set. When in 1813 Schleiermacher suggested 'ein eignes Sprachgebiet [...] für die Uebersezungen' [a special area of language for translations] (Störig, p. 70) he was voicing something long inherent in the German tradition: Voss's Homer, the paradigmatic translation, presented an aspect of the tension, the difference and resemblance, that existed between German and Greek. In that tension the otherness of a different age, civilization and language is intimated, and this can only truly be perceived if the receiving language is itself made new, altered.

Thinkers about translation in Germany were aware of the incision it made in the history of the language, the literature and even the nation, and tried to make the most of this. The coincidence between the growth of such an awareness and the date of the French Revolution is not fortuitous. Perhaps partly for geographical and political reasons, Britain was just not as sensitive to the potential lying in translation, and so not so disposed to develop its significance out beyond the purely literary sphere.

The German Romantics

In the hands of the German Romantics this potential was realized explosively, or perhaps it would be better to say that it was charged to the highest possible degree—the importance of the activity and the scope of the concept expand and ramify as never before or since. The early Romantics were highly conscious of living at a point in time ('wahre *Epoche* in der Übersetzungskunst' [a true turning-point in the

---

[54] Which brings it in line with Herder's reflections. Cf. Paulin, 255.

art of translation][55]) and in a particular place which both needed and favoured translation as such:

Ich glaube man ist auf dem Wege, die wahre poetische Uebersetzungskunst zu erfinden; dieser Ruhm war den Deutschen vorbehalten. Es ist seit kurzem hierin so viel und mancherley geschehen.[56]

[I think we are in the process of establishing the true poetic art of translation; this honour was bound to fall to the Germans. Recently so much has happened in this field, and with such variety.]

The Schlegel brothers and Novalis all had a very high regard for translation: with them there is a focus on the benefits, on what it is the peculiar nature of translation to effect. This focus is related to the Romantics' understanding of poetry *tout court*: translation shares with what may be called Romanticism's characteristic genre, the fragment, a peculiar relation to the idea of a finished or classical work—they both limit themselves to certain aspects, but they contain the potential to transcend the limits of a rounded, complete work.[57] They both occupy uncertain ground in that they have no accepted status; they are both dependent, the translation on its original, and the fragment dually on the notion it inspires, through its frequent character of a project, of a whole work, and on the other fragments with which, as part of a collection, it forms a different kind of whole. There *is* a sort of nostalgia here,[58] but this is overcome or made productive in the case of translation because it is seen as developing possibilities inherent in the original work which would otherwise have remained untouched. Translation is thus seen positively, really for the first time, if we discount Enlightenment ideas of 'improvement' (Tytler's praise of Pope), which stem from an underestimation of the originals. It is only now that translation is not haunted by a sense of loss. Even Herder, who is near the roots of the Romantics' understanding of translation as a category of thought, falls back into laments that a text can only be grasped in the original language.[59] The Romantics were sensible to the understanding that only a translation can give.

[55]   Friedrich Schlegel, quoted in Andreas Huyssen, *Die frühromantische Konzeption von Übersetzung und Aneignung: Studien zur frühromantischen Utopie einer deutschen Weltliteratur* (Zürich, 1969), 112.
[56]   August Wilhelm Schlegel, *Sämmtliche Werke*, ed. Eduard Böcking, 12 vols. (1846–7), iv 126.
[57]   Berman, *L'Epreuve de l'étranger*, 114–15.   [58] As Berman points out, 114.
[59]   E.g.: 'Ihr leset nicht mehr Homer [...]' (Herder, i 177).

Among the Romantics, though they all translated a little at some time, there is one great translator, August Wilhelm Schlegel, and he was immediately recognized as such by his friends. Novalis's letter to him of 30 November 1797, when the first of Schlegel's Shakespeare translations had appeared, is an amazing document of the expectations and significance attached to translation both, in one breath, as a literary activity and as a larger movement with specific relevance to Germany:

Der Recensent ihres Shakespear ist ein gutmeynender Mensch. Seine Recension ist aber wahrhaftig keine Poësie. Was hätte sich nicht über Ihren Shakespeare, besonders in Beziehung *auf das Ganze*, sagen lassen. Er ist unter den Übersetzungen, was W[ilhelm] Meister unter den Romanen ist. Giebts denn schon eine Ähnliche? So lange wir Deutschen übersetzen, so national dieser Hang des Übersetzens ist, indem es fast keinen deutschen Schriftsteller von Bedeutung giebt—der nicht übersezt hätte, und warlich darauf soviel sich einbildet, als auf Originalwercke, so scheint man doch über nichts unbelehrter zu seyn, als über das Übersetzen. Bey uns kann es zur Wissenschaft und zur Kunst werden. Ihr Shakespear ist ein trefflicher Canon für den wissenschaftlichen Beobachter. Außer den Römern sind wir die einzige Nation, die den Trieb des Übersetzens so unwiederstehlich gefühlt, und ihm so unendlich viel Bildung schuldig sind. Daher manche Aehnlichkeit unsrer und der spätrömischen litterairischen Kultur. Dieser Trieb ist eine Indication des sehr hohen, ursprünglichen Karacters des deutschen Volks. Deutschheit ist Kosmopolitismus mit der kräftigsten Individualitaet gemischt. Nur für uns sind Übersetzungen Erweiterungen gewesen. Es gehört poëtische Moralität, Aufopferung der Neigung, dazu, um sich einer wahren Übersetzung zu unterziehen—Man übersezt aus ächter Liebe zum Schönen, und zur vaterländischen Litteratur. Übersetzen ist so gut dichten, als eigne Wercke zu stande bringen—und schwerer, seltner. Am Ende ist alle Poësie Übersetzung. Ich bin überzeugt, daß der deutsche Shakespeare jezt besser, als der Englische ist. Auf den Hamlet freue ich mich, wie ein Kind.[60]

[The reviewer of your Shakespeare is a well-meaning fellow. But his review is hardly poetry. There would have been so much to say about your Shakespeare, particularly taken *as a whole*. Among translations it is what *Wilhelm Meisters Lehrjahre* is among novels. Is there anything else like it? We Germans have been translating for ages, this penchant for translating is part of our national character—there is hardly a German writer of importance who doesn't translate, making just the same claims for his translations as for

[60] Novalis, *Schriften*, ed. Paul Kluckhohn and Richard Samuel, 3rd edn., 5 vols. (Stuttgart, 1977–88), iv 237.

original works—and yet there seems to be nothing we know less about than translation. In Germany it will become a science and an art. Your Shakespeare is an excellent object of study for those with an academic interest. Apart from the Romans we are the only nation to feel such an irresistible urge to translate, and to owe so much in our development to translation. That's why there are many points in common between the literary culture of late Rome and our own. This urge is a sign of the great and original character of the German people. Germanness is cosmopolitanism mixed with the most powerful individuality. Only for us have translations been expansions. It needs poetic morality, self-sacrifice, to arrive at a true translation. One translates out of genuine love of beauty and of the literature of one's country. To translate is to write, no less so than creating your own works—and harder, rarer.
In the end all poetry is translation. I am convinced that the German Shakespeare is now better than the English. I am as excited as a child at the idea of *Hamlet*.]

Several statements here seem amazing at first. But once we understand the assumptions behind them which Novalis and Schlegel share, they all fit together and illuminate each other. Underlying the letter is the whole conception of 'romantische Poesie', and Friedrich Schlegel's *Athenaeum* Fragment 116 is perhaps the best commentary on it. But much of what Friedrich Schlegel formulates there could also be gathered from Novalis's letter, were that necessary. And Novalis also makes the understanding of the fragment easier—in fact translation will seem to provide a good pattern for the essential traits of the Romantic undertaking.

Poetry for Schlegel, 'romantic poetry', is characterized by two main qualities: it is always extending itself, always under way; and it is always attempting to bring together what is disparate—it is 'eine progressive Universalpoesie' [a progressive universal poetry].[61] These complementary tendencies are in a way quantitative: the greater the exuberance and the conjoining, the more Romantic poetry will be. This unfolding is effected by poetry's being self-reflexive: the relationship between poetry and the empirical world is already one of reflection, and this reflection must not be static but dynamized by the poetry, 'potentiated', multiplied 'wie in einer endlosen Reihe von Spiegeln' [as in an endless series of mirrors]. An unlimited expanse is opened, a state of receptivity and passage: 'Die romantische Poesie [...]

[61] F. Schlegel, *KA*, ii 182–3 (*Athenaeum* Fr. 116). The next two quotations in this paragraph are from the same fragment.

ist der höchsten und der allseitigsten Bildung fähig; nicht bloß von innen heraus, sondern auch von außen hinein' [Romantic poetry is capable of the highest and most various development; not just outwards, from within, but inwards, from without].

Novalis compares A. W. Schlegel's Shakespeare with Goethe's *Wilhelm Meisters Lehrjahre*; that is, he believes that Schlegel has done for translation what Goethe did for the novel. And Novalis saw *Wilhelm Meister* to have introduced to the genre precisely the element of self-reflexivity which made it the prototype of Romantic writing: through its narrative structure,[62] and through its irony, it initiated that movement of self-transcendence which the Romantics thought essential to 'die romantische Poesie'. For Novalis, Schlegel's translation has done the same to Shakespeare, taken him up and transmuted him into a continuum, extended his reach, introduced that self-reflexivity which unsettles the finished work (and thus the 'classical' work) and exposes it. Translation is thus understood as virtually cognate with the nature of poetry as the Romantics propound it; it is an instance of 'Bildung [...] von außen hinein' [development inwards, from without] (Fr. 116), a kind of abstract of the Romantic mode. But it has a special relevance of its own: what Friedrich Schlegel seems to suggest is that the classical genres should be romanticized to produce 'eine grenzenlos wachsende Klassizität' [a limitlessly growing classicism] (Fr. 116), a kind of oxymoron which is a radical unanchoring of classicism. Translation can function similarly, but with classical *works*: it can transform them into a combination of classical and Romantic modes where the classical is subsumed in the Romantic, and thus renewed: 'Jede Uebersetzung ist *Verpflanzung* oder *Verwandlung* oder beides [...] Jede wahre Ueb[ersetzung] muß eine Verjüngung sein' [Every translation is a *replanting* or a *transformation* or both. Every true translation must be a rejuvenation].[63]

This is why Novalis can claim the German Shakespeare is better than the English—it is better because it is a translation, though this must be understood in its context of the Romantics' awareness that a new kind of precise, 'poetic' translation has evolved.[64] The other categorical statements Novalis makes in the letter fall into place, and

---

[62] Cf. a note of F. Schlegel's: 'Die *Bestimmung* des Menschen vielleicht nur als Uebersetzung zu betrachten' (*KA*, xviii 459).

[63] F. Schlegel, *KA*, xviii 204.   [64] Berman, *L'Epreuve de l'étranger*, 170.

they are fundamental to the Romantic way of thinking: translation is poetry ('Übersetzen ist so gut dichten...') and poetry is translation ('Am Ende ist alle Poësie Übersetzung'). It becomes clear why translation is taken so seriously and why the Romantics (A. W. Schlegel, Tieck, Schleiermacher) achieved so much in that quarter. In another definition, Friedrich Schlegel says that a work should be 'zugleich Poesie und Poesie der Poesie' [at once poetry and poetry of poetry], that is it should be 'critical' in a Kantian sense, examining its own premisses.[65] A translation by its nature keeps to that because it is at once a work itself ('Poesie') and a manifestation of a work ('Poesie der Poesie') and, intrinsically, constitutes a review of the original. The Romantics were remarkably alive to the exact complexion of translation, its particular power. It was in a sense their peculiar domain: as a concrete practice, translation could provide a model for that most abstract of Romantic enterprises, the transformation, the 'romanticization', of the world.[66]

Given the importance of translation, it is surprising that it is mentioned seldom and that neither Novalis nor the Schlegels wrote anything extensive on the subject. This is partly because the person best equipped to do this, A. W. Schlegel, devoted his energies to practice, and though he intended some form of treatise,[67] he later became too aware of the insufficiency of theory when confronted with the specifics of the actual text: 'Alles, selbst der Begriff der Treue, bestimmt sich nach der Natur des Werkes, womit man es zu thun hat, und nach dem Verhältniß der beiden Sprachen' [Everything, even the idea of fidelity, gains definition from the nature of the work in hand, and from the relationship between the two languages].[68] He seemed to know that his practice was superior to theory. But the marginalization is also due to much of the reflection on translation's being absorbed by comment on the nature and function of criticism.[69]

---

[65]   KA, ii 204 (*Athenaeum* Fr. 238).
[66]   'Die Welt muß romantisirt werden. So findet man den urspr[ünglichen] Sinn wieder. Romantisiren ist nichts, als eine qualit[ative] Potenzirung' (Novalis, ii 545).
[67]   *Sämmtliche Werke*, iv 126–7.
[68]   'Über die Bhagavad-Gita', in Störig, 97–100 (99).
[69]   Probably the first to realize this was Walter Benjamin (iv 15): 'Diese [die Romantiker] haben vor andern Einsicht in das Leben der Werke besessen, von welchem die Übersetzung eine höchste Bezeugung ist. Freilich haben sie diese als solche kaum erkannt, vielmehr ihre ganze Aufmerksamkeit der Kritik zugewendet, die ebenfalls ein wenn auch geringeres Moment im Fortleben der Werke darstellt.'

The two are often mentioned in the same breath by Friedrich Schlegel.[70] He tended to see in both of them the ideal of the perfect description of a work.[71] Criticism, as a vital part of the Romantics' achievement, was seen as a creative act, contributing to the life of a work and heightening it as translation could. Friedrich Schlegel went so far as to call his review of *Wilhelm Meister* an 'Übermeister' [a Supermeister].[72] This explains Novalis's otherwise odd remark in his letter to A. W. Schlegel that the review of his Shakespeare is 'wahrhaftig keine Poësie' [hardly poetry]. It should have been a redoubling of the creative extension already realized by Schlegel's translation.

Schlegel's work at Shakespeare went on until 1810, during which period he found the time to translate from Italian, Portuguese and Spanish as well. Then later he started translating Sanskrit into Latin. In sharp contrast to the other early Romantics he produced important works which were not overt fragments. But apart from the obvious sense in which translation is always fragmentary, his achievement necessarily falls short of completeness once set in the context of his desire to do 'alles im Deutschen Tunliche' [everything that can be done in German],[73] to translate *everything* 'in seiner Form und Eigenthümlichkeit' [in its form and peculiarity].[74] He confesses to being a translator by compulsion:

leider kann ich meines Nächsten Poesie nicht ansehen, ohne ihrer zu begehren in meinem Herzen, und bin also in einem beständigen poetischen Ehebruche begriffen.[75]

[unfortunately I cannot look at my neighbour's poetry without coveting it in my heart, and am thus involved in constant poetic adultery.]

Nevertheless Schlegel is selective as to whom he commits adultery with: he translated hardly any contemporary works and very few from antiquity, preferring medieval and Renaissance writers, writers who in fact could be described as Romantic, close to his own frame of

---

[70]   *KA*, ii 303 for example.

[71]   Cf. too Novalis, speaking of 'mythische Übersetzungen': 'Noch existirt wie ich glaube, kein ganzes Muster derselben. Im Geist mancher Kritiken und Beschreibungen von Kunstwerken trifft man aber helle Spuren davon' (Novalis, ii 439).

[72]   Huyssen, 110.

[73]   August Wilhelm Schlegel, *Kritische Schriften und Briefe*, ed. Edgar Lohner, 7 vols. (Stuttgart, 1962–74), i 117.

[74]   *Sämmtliche Werke*, iv 127.   [75]   *Sämmtliche Werke*, iv 127.

mind, such as Petrarch.[76] There is nothing wrong with this, but it is an aspect of Romanticism's self-reflexivity which indicates its limits; it is significant that the only time Schlegel really confronted something of a quite foreign nature, the *Bhagavad Gita*, he translated it into Latin, thus avoiding a true encounter. There is a similar evasion, or discrepancy, in his method of translating: most of his pronouncements proclaim the desire to translate warts and all—he talks of the *aerugo nobilis* found on coins which is a guarantor of their value: it should be preserved, rather than trying to turn out 'den nunmehr blanken Schaupfennig' [a shiny display coin][77]—and he is always at pains to stress the importance of form, reproducing very complex metrical schemes. But he is far less willing than Voss to test and alter German grammar and usage by exposing them to the foreign, and his Shakespeare translation occasionally skates over some of the earthier aspects of the plays and heightens or 'poeticizes' the tone. The fact that the first play he tackled was *Romeo and Juliet* gives an indication of the general tendency. It was of course in line with the Romantic principle of 'Erweiterung' [expansion],[78] of a piece with the arc from 'Natursprache' [language of nature] to 'Kunstsprache' [language of art] that art was to describe. But that Schlegel did translate with a special bias meant he came closer to the 'French', assimilative tradition he constantly criticized than did Voss (though his brother Friedrich noted that Voss made of Homer a 'Vosside'[79]) or Hölderlin. His emphasis on form meant above all metrical form, and the words of his originals, their exact connotations, hold for him less fascination than for Voss. Hölderlin's translation of Sophocles is in some respects the inverse of Schlegel's technique: early on he gave up trying to follow the Greek metres, but tracked every word in its exact resonance.

Despite the consonance between Schlegel's translations and the Romantic undertaking as a whole, there is a gap between the speculative conceiving of translation as an all-embracing category and A. W. Schlegel's, the practitioner's, consciousness that larger derivations from the business of literary translation would almost inevitably lose their particularity and become meaningless. For a study like this one, which intends to examine the significance of translation

---

[76] Cf. Berman, *L'Epreuve de l'étranger*, 218: 'La traduction romantique ne traduit que des oeuvres romantiques, que le 'même'. L'expérience de l'étranger comme étranger lui est étrangère.'

[77] *Kritische Schriften*, i 86.   [78] Novalis, iv 237.   [79] *KA*, ii 161.

beyond the confines of the literary act, there is much to be learnt from the failure of the German Romantics to bridge this gap. Even Schleiermacher's lecture, which, though much later, arises from his Plato translation and contact with Friedrich Schlegel, is more of a systematic, philosophical investigation of literary translation itself than a development beyond that, though he clearly states that all communication is translation (Störig, p. 39). There is no doubt that a metaphorical understanding of translation is valid and tallies with something in experience, but if it is not limited it becomes so vague as to ignore all the differences which are as important to definition as similarities. Literary translation itself must always provide the measure whereby translation in a larger sense can retain meaningful proportions, translation as a concept must have for its ground the precise anatomy of a specific practice. This is why useful studies of the relation between translation and poetry, for example, probably have to be restricted to one writer. It is because the Romantics did not carry out this anatomy of their own practice that their speculations lose definition, though as provocations and suggestions they are very rich, and they have the merit of having taken these reflections to their extreme. This extreme is most apparent in Novalis's 68th 'Blüthenstaub' fragment, which, oddly, is the only classification of literary translations to be found among the Romantics apart from Schleiermacher's:

Eine Übersetzung ist entweder grammatisch, oder verändernd, oder mythisch. Mythische Übersetzungen sind Übersetzungen im höchsten Styl. Sie stellen den reinen, vollendeten Karakter des individuellen Kunstwerks dar. Sie geben uns nicht das wirkliche Kunstwerk, sondern das Ideal desselben. Noch existirt wie ich glaube kein ganzes Muster derselben. Im Geist mancher Kritiken und Beschreibungen von Kunstwerken trifft man aber helle Spuren davon. Es gehört ein Kopf dazu, in dem sich poetischer Geist und philosophischer Geist in ihrer ganzen Fülle durchdrungen haben. Die griechische Mythologie ist zum Theil eine solche Übersetzung einer Nazionalreligion. Auch die moderne Madonna ist ein solcher Mythus.
Grammatische Übersetzungen sind die Übersetzungen im gewöhnlichen Sinn. Sie erfordern sehr viel Gelehrsamkeit, aber nur diskursive Fähigkeiten. Zu den verändernden Übersetzungen gehört, wenn sie ächt seyn sollen, der höchste poetische Geist. Sie fallen leicht ins Travestiren, wie Bürgers Homer in Jamben, Popens Homer, die Französischen Übersetzungen insgesamt. Der wahre Übersetzer dieser Art muß in der That der Künstler selbst seyn, und die Idee des Ganzen beliebig so oder so geben können. Er muß der Dichter des Dichters seyn und ihn also nach seiner und des Dichters eigner Idee

zugleich reden lassen können. In einem ähnlichen Verhältnisse steht der Genius der Menschheit mit jedem einzelnen Menschen.
Nicht blos Bücher, alles kann auf diese drey Arten übersetzt werden.[80]

[A translation is either grammatical, or modifying, or mythical. Mythical translations are translations in the highest style. They present the pure, complete character of the individual work of art. They do not give us the real work of art, but the ideal of it. As yet there is I think no full example of this type. But in the spirit of many pieces of criticism and descriptions of works of art one comes across clear traces of it. For such a translation a mind is required in which poetic spirit and philosophical spirit have penetrated each other in all their fullness. Greek mythology is in part such a translation of a national religion. The modern madonna is also a myth of this kind.
Grammatical translations are translations in the ordinary sense. They demand a great deal of learning, but only discursive qualities.
For modifying translations, if they are to be genuine, the highest poetic spirit is required. They easily fall into travesty, like Bürger's Homer in blank verse, Pope's Homer, or all French translations. The true translator of this sort must indeed be an artist himself, and be able to render the idea of the whole in whatever way he wishes. He must be the poet's poet and thus be able to make him speak according to his lights and the poet's own at the same time. The genius of mankind stands in a similar relationship to every individual person. Not only books, everything can be translated in these three ways.]

As with Goethe, this schema is tripartite, and though the dividing lines are not drawn in the same places, there is a similar progression (Goethe: 'schlicht-prosaisch'—'parodistisch'—'identisch';[81] Novalis: 'grammatisch'—'verändernd'—'mythisch') in each case. If we look at the stages in the order shown above, the first terms ('plain prose' and 'grammatical') do correspond. The second set overlap: Novalis's category includes Goethe's (this is clear in the way they both refer to French translations), but also seems to encompass translation in A. W. Schlegel's mode, which Goethe obliquely includes in his last category along with Voss.[82] Novalis's second category is parallel to Friedrich Schlegel's *Athenaeum* Fragment 393:

Um aus den Alten ins Moderne vollkommen übersetzen zu können, müßte der Übersetzer desselben so mächtig sein, daß er allenfalls alles Moderne machen könnte; zugleich aber das Antike so verstehn, daß ers nicht bloß nachmachen, sondern allenfalls wiederschaffen könnte.[83]

---

[80] Novalis, ii 439/41.   [81] Goethe, ii 255–6.   [82] Goethe, ii 256.
[83] KA, ii 239. See also Novalis's own fragment from the *Athenaeum* (No. 287): 'Nur dann zeig ich, daß ich einen Schriftsteller verstanden habe, wenn ich in seinem

[In order to be able to translate perfectly from the ancients into the modern idiom, the translator should master the latter well enough to do anything modern if need be; but at the same time understand antiquity well enough to be able to recreate it, and not just copy it.]

The third pair are alike in that they represent a *non plus ultra*, but the similarities end there. Where Goethe can list examples of his last stage, Novalis tells us he doesn't think any 'mythical translations' yet exist.[84] He seems to envisage the possibility of literary translation of this order ('Es gehört ein Kopf dazu, in dem sich poetischer Geist und philosophischer Geist in ihrer ganzen Fülle durchdrungen haben'— perhaps a last-ditch attempt to relate his term to something concrete), but he is really talking about an ideal, making of translation myth itself, which can elicit an abstract or essence, like the 'divinatorische Kritik' [divinatory criticism] Schlegel speaks of in Athenaeum Fragment 116, which also aims at the 'Ideal'. It is in the end something not purely literary, it becomes identified with the ideal it is meant to disclose, located itself in an ideal future and only apparent in rare traces, like Paradise:

Das Paradies ist gleichsam üb[er] d[ie] ganze Erde *verstreut* und daher so unkenntlich etc. geworden—Seine zerstreuten Züge sollen vereinigt—sein Skelett soll ausgefüllt werden. Regeneration des Paradieses.[85]

[Paradise is as it were *strewn* over the whole earth and for that reason has become so hard to see etc.—Its scattered lineaments should be reassembled— its skeleton fleshed out. Regeneration of paradise.]

In its most utopian incarnation, translation can partake of the movement towards the unreachable goal of the Romantic project: the realization of a second Golden Age through the unification of what is now dispersed.[86] In this light, translation appears as an activity peculiarly fit for our time, which for Hölderlin too is in essence a time of transition. Even A. W. Schlegel's painful awareness that the best translation can only be an 'Annäherung in unbestimmbaren Graden' [a gradual, indeterminate approximation] is of a piece with this train of thought, since the proper activity of the moment must always fall short of the ideal.[87]

Geiste handeln kann, wenn ich ihn, ohne seine Individualitaet zu schmälern, übersetzen, und mannichfach verändern kann' (Novalis, ii 424).

[84] Cf. 'Die Welt muß romantisirt werden. [...] Diese Operation ist noch ganz unbekannt' (Novalis, ii 545).

[85] Novalis, iii 447.   [86] Cf. Huyssen, 168–71.   [87] *Kritische Schriften*, iii 18.

Novalis ends his fragment by saying that 'Nicht blos Bücher, alles kann auf diese drey Arten übersezt werden.' Similar all-encompassing statements can be found in Friedrich ('Wie es eine Geographie und Char[akteristik] d[es] Universums giebt, so muß es auch eine *Uebersetzung* d[es] Universums geben' [Just as there exists a geography and description of the universe, so there must also be a *translation* of the universe]) and in A. W. Schlegel ('wenn jemand sagt, man solle gar nicht übersetzen, so setzt man ihm entgegen: der menschliche Geist könne eigentlich nichts als übersetzen, alle seine Tätigkeit bestehe darin' [if anyone says one should not translate at all the correct reply runs: really, the human mind can do nothing but translate, its whole activity consists of translation]).[88] They represent at once the strengths and the final limits of Romantic and of all thinking on translation. It is fair to say that such thinking arrived at its acme with the German Romantics; it could be enriched and more and more subtly and precisely defined (it has been), but it could not go further in absolute terms.

Schleiermacher and Humboldt

One of the most important amplifications, in a sense the essay on translation the Romantics never wrote, is Friedrich Schleiermacher's masterly 'Ueber die verschiedenen Methoden des Uebersezens' of 1813. George Steiner sees it as initiating a new stage in writing on translation, 'one of theory and hermeneutic inquiry'.[89] With Schleiermacher, translation is taken in the framework of a theory of understanding, of epistemology. Rigorously, he deduces a philosophically viable mode of translation based on the premiss that all communication is engaged in it, and deriving out of his awareness of the nature of language, an awareness he shares with Wilhelm von Humboldt:

Alle Sprachformen sind Symbole, nicht die Dinge selbst, nicht verabredete Zeichen, sondern Laute, welche mit den Dingen und Begriffen, die sie darstellen, durch den Geist, in dem sie entstanden sind, und immerfort entstehen, sich in wirklichem, wenn man es so nennen will, mystischem Zusammenhange befinden, welche die Gegenstände der Wirklichkeit gleichsam aufgelöst in Ideen enthalten, und nun auf eine Weise, der keine

---

[88]   *KA*, xviii 235 and *Kritische Schriften*, iv 35.
[89]   George Steiner, *After Babel* (Oxford, 1975), 237.

Gränze gedacht werden kann, verändern, bestimmen, trennen und verbinden können.[90]

[All linguistic forms are symbols, not the things themselves, not conventional signs, but sounds which by virtue of the spirit in which they have evolved and continue to evolve have a real, or if you like, mystical connexion with the things and concepts they represent; and which contain the objects of reality, as it were dissolved into ideas, and can change, determine, separate and join them in a manner which has no imaginable limits.]

In this understanding there can be no separation of thought and expression, they combine symbolically: words are no longer instruments, as they were for Leibniz, but the very stuff of our experience.

Any theory of translation must, says Schleiermacher, take this into account. The result is that he shows the 'Vossian' method, which transmits the foreignness of the original text, to be the only true one, because the counterpart, essentially what Goethe calls the 'parodistic' method as practised by Wieland, rests on the flawed principle that the translation should be as the author would have written it had he spoken the language of the translator. Schleiermacher sees that he would then have written, indeed been, something quite different:

Ja was will man einwenden, wenn ein Uebersezer dem Leser sagt, Hier bringe ich dir das Buch, wie der Mann es würde geschrieben haben, wenn er es deutsch geschrieben hätte; und der Leser ihm antwortet, Ich bin dir eben so verbunden, als ob du mir des Mannes Bild gebracht hättest, wie er aussehen würde, wenn seine Mutter ihn mit einem andern Vater erzeugt hätte? Denn wenn von Werken, die in einem höheren Sinne der Wissenschaft und Kunst angehören, der eigenthümliche Geist des Verfassers die Mutter ist: so ist seine vaterländische Sprache der Vater dazu. (Störig, p. 65)

[How can one not applaud if to a translator who tells his reader: 'Here is the book as the author would have written it had he written it in German' the reader replies: 'I am as grateful to you as if you had brought me a portrait of how he would have looked if his mother had had him with a different father'? For if the mother of works of art and learning in the higher sense is the particularity of the author's mind, then his mother-tongue is the father.]

At bottom the true method is one that admits and communicates all the differences between author and translator to the reader.[91] This is

[90] Humboldt, *Gesammelte Schriften*, viii 131.
[91] In general, Schleiermacher's essay marks a shift away from the earlier Romantic

the only way real communication can take place, through a kind of friction where the language shows the effects of its experience, leading to 'eine Haltung der Sprache, die nicht nur nicht alltäglich ist, sondern die auch ahnden läßt, daß sie nicht ganz frei gewachsen, vielmehr zu einer fremden Aehnlichkeit hinübergebogen sei' [an attitude of language which is not only not everyday but leads one to suspect that it has not been allowed full freedom of growth, that it has been compelled to style itself to something foreign to it (Störig, p. 55)]. Schleiermacher is conscious of the dangers in this, and of the self-effacement it entails—'der wunderbarste Stand der Erniedrigung' [a most curious state of abasement (Störig, p. 55)]—but he insists that the risks must be run and all tact and art employed to observe 'die feinste Linie' [a very fine line] so that 'das heimische Wohlbefinden der Sprache' [the at-homeness of language] is not troubled (Störig, p. 56). Humboldt agrees that the opposed method is unviable, and that 'eine gewisse Farbe der Fremdheit' [a certain foreign colour] should be conveyed, but by making a distinction between 'die Fremdheit' [foreignness] and 'das Fremde' [the foreign] he feels certain where the line should be drawn:

Solange nicht die Fremdheit, sondern das Fremde gefühlt wird, hat die Uebersetzung ihre höchsten Zwecke erreicht; wo aber die Fremdheit an sich erscheint, und vielleicht gar das Fremde verdunkelt, da verräth der Uebersetzer, dass er seinem Original nicht gewachsen ist.[92]

[So long as the foreign, and not foreignness, is felt in a translation it has attained its highest goal. But if foreignness itself appears, perhaps even obscuring the foreign, the translator has revealed that he is not up to his original.]

Though the terms are vague, this ordinance is potentially very constrictive because the only way of distinguishing between 'Fremdes' and 'Fremdheit' is through taste, which is also how the French had come to translate in such a way that, according to Schleiermacher, they could not claim to have translated anything from the languages of antiquity at all (Störig, p. 69). Moreover, it disables that faculty for productive development via encounter with the foreign which Schleiermacher affirms once again, and most clearly and expressly, to be the peculiar property of the Germans:

---

focus on the *work* towards concern for the *reader*. The translator is seen as a mediator.
[92] Humboldt, *Gesammelte Schriften*, viii 132.

Eine innere Nothwendigkeit, in der sich ein eigenthümlicher Beruf unseres Volkes deutlich genug ausspricht, hat uns auf das Uebersezen in Masse getrieben; wir können nicht zurükk und müssen durch. Wie vielleicht erst durch vielfältiges Hineinverpflanzen fremder Gewächse unser Boden selbst reicher und fruchtbarer geworden ist, und unser Klima anmuthiger und milder: so fühlen wir auch, daß unsere Sprache, weil wir sie der nordischen Trägheit wegen weniger selbst bewegen, nur durch die vielseitigste Berührung mit dem fremden recht frisch gedeihen und ihre eigne Kraft vollkommen entwikkeln kann. Und damit scheint zusammenzutreffen, daß wegen seiner Achtung für das fremde und seiner vermittelnden Natur unser Volk bestimmt sein mag, alle Schäze fremder Wissenschaft und Kunst mit seinen eignen zugleich in seiner Sprache gleichsam zu einem großen geschichtlichen Ganzen zu vereinigen, das im Mittelpunkt und Herzen von Europa verwahrt werde, damit nun durch Hülfe unserer Sprache, was die verschiedensten Zeiten schönes gebracht haben, jeder so rein und vollkommen genießen könne, als es dem Fremdling nur möglich ist. Dies scheint in der That der wahre geschichtliche Zwekk des Uebersezens im großen, wie es bei uns nun einheimisch ist. (Störig, p. 69)

[An inner necessity, in which a calling peculiar to our people can unquestionably be discerned, has drawn us *en masse* to translation; we cannot turn back and must go on. Perhaps our native soil has only become richer and more fertile, our climate more mild and pleasant, after intensive and varied transplantation of foreign plants. In the same way we may feel that our language, since in our northern sluggishness we do not exercise it much ourselves, can only flourish properly and develop its own full strength through the broadest possible contact with the foreign. And this seems to correspond to the fact that on account of our mediatory nature and the place we accord the foreign we Germans are perhaps destined to combine in our language all the treasures of foreign learning and art with our own to form a great historical whole, which will be preserved at the very heart of Europe. Thus, through the medium of our language, everyone will be able to enjoy the fine products of many different ages as purely and completely as it is possible for a foreigner to do. Indeed, this seems to be the true historical goal of mass translation as the practice has now become established in Germany.]

This belief that German was becoming a *lingua franca* of translation was shared by Goethe in his old age, it was something he thought he saw happening before his eyes.[93]

---

[93] See e.g. Goethe, xii 353.

Practice: The Example of Pindar

Certainly there were quantities of translation going on throughout the period. 'Unsere Übersetzer arbeiten noch frisch von der Faust weg. Was haben sie nicht schon alles übersetzt, und was werden sie nicht noch übersetzen' [Our translators show no signs of letting up. They've translated all sorts of things already, and there are no limits to what they'll go on to do], wrote Lessing in 1759.[94] Most was in prose. There were many versions of the English and French novelists, particularly Defoe and Richardson; important translations of Montaigne and Sterne by J. J. C. Bode (who invented the word 'empfindsam' for the German language, from Sterne's 'sentimental'); and many attempts at Shakespeare before A. W. Schlegel's. Ossian was also widely translated, by, among others, a friend of Hölderlin's, Franz Wilhelm Jung, who sent his version to Hölderlin to look through.[95] Translation seemed to become a pastime which any young man or woman with an interest in literature would indulge in at some point or other. The most representative of Goethe's characters—Werther, Wilhelm Meister and Faust—all translate (Ossian, *Hamlet* and John's Gospel respectively), and it is particularly interesting that Werther, who incorporates and crystallizes so many habits of mind and fashions of his time, should do so and that a translation should provoke the climax of the novel.

Nearly all the journals dealt with translation and the problems of translation. Lessing's remarks in the *Briefe, die neueste Literatur betreffend* expose the low quality of much of what was churned out, though he also singles out one Meinhard as being such a good translator (from the Italian) as to deserve the status of an 'Original'.[96] He devotes special attention to the problem of translating Pindar, the ultimate test, and gives examples by 'einen jungen kühnen Geist' [a bold young mind] from Switzerland, Johann Jakob Steinbrüchel.[97] What now follows are some specimens of Pindar translations, including Hölderlin's, from the second half of the eighteenth century. They will serve to concentrate more on the actual practice of translation, and to give an idea of the context round Hölderlin's versions, of what made them exceptions.

[94] Gotthold Ephraim Lessing, *Werke*, ed. H. G. Göpfert, 8 vols. (Munich, 1970–9), v 32.
[95] See vi/338 and vii, 2/59–60, 118–20.
[96] Lessing, v 324. [97] Lessing, v 94.

Steinbrüchel's versions are in prose, which Lessing finds entirely natural, especially as he perceives German to be capable of an endlessly 'poetic' prose which does not need metre to secure its effects and has the advantage of permitting greater fidelity in translation.[98] Lessing also approves of the fact that Steinbrüchel does not translate literally (though he does stay close), quoting Abraham Cowley: 'If a man should undertake to translate *Pindar* word for word, it would be thought that *one Mad-man* had translated another'.[99] Steinbrüchel's translations of Pindar started coming out in 1759. They were followed by several prose versions, and in 1777 Voss initiated a series of attempts to do him into verse with his rendition of P1 in the style of Klopstock. But in 1803 Herder was still calling for 'eine echte rhythmische Übersetzung Pindars' [a genuine rhythmical translation of Pindar], by which he means one in verse, 'denn bei einem musikalischen Dichter erreicht die beste poetische Prose den Accent und Gang seines Gesanges nicht' [for even the best poetic prose cannot attain the lift and movement of truly musical poetry].[100] By then Wilhelm von Humboldt had made several attempts, including strictly metrical ones, and A. W. Schlegel and others had tried their hand. Lessing quotes in full Steinbrüchel's versions of O1, O4 and O11. Of these Hölderlin translated only O11.[101] Here is the first strophe of that ode in Steinbrüchel's prose:

Nach Winden schmachtet der Schiffer oft, und der Landmann nach Regen, den himmelträufelnden Söhnen der Wolken.—Aber wem Heldenarbeit gelang, dem sind honigtriefende Hymnen Quellen des Nachruhms, und ein Pfand der Unsterblichkeit erhabener Taten.[102]

[The sailor often yearns for winds, and the husbandman for rains, the cloud-sons that trickle from the sky.—But for him who has achieved the work of heroes hymns running with honey are sources of fame after death, and a pledge of the immortality of sublime deeds.]

And here is a version by Friedrich Gedike, whose edition of Pindar's *Olympische Siegshymnen* translated Hölderlin owned:

[98] Lessing, v 95.

[99] Abraham Cowley, 'Preface' to *Pindarique Odes*, in: *Poems* (London, 1656).

[100] Quoted in Norbert von Hellingrath, *Pindarübertragungen von Hölderlin: Prolegomena zu einer Erstausgabe* (Jena, 1911), 14.

[101] A translation of the first ten lines of O1 interrupts the essay 'Über die verschiednen Arten, zu dichten'. See v/40.

[102] As quoted in Lessing, v 100.

Nöthig ist oft dem Menschen das Wehen des Windes; nöthig oft wieder das Tröpfeln der Wolkentochter, der Waßer des Himmels. Aber wenn jemand herrliche Thaten verrichtet, dem wird der Hymnen Honigmund Quelle des Nachruhms und seiner erhabenen Tugenden sicheres Unterpfand.[103]

[Man often needs the blowing of the wind; and again he often needs the dripping of the cloud-daughters, the waters of the sky. But if someone carries out glorious deeds the honeyed lips of hymns become the source of fame after death and a safe earnest of sublime virtues.]

And by Hölderlin:

> Es sind den Menschen Winde das gröste
> Bedürfniß, auch sind es himmlische Wasser
> Reegnende, die Kinder der Wolke.
> Wenn aber mit Arbeit einer wohlverfährt, sind süßgestimmte Hymnen
> Des Nachruhms Anfang; es gehet
> Auch treuer Eidschwur großen Tugenden auf.
>
>   (O11 1–6)

[For human beings winds are the greatest
Need, and also waters from the sky,
Rains, the children of the clouds.
If though a man proceeds well in his work, sweet-voiced hymns
Are the beginning of fame after death; and
A loyal oath is sworn of great virtues.]

Hölderlin's version is very closely patterned on the Greek, so closely, and in this case accurately, that, set alongside, Steinbrüchel's embellishment and rationalizing of the original are immediately visible, and even Gedike's more subdued translation seems ornate. Steinbrüchel explains—why wind and rain are needed, and of what consists the pledge of hymns ('immortality'). But Pindar's Greek itself is gnomic and ungiving, the argument has to be worked out or seized instinctively. As Hellingrath suggests, Hölderlin has helped us 'einzusehen, wie dunkel die klassischen Texte sind' [to see how obscure the classical texts are][104] (Cowley called Pindar 'unnavigable'); but also to realize how Pindar functions as poetry. Steinbrüchel adorns—a need becomes yearning ('schmachtet'), work well done 'Heldenarbeit', and μελιγάρυες ('sweet-voiced') 'honigtriefende' (Gedike also elaborates at these points). They are fairly small shifts in

---

[103] *Pindars Olympische Siegshymnen, verdeutscht von Friedrich Gedike* (Berlin, 1777), 119.   [104] Hellingrath, *Pindarübertragungen von Hölderlin*, 6.

themselves, but they amount to a constant burdening of the tone. Against this, Hölderlin respects the tone and also the general rhythm of Pindar's lines, especially in the first three. Only 'Eidschwur', the first dictionary meaning of ὅρκιον, is out of place; Steinbrüchel's 'Pfand' fits the context better. But this kind of comparison has little sense, since Hölderlin was not primarily concerned with literal meaning. Here I want to do little more than give examples of actual translations next to Hölderlin's, as the best way of commenting on them. This becomes more illuminating when the examples are in verse.[105]

Voss published his translation of P1 in a magazine in 1777. It was the first into verse, and meant as a sample of more to come. Voss does not preserve the division into strophes, antistrophes and epodes. This is his first stanza:

> Goldne Harfe Apollons,
> Der violenlockigen Musen Lenkerin ihm!
> Welcher der Tanz, der Freudenfürst,
> Und der mitertönende Chor gehorcht,
> Wann du den Reigengesängen
> Mit Herrscherstimme voranhallst:
> Selbst den zuckenden Stral
> Des ewigen Feuers löschest du;
> Und auf dem Stabe Zeus schläft der Adler,
> Die gewaltigen Schwingen beyde herabgebreitet,
> Der Vögel König![106]

> [Golden harp of Apollo,
> His guide belonging to the violet-curled Muses.
> Which the dance, the prince of joy,
> And the consonant choir obeys
> When you introduce the round
> Of songs with your sovereign voice:
> Even the flickering flash

---

[105] I quote these prose versions because Hölderlin possessed Gedike's book, and Steinbrüchel's singling out in the *Literaturbriefe* gave him unusual currency. For a comparison of Hölderlin's Sophocles translations with contemporary and later versions see Wolfgang Schadewaldt, 'Hölderlins Übersetzung des Sophokles', in: *Hellas und Hesperien*, 2 vols. (Zürich, 1970), ii 275–332 (316–22).

[106] Johann Heinrich Voss, 'Pindaros erster püthischer Chor; nebst einem Briefe an Herrn Hofrath Heyne', *Deutsches Museum*, 1 (1777), 78–93 (78).

Of eternal fire you put out;
And on Zeus's staff the eagle sleeps
Both mighty wings spread downwards,
The king of the birds!]

Against Voss, Humboldt, after careful study of Pindar's metres, attempted a metrical version:

1. Strophe

Goldne Leier, Phoebos und der
Musen mit wallenden Locken
ewig süss begleitender Schmuck.
Du gebietst dem Tanz, dem Beginner des Freudenfests,
Deinem Wink gehorcht der Sänger, wenn
Du des reigenführenden Liedes Erstlings-
Töne Deinen bebenden Saiten entlockst.
Dann erlischt des Blitzes ewig rastlose,
drohende Flamme, und es
schlummert, eingewiegt auf dem Scepter, Kronions
Adler, und senkt zu beiden Seiten nieder den
schnellen Fittig,

1. Antistrophe

des Geflügels Herrscher.[107]

[1st strophe

Golden lyre, Phoebus' and the
Muses' with full-flowing curls
always sweetly present adornment.
You direct the dance, the beginner of festive joy,
the singer obeys your beckoning,
when you coax the initial notes of the song
that leads the round from out of your trembling strings.
Then the always tireless and threatening flame
of lightning goes out, and lulled
to sleep on the sceptre, Kronion's eagle slumbers
there and lets its rapid pinions hang downwards
on either side,

1st antistrophe

the ruler of the birds.]

---

[107] Humboldt, *Gesammelte Schriften*, viii 67; written 1794, not published until 1841.

A. W. Schlegel's version is also metrical:

Strophe

Goldnes Kleinod, Laut'! Apollons
Gleichwie der Musen, viol-
farbumlockt, mitwaltendes Gut!
Dich vernimmt, anhebend die Feier, der Tritt; gern lauscht
Gleichfalls wer Gesang übt, deinem Wink,
Chorführender Weisen zuerst Vorspiele noch,
Wann du die anstimmest im Wirbelgetön.
Ja, dir lischt auch, ew'ger Glut voll, aus der viel-
zackige Donner, es schläft
Ein auf Zeus Goldscepter der Adler, gesenkt
Rasch eilender Fittige Paar
Rechts und links hin,

Gegenstrophe

Er, des Luftvolks Oberherr.[108]

[Strophe

Golden treasure, lute! Apollo's
And the Muses' also, curled
Round with violet, co-regnant thing!
You the dance-step, starting the celebration, hears;
Whoever sings is gladly beckoned
By you, the prelude to the tunes that lead the choir,
When you start playing them in a whirl of sound.
And you make the many-pronged thunder go out,
Glowing with eternal heat,
The eagle goes to sleep on Zeus' gold sceptre
Both hurrying pinions hanging down
To left and right,

Antistrophe

The airy race's sovereign.]

These two versions adopt exactly or very closely the syllable-count of
Pindar's poem, and then retain their equivalents throughout; that is,
all strophes and antistrophes follow the same metrical scheme, and all
epodes another scheme, as Hölderlin set out to do in his poem 'Wie
wenn am Feiertage...'. That accounts for fillers such as Humboldt's
'ewig süss' (l. 3) or Schlegel's 'Kleinod' (l. 1) which have no

---

[108] Schlegel, *Sämmtliche Werke*, iii 131.

counterpart in the Greek. In contrast Hölderlin's translation seems much sparser:

> Goldne Leier Apollons
> Und der dunkelgelokten
> Beistimmendes der Musen Eigentum;
> Welche höret der Tanz, der Heiterkeit Anfang,
> Es gehorchen aber die Sänger den Zeichen,
> Des reigenführenden, wenn des Eingangs
> Zögerungen machest erschüttert,
> Und den scharfen Bliz auslöschest
> Des unaufhörlichen Feuers. Es schläft aber
> Über dem Zepter Jupiters der Adler, den schnellen
> Flügel auf beiden Seiten niedersenkend,
>
> Der Herr der Vögel.
>   (P1 1–12)

> [Golden lyre of Apollo
> And of the dark-curled Muses,
> Their property in agreement;
> Which the dance hears, the beginning of gaiety,
> But the singers obey the sign,
> When of the opening that leads the round
> You set the hesitations shaking,
> And extinguish the sharp lightning
> Of incessant fire. The eagle sleeps
> Though over the sceptre of Jupiter, letting
> On both sides the rapid wing hang down,
>
> The lord of the birds.]

Voss and Hölderlin simply use fewer words. But otherwise there is a great deal of homogeneity between the four translations: certainly they are all that—close translations rather than imitations. Though Hölderlin follows Pindar's word-order exactly, his German does not diverge from normal usage significantly more than the others', except perhaps in lines 3 and 6. It is true there are passages far more contorted than this one, but still it can be seen that there is a climate of translation favourable to Hölderlin, even if he grows into something strange and overreaching.[109] Probably none of the versions would have turned out thus without the revolution in poetic diction

---

[109] Cf. Hellingrath, *Pindarübertragungen von Hölderlin*, 20–1.

performed by Klopstock. In general it can be said that as a translator Hölderlin fits into a contemporary context (dominated by Voss) but at the same time far exceeds it.

This background is, I think, helpful for understanding Hölderlin's position when he comes to translate himself. His few comments on translation, and his practice too, may be seen to derive from, and are illumined by, the tendencies in translation current during the time he was writing. It is easier to make out that his translations from the Greek are indebted to Voss and to that side of the translation debate, however different they are, than it is to find a real precedent for Voss himself, other than the general influence and obvious relevance of biblical translation, represented here by the extreme example of Junckherrott.

But though Hölderlin's translations are very much of their time, they develop with a frightening logic certain of the traits I have mentioned and spin them out and intensify them to an extreme which far outstrips the potential they held for anybody else. And then Hölderlin was a great poet, which none other of the great translators—Schlegel or Voss—were, and his work as a translator, though it is not the same work, is inseparable from the course taken by his poetry. With Hölderlin, poetry and translation went hand in hand as with probably no other writer, and not just theoretically, as in the case of Novalis and the Schlegels, but in the concrete workings of actual poems and versions.

CHAPTER 2

Hölderlin on Translation

Jezt hab' ich, da ein Dichter bei uns auch sonst etwas zum
Nöthigen oder zum Angenehmen thun muß, diß Geschäft
gewählt, weil es zwar in fremden, aber festen und historischen
Gesezen gebunden ist.

(HÖLDERLIN, dedication of his Sophocles to the princess of Homburg)

For someone who made translations all his writing life and, when it
came to poetry, reflected intensely on the premises and nature of
composition, Hölderlin wrote surprisingly little about translation.
The essays do not even mention it in passing, except for a brief
reference to Voss. Similarly, Hölderlin's programme for *Iduna*, the
literary journal he intended to edit, makes no provision for promoting
translation as such, though it does aim to focus on classical writers and
on moderns such as Shakespeare and Rousseau, as Hölderlin
explained to Neuffer in a letter of 4 June 1799 (vi/323–5).

Different reasons might be discovered for this, but the first point to
be made is that Hölderlin's apparent disinclination to theorize about
translation is by no means at odds with the drift of the period. Neither
of the other two great translators of the time, Voss and A. W. Schlegel,
contributed anything substantial to thinking on translation except
through their practice, and we have seen that Schlegel was at pains to
emphasize that theory was not much use as far as translation was
concerned; his conviction that it was essentially a practical business is
upheld by Hölderlin's work.[1] The great achievements of German
translation were only followed, and not preceded, by extended

---

[1] Cf. the comment of a modern practitioner, Elaine Feinstein: 'I am not sure ...
how far a discussion of methods of translation attracts much useful reflection.... Poems
are not translated *consistently*. Every line proposes a new set of possibilities' (quoted in
Charles Tomlinson (ed.), *The Oxford Book of Verse in English Translation* (Oxford,

reflection on the subject. Before Schleiermacher's lecture, most pronouncements on translation were incidental and summary; only drawn together do they form a coherent horizon within which certain points and paths of thought can be made out. The same is true of the few occasions on which Hölderlin addresses the question of translation, and it is obviously the case that nothing he says approaches the insights into its dynamics afforded by the translations themselves. Still, it is interesting to look at these remarks in isolation to see what general notions emerge, and to let them appear against the ideas current among Hölderlin's contemporaries as outlined in the first chapter. The real importance of translation for Hölderlin lies elsewhere, but the discrepancy between the paucity of comment and the central, structuring, part translation plays at the heart of Hölderlin's undertaking is itself instructive.

The few remarks (nearly all in letters) are the apparent tip of something much larger and deeper-running, which is to say that much of Hölderlin's thought on translation is hidden. I think that, as with the German Romantics, it is partly subsumed by and diverted into other of his concerns, such as tragedy and his thinking about the Greeks. Translation was something Hölderlin must have worked at more or less constantly—there is no real reason to discredit the claims of the publisher's advertisement for the Sophocles translations that 'der Verfasser dieser klassischen Übersetzung [...] hat 10 Jahre an derselben gefeilt' [the author of this classical translation has been filing at it for 10 years] (v/450). Yet he barely mentions translation in his letters, and when he does, it is always in direct relation to a particular translation, either one of his own or a friend's. Only once does such an initial remark develop into something more general, to be understood as referring to all translation. Hölderlin never alludes to his translation of Pindar (many of Hölderlin's letters have disappeared, of course), but we hear a good deal about 'das innigere Studium der Griechen' [intense study of the Greeks] (vi/381) and his labouring to attain 'die wahre Erkentniß der poëtischen Formen' [true knowledge of poetic forms] (vi/380): 'Ich habe mich seit Jahren fast ununterbrochen mit der griechischen Literatur beschäfftiget' [For years, almost without a break, my main preoccupation has been Greek literature] (vi/422), he

1980), p. xii). Also, C. H. Sisson on what metre to use when translating verse: 'I would say that there is no way of knowing except by doing it, and that all theory about the proper measures for a translation is out of place', in *In the Trojan Ditch: Collected Poems and Selected Translations* (Cheadle, 1974), 160.

tells Schiller in 1801. Translation was the main form the study took; it is a kind of intense reading, and to translate was to apply an instrument of knowledge, a kind of theory in practice, where the root sense of the Greek θεωρία, a viewing, a contemplation, intimates the process. Translation was Hölderlin's angle of incidence on the Greeks most immediately necessary to him. It was a form of looking that enabled him to see 'den durch und durch bestimmten und überdachten Gang der alten Kunstwerke' [the thoroughly considered and purposeful course of ancient works of art] (vi/380), an inquiry through writing like the Homburg essays. At least until the Pindar translation this is the status translation has in Hölderlin's work—an auxiliary, investigative one; it is an activity secondary to the writing of poetry or tragedy or the novel, a method of learning and a preparation for something else. In the only period in which Hölderlin explored his work through analytic prose, translation was itself part of the process of analysis and discovery and so did not receive its attentions. Later, translation became a primary activity with its own independent role within the work, but by then Hölderlin had almost abandoned theoretical inquiry outside the work itself, and its premises were not, so far as we know, examined in prose. Perhaps the planned introduction to the translation of Sophocles' tragedies would have included something on translation and the particularities of Hölderlin's method, an enlargement of the brief annotations in the 'Anmerkungen' to the plays. Hölderlin says nothing of this to Wilmans. The lack of theoretical statement, however it is explained, only underlines the fact that by far the greater part of what Hölderlin can tell us about translation in general and his own translations in particular is to be extracted from the translations themselves, from the practice, or rather, experienced in them. Next to the translations, the few comments I discuss below carry very little weight indeed.

They are still of great intrinsic interest. Hölderlin's pronouncements fall into two very different groups. The first consists of early remarks to Neuffer in letters written to him from 1794 to 1796; they are about either Neuffer's various translations or Hölderlin's own attempts to translate the Phaethon episode from Ovid's *Metamorphoses* into regular stanzas, a job given him by Schiller and which he ended up considering an 'albernes Problem' [silly problem] (vi/205) though he had originally spoken of being engrossed by 'die Musik der Versification' [the music of the versification] (vi/169). The second group concerns the last stages of the Sophocles translations, particularly *Antigonä*: letters to the publisher, a few lines of the notes he appended to his translations (the 'Anmerkungen'), and the dedication of the tragedies to Princess Auguste of Homburg. There is a gap of more than seven years between these two groups, and in those seven years Hölderlin wrote most of his best poems and virtually all his translations. They are thus almost incommensurable.

Hölderlin's friend Neuffer spent years on a translation of the *Aeneid*. Hölderlin took an interest in this, as did Schiller, who approved of the 'Rastlosigkeit' [untiringness] with which Neuffer went about his work (vi/152). To translate Virgil was to invite comparison with Voss's versions of Homer, the status of which was as discouraging as encouraging to a translator of classical epic verse. Hölderlin urges Neuffer not to be daunted: 'Laß Dich doch durch Voß nicht abschröken. Tritt kühn heraus, u. laß die Leute sich wundern, über den Menschen, der sich mit Vossen messen wollte. Desto besser für Dich!' [Don't let Voss put you off. Come out into the open, that people may marvel at the man who dared compete with Voss. All the better for you!] (vi/152). Hölderlin understands Neuffer's efforts conventionally as an exercise, a toning of his language which will prepare it for something else: the writing of original poetry. Translation is secondary, something for fallow intervals. 'Der Geist des hohen Römers muß den Deinen wunderbar stärken. Deine Sprache muß im Kampfe mit der seinigen immer mer an Gewandtheit und Stärke gewinnen' [The spirit of the great Roman will strengthen yours wonderfully. In the struggle with his, your language will gain more and more strength and agility] (vi/109–10), Hölderlin says. It is the classical idea of improvement through translation, with a double emphasis on following through the thoughts of an acknowledged master and wrestling with the complexities of a foreign language. Perhaps the stress on conflict ('im Kampfe') and resultant strength ('stärken', 'Stärke') *is* more unusual, though it probably stems, ultimately, from Quintilian's 'certamen atque aemulatio'.[2] The agonistic element he identifies in translation is also explored in his ideas about poetry, and the violence it entails is something his own translations of Pindar and Sophocles make their peculiar prerogative.

---

[2] 'Wrestling and vying'. Quintilian, *Institutio Oratoria*, with an Eng. tr. by H. E. Butler, 4 vols. (London, 1968), iv 114.

These less common notions of translation which, even though their full consequences had not yet emerged, will partly have arisen from Hölderlin's own experience, reappear in another letter to Neuffer. This time the point of departure is Neuffer's translation of Sallust's *Catiline*. It gives rise to the most extended utterance on translation Hölderlin ever made, an uncanny proleptic evocation of the whole of his development as a translator. The distinction between 'Geist' and 'Sprache' made before is retained and the ideas of conflict and training merge in the figure of 'foreign service', recalling Herder's images for translation[3]:

Deine Übersezung des Katilina interessirt mich um so mer, da ich noch von vorigem Jare, wo ich ihn las, mit ihm bekannt bin. Es ist recht ein Geschäft zu seiner Zeit. Du hast recht, das Übersezen ist eine heilsame Gymnastik für die Sprache. Sie wird hübsch geschmeidig, wenn sie sich so nach fremder Schönheit und Größe, oft auch nach fremden Launen bequemen mus. Aber, so ser ich Dich bewundere, daß Du mit solcher Beharrlichkeit das Mittel zu Deinem Zweke vorbereiten kannst, so werd' ich Dir doch einen Fehdebrief schiken, wenn Du nach Vollendung beider Arbeiten, die Du jezt unter den Händen hast, eine neue der Art anfängst. Die Sprache ist Organ *unseres* Kopfs, *unseres* Herzens, Zeichen *unserer* Phantasien, *unserer* Ideen; *uns* mus sie gehorchen. Hat sie nun zu lange in fremdem Dienste gelebt, so, denk' ich, ist fast zu fürchten, daß sie nie mer ganz der freie reine, durch gar nichts, als durch das Innre, so und nicht anders gestaltete Ausdruk unseres Geistes werde. Ich würde mich gerne näher darüber erklären. (vi/125)

[Your translation of the *Catiline* is of particular interest to me because it is still familiar from last year, when I read it. It is just the thing to be doing at the moment. You are right, translation is like gymnastics, and does the language a lot of good. It becomes nice and supple when it has to adapt to foreign beauty and grandeur, and often to foreign whims too. But though I have a great deal of admiration for your ability to prepare the means to your end so doggedly, I warn you I'll have a few words to say if you start a new translation once you have finished the two you are on now. Language is the organ of *our* minds, *our* hearts, the sign of *our* imaginings, *our* ideas; it must obey *us*. If it has lived too long in foreign service there is, I think, the danger that it will never again become quite the free and pure expression of our minds, shaped entirely from within, that it should be. I would gladly go into this in more detail.]

Translation is understood to be 'recht ein Geschäft zu seiner Zeit', which, though primarily referring to the subject-matter of the

---

[3] Cf. p. 24 above.

Catiline and its relevance to a world after the French Revolution, may possibly also indicate a consciousness of the importance translation had at the time. The extension and enrichment of a language as it comes into contact with the foreign and is stretched into a new suppleness is seen as 'heilsam' because by breaking the limits it inhabits at a given point in time it reaches or retrieves a wholeness until then denied. This occurs through the encounter with the foreign as other, not only in its 'Schönheit und Größe', but also in its 'Launen', and thus far Hölderlin's comments are essentially an elaboration on his earlier ones and constitute a particular restatement of current ideas. Hölderlin now issues his warning: the process of extension and 'experience abroad' can be overdone and the native language become irrevocably estranged. The danger, Hölderlin maintains, is that the language which has undergone foreign influence might lose its organic relation with the mind that bodies it forth: 'daß sie nie mer ganz der freie reine, durch gar nichts, als durch das Innre, so und nicht anders gestaltete Ausdruk unseres Geistes werde'. Hölderlin conceives of the relationship between writer and language as one of control and mastery—'*uns* mus sie gehorchen'—and the stretching a home language undergoes in the process of translation has to be kept within limits set by the translator. The language can be expanded only up to a certain point if the return home is to be made.

The letter seems to contain an idea of the relationship between poetry and translation which is rendered much more complex by Hölderlin's later practice. If the hidden possibilities of a language are to be discovered through encounter with the foreign the poet must relinquish his mastery to some extent to allow the unknown to act. His position is more one of servant to language than of master. The letter gives a negative description of this, the course of Hölderlin's poetry: once Hölderlin's language had been through the Pindar translation it was never the same again (by the standards of the letter, it did spend too long in foreign service). But those standards are not appropriate to Hölderlin's poems, nor probably to poetry in general. The suggestion that a poetic language should be shaped by 'das Innre' alone is countered by the diction of the Pindar translation, which is produced out of a tension between the writing self, and what of his language he is heir to, and the new deflections prompted by another language, Greek. And in Hölderlin's later poems some words seem to have been jolted so far out of their natural idiom that they hardly function at all within the parameters of the language they ostensibly belong to; the tension from the pole of German is at its most weak, weaker even than in Voss's Homer, Klopstock, or Goethe's 'Greek' fragments, *Nausikaa*, *Achilleis* and *Pandora*. But the pull from outside, from the Greek, is by then rendering the structures and conventions of German into a form which, as a poem, alters them irrevocably and begins to incorporate them into the fund of the language. The line the letter draws, which is also a segregation of translation and poetry, into 'Mittel' and 'Zwek' [means and ends], is overridden by a much more intricate relationship that allows the dynamics of translation to operate in the poems and the writing of translations that partake in the full intention of the poems. A work such as the Sophocles translation, doing unheard-of things with German but founding them in a living language in contact with its deepest resources, confounds the hierarchical notions of the letter.

What Hölderlin has to say about translation later all relates to his versions of *Oedipus the King* and *Antigone*, published by Wilmans in spring 1804. The Pindar translation, as I said, is passed over in silence. The comments on the Sophocles translations are not intended to have any significance outside their immediate context, and to look at them separately, as about translation in general and not just about the translations of the tragedies, has limited point. It does allow the changes in Hölderlin's thinking about translation to appear very clearly. The gist of the new orientation comes in Hölderlin's first letter to Wilmans, of 28 September 1803.

Ich hoffe, die griechische Kunst, die uns fremd ist, durch Nationalkonvenienz und Fehler, mit denen sie sich immer herum beholfen hat, dadurch lebendiger, als gewöhnlich dem Publikum darzustellen, daß ich das Orientalische, das sie verläugnet hat, mehr heraushebe, und ihren Kunstfehler, wo er vorkommt, verbessere. (vi/434)

[Greek art is foreign to us because of the national convenience and bias it has always relied on, and I hope to present it to the public in a more lively manner than usual by bringing out further the oriental element it has denied and correcting its artistic bias wherever it occurs.]

This is an astonishing statement, especially in the context of a letter written to someone Hölderlin does not know and which is otherwise concerned to thank Wilmans for his offer of publication and accept it. He was lucky he did not scare his publisher off. But at this stage everything Hölderlin wrote was part of a necessary act, with a kind of visionary intensity and seriousness. The letter ends on the same uncompromising tone, in which the near-esoteric becomes the self-evident: 'jezt, da ich mehr aus dem Sinne der Natur und mehr des Vaterlandes schreiben kann als sonst' [now that I am more able than usual to write for and with nature and my country] (vi/434).

What Hölderlin writes about the intentions of his translation encompasses a dense and controversial understanding of Greek art and of the distance which separates it from the modern reader. Oddly, the main impediment, and the one that is central to translation, the (foreign) language, is ignored: Greek art is 'uns fremd', alien, not because it is written in a 'dead' tongue but because of the (Greek) 'Nationalkonvenienz und Fehler' it labours under. Hölderlin will correct this by bringing out 'das Orientalische', which has been repressed. It is in this repression that the defect or bias[4] of Greek art consists, and Hölderlin seeks to redress the balance. The balance needs redressing, as Hölderlin sees it, so that Sophocles' tragedies may make their full pressure felt now, in modernity. What appears as a fault (and in need of rectifying) to our modern eyes is not an intrinsic blemish but a necessary function of the particular historical nexus in which the plays arose. To Hölderlin a 'Kunstfehler', to the Greeks it was simply necessary, right form. The strange word 'Kunstfehler' is bifocal: it means a twist applied by 'too much art', something approaching the modern sense of a 'professional error' (Hölderlin's viewpoint); but it also suggests, by analogy with words such as 'Kunststück', a deviation made in the name of and as part of art, for art's sake (the Greeks' viewpoint as imagined by Hölderlin). The pinpointing of 'errors' in the Greek is a necessary consequence of the difference in viewpoint. In proposing correction, Hölderlin is proposing a vital, reciprocal act of reading, in which the dialectic between two historical situations, ancient and modern, is argued out.

This can be better understood by turning to the letter Hölderlin wrote to Böhlendorff on leaving Germany for Bordeaux, on 4 December 1801.[5] What he means by 'das Orientalische', and what the tendency is that covers it up, emerges from his theory, an anthropological theory, about the nature of the Greeks:

---

[4] David Constantine's word: *Hölderlin* (Oxford, 1988), 386.
[5] On which see Peter Szondi, 'Überwindung des Klassizismus: Der Brief an Böhlendorff vom 4. Dezember 1801', in: *Hölderlin-Studien* (Frankfurt a. M., 1970), 95–118.

Es klingt paradox. Aber ich behaupt' es noch einmal, und stelle es Deiner Prüfung und Deinem Gebrauche frei; das eigentliche nationelle wird im Fortschritt der Bildung immer der geringere Vorzug werden. Deßwegen sind die Griechen des heiligen Pathos weniger Meister, weil es ihnen angeboren war, hingegen sind sie vorzüglich in Darstellungsgaabe, von Homer an, weil dieser außerordentliche Mensch seelenvoll genug war, um die abendländische *Junonische Nüchternheit* für sein Apollonsreich zu erbeuten, und so wahrhaft das fremde sich anzueignen. (vi/426)

[It sounds paradoxical. But I'll make my point again and leave it to you to test it and make what use of it you can. The things we are born with, our national qualities, will always become less and less advantageous in the course of our development. That is why the Greeks do not master holy pathos well: it is innate in them; on the other hand they excel in the art of depiction, beginning with Homer, because this extraordinary man was inspirited enough to capture the *Junonian sobriety* of the Occident for his Apolline realm, and thus appropriate the foreign and make it truly his own.]

Hölderlin distinguishes between 'das eigentliche' or 'nationelle' or 'eigene' and 'das fremde': 'Das eigene muß so gut gelernt seyn, wie das Fremde' [One needs to learn what is proper to one just as much as what is foreign] (vi/426). But it is far harder to learn what is inborn and proper, and easier to learn what is other, which process is itself an education and a preparation for dealing with one's origins. Thus the Greeks excelled 'in the art of depiction', they mastered clarity and plasticity because these qualities were diametrically opposed to their true nature, which is something without form, 'das Feuer vom Himmel' [fire from the heavens] (vi/426). To counteract this threat of formlessness they worked in the other direction, towards '*Junonische Nüchternheit*', and appropriated what was alien to them. Hölderlin puts this movement at the heart of artistic creation, so that we can identify 'das Orientalische' in his comments to Wilmans with 'das heilige Pathos', the element which the Greeks were obliged to counterbalance by its polar opposite to achieve 'das lebendige Verhältniß und Geschik' [living craft and proportion] (vi/426), which he sees as a universal requisite of art. It is often pointed out that this pairing bears a strong resemblance to Nietzsche's concepts of the Apollonian and the Dionysian, which also find their perfect balance and resolution in Attic tragedy. The Dionysian origins of Greek life have been held in check, given form, by the structuring force of the Apollonian impulse, which Hölderlin calls '*Junonische Nüchternheit*'.

'Bei uns' though, Hölderlin goes on to say, 'ists umgekehrt' [With us it is the other way round] (vi/426). 'Die Klarheit der Darstellung' [clarity of depiction] (vi/425–6) is our innate characteristic, and thus we must tend towards 'heiliges Pathos'; it is in this, as other to us, that we may have a hope of surpassing the Greeks. Because the dialectical tension Hölderlin identifies in the Greeks is the same, but inverted, in us, Greek art needs to be read obliquely; from our perspective the realization made in Sophocles' text has to be reignited and the balance achieved there shifted. Our sluggish selves need the flame the Greek contains but occludes.

The 'correction' of which Hölderlin speaks in his letter to Wilmans thus involves a piercing of the propriety the Greeks observed to control their dangerously inflammatory nature, and an exposure of that nature, which is here called 'das Orientalische' in line with the theory, given wide currency by Herder, of a movement of culture from east to west. Implicitly, though it is interesting that Hölderlin does not say so in all explicitness, the means of emphasizing 'das Orientalische' is translation, translation which estranges the Greek from its habitual form and brings it closer to its origins.[6] In doing this it unfolds the Sophocles from itself, and in this sense translation is understood in a way similar to the Romantics' understanding: it extends and continues the work. But it is much more violent, since it involves the destruction of the classical wholeness and poise Sophocles had constructed and which the conventional view of him sought to perpetuate. It salvages something behind the original, gives it a new emphasis; and in so doing it recovers the whole work for modernity by reading it in stringent relation to the nature of the modern as Hölderlin grasps it. This undertaking—translation as a new manifestation of the grounds of the original—throws into relief the fact that translation is always itself a mode of manifestation, that what it gives is a new work in itself, dependent on, but different from, the original. But how in practice can the (concealed) grounds of a work be elicited? Are they not unknowable? Sophocles' Greek has a particular form which makes it what it is—all there is is the text, marked by 'Nationalkonvenienz und Fehler' (vi/434). Hölderlin's

---

[6] Karl Reinhardt defines 'das Orientalische' as 'das Nicht-Griechische', but in a sense there is nothing *more* Greek: 'Hölderlin und Sophokles', in: Alfred Kelletat (ed.), *Hölderlin: Beiträge zu seinem Verständnis in unserm Jahrhundert* (Tübingen, 1961), 286–303 (293).

desire to reveal 'das Orientalische' is a desire to have access to
something largely outside the text, present if it is present at all only in
traces which the translator must track down and give prominence to
(Hölderlin says 'daß ich das Orientalische [...] *mehr* heraushebe'
(vi/434),[7] suggesting that it is present in some measure). Translation
becomes akin to divination, attempting to tap into something other
than, beyond, the text; to 'correct' Sophocles is a temerarious move
to say what he left unsaid, to say what he 'really meant'.

Yet this is not true in an absolute sense. It is only from our modern,
complementary perspective that we can feel that Sophocles' plays are
hiding something, that they are not quite speaking the truth. To the
Greeks, in their time, the plays were finished works of art. Their
tendency to exclude an element natural to the Greeks was a danger to
which Hölderlin thought in the fragment '..meinest du/Es solle
gehen...' (ii/228) Greece had finally succumbed, but to which
Sophocles did not succumb. Sophocles provided the balance the
Greeks needed: no work can be universal, it must always leave
something unsaid, and Sophocles had only left unsaid what the Greeks
compensated for by their emotional, psychic make-up and 'direction'.
By apparently upsetting the Greek balance, Hölderlin is attempting to
reconstitute an Hesperian one, so as to arrive at 'was bei den Griechen
und uns das höchste seyn muß, nemlich [das] lebendig[e] Verhältniß
und Geschik' [what must be the supreme thing with the Greeks and
with us: living craft and proportion] (vi/426).

This becomes clear in another letter to Wilmans, of 2 April 1804,
in which Hölderlin defines his procedure:

Ich glaube durchaus gegen die exzentrische Begeisterung geschrieben zu
haben und so die griechische Einfalt erreicht; ich hoffe auch ferner, auf
diesem Prinzipium zu bleiben, auch wenn ich das, was dem Dichter
verboten ist, kühner exponiren sollte, gegen die exzentrische Begeisterung.
(vi/439)

[I am certain I have written in the direction of eccentric enthusiasm and thus
reached Greek simplicity; I hope to continue to stick to this principle, even
if that means drawing more attention to what was forbidden to the original
poet, precisely by going in the direction of eccentric enthusiasm.]

Beissner first pointed out that 'gegen' must mean 'towards' rather than
'against'.[8] It does not seem like Hölderlin for 'exzentrische

---

[7]   My italics.
[8]   Friedrich Beissner, *Hölderlins Übersetzungen aus dem Griechischen* (Stuttgart, 1933;

Begeisterung' to be something to be aimed for, the phrase recalls 'ins Ungebundene gehet eine Sehnsucht' [there is a longing for undoing] (ii/197), an urge to be resisted; but the sentence can only really be read if 'gegen' is so understood, and when read this way it yields a sense perfectly congruent with the letter to Böhlendorff. 'Griechische Einfalt' I take to be the 'lebendiges Verhältniß und Geschik' which all works should achieve, called Greek because it is so evident in Greek productions. Hölderlin says he has attained this in his Hesperian translation by writing 'gegen die exzentrische Begeisterung', that is, by concentrating on what is foreign to the modern sensibility, on 'heiliges Pathos' in the words to Böhlendorff. (The word 'gegen' illustrates an important facet of Hölderlin's theory of the complementary relationship between ancient and modern—that the directions (towards or away from sobriety) are tendencies.) The other tragedies ('ferner') Hölderlin also wanted to translate according to this principle, going beyond the constraints that Sophocles ('dem Dichter') imposed.[9] Hölderlin's thinking about the function of writing was always related to a readership, as in the 'Preface' to *Hyperion*, and he hoped that his course towards 'exzentrische Begeisterung' would offset the opposite, staid propensity he considered specific to his time. He released the translation eagerly expectant of the reactions it would provoke: 'Ich wünsche, daß die Ideen und Berührungspuncte, welche dieses Buch in Umlauf bringen, so schnell, wie möglich sich berühren mögen' [It is my wish that the ideas and points of contact which are the cause of this book may come into contact as quickly as possible] (vi/439).

Details of a reorientation of Sophocles appear in the 'Anmerkungen zur Antigonä'. Certain points of Hölderlin's bending of 'straightforward' Greek sense are justified and explained, though in a manner that compounds their complexity rather than leading outwards to immediate clarity. Hölderlin is almost certainly annotating passages he reworked at a late stage, during the period of the letters to Wilmans, in one of which (8 December 1803) he says he intends to alter a few things as 'die Sprache in der Antigonä schien mir nicht lebendig genug' [the language in the *Antigonä* didn't seem lively enough] (vi/435).

repr. 1961), 168. It could perhaps mean against the flow issuing from the (Greek) source of 'Begeisterung'.

[9] Beck seems wrong to me when he says the poet here is 'natürlich nicht etwa mit Sophokles gleichzusetzen' (vi/1099).

Kreon
Wenn meinem Uranfang' ich treu beistehe, lüg' ich?
Hämon
Das bist du nicht, hältst du nicht heilig <u>Gottes Nahmen</u>.

statt: trittst du der Götter Ehre. Es war wohl nöthig, hier den heiligen Ausdruk zu ändern, da er in der Mitte bedeutend ist, als Ernst und selbständiges Wort, an dem sich alles übrige objectiviret und verklärt. (v/266–7)

[**Creon**
If I stand by my beginning, faithfully, is that a lie?
Haemon
You aren't, if you do not keep holy the <u>name of God</u>.

in place of: if you spurn the honour of the gods. It was probably necessary to alter the holy expression here, as being at the centre it is significant, in its gravity and as independent words which everything else is objectified and transfigured around.]

The exchange could be said to be 'in der Mitte'—the phrase echoes 'der kühnste Moment eines Taglaufs oder Kunstwerks [...] da, wo die zweite Hälfte angehet' [the boldest moment in the course of the day or a work of art, when the second half begins] (v/266)—in that it occurs near the actual middle of the play (ll. 773–4 of 1402) and is a pivot which articulates perhaps its cardinal controversy—over the nature of authority as it is underwritten by different conceptions of the gods. Hölderlin's alteration gives the line a strong Christian flavour which this is not the place to go into, except to point out that Hölderlin's designs on Sophocles do not restrict themselves to extracting 'das Orientalische'.

A second gloss seems to combine these two tendencies, which can be understood together as a process of 'hesperization':

Sie zählete dem Vater der Zeit
Die Stundenschläge, die goldnen.

statt: verwaltete dem Zeus das goldenströmende Werden. Um es unserer Vorstellungsart mehr zu nähern. Im Bestimmteren oder Unbestimmteren muß wohl Zeus gesagt werden. <u>Im Ernste</u> lieber: Vater der Zeit oder: Vater der Erde, weil sein Karakter ist, der ewigen Tendenz entgegen, das Streben aus dieser Welt in die andre zu kehren zu einem Streben aus einer andern Welt in diese. Wir müssen die Mythe nemlich überall <u>beweisbarer</u> darstellen. (v/268)

[She counted out to the Father of Time
The strokes of the hours, golden.

in place of: looked after for Zeus the golden-flowing becoming. To bring it closer to our
way of thinking. In more or less precise terms one would probably have to say Zeus.
But in earnest rather: Father of Time or Father of the Earth, because it is his character,
against the eternal tendency, to turn the striving out of this world into the other
into a striving out of another world into this. *That is, we must present the myth*
at every point in a more demonstrable form.]

As in the first passage, it is in the name of seriousness ('Ernst') that
Hölderlin translates Zeus into 'Vater der Zeit', and this is part of a
movement to bring the play closer to our way of thinking ('um es
unserer Vorstellungsart mehr zu nähern') and make the myth more
palpable and incontrovertible ('die Mythe [...] überall beweisbarer
darstellen').[10] What he then says about the 'Karakter' of the 'Vater der
Zeit oder: Vater der Erde' can be read in relation to the letter to
Böhlendorff. The 'Streben aus dieser Welt in die andre' is the
fundamental urge of the Greeks, which they counter by finding a hold
in sobriety, cultivating a 'Streben aus einer andern Welt in diese'. This
characteristic then becomes the defining attribute of Hesperians, who
must counter it in their turn by espousing 'Leidenschaft' [passion]
(vi/426). For Hölderlin *Antigone* marks a historical turning-point, and
through his interpretative translation of Zeus he sets a new god over
the transition from the '*orbis* der Alten' [*orbis* of the ancients] to the
'hesperischer *orbis*' [Hesperian *orbis*] (ii/876) as an intrinsic, operative
part of that transition.[11]

In the 'Anmerkungen' Hölderlin does not specifically talk about
translation as a translingual negotiation at all. When he refers to a
dictionary understanding of the Greek text he cites it already
translated into German. He seems to think of his dealings with the
Sophoclean text as a *rewriting* of the original, whose language, though
on one level it is clearly crucial that it be Greek, is curiously
indeterminate and abstract, as if its specificity had already been
dissolved into a reservoir of numerous possibilities.

[10] Reinhardt (299) writes of the seriousness: 'das bedeutet: in Vorbereitung der
Wiederkehr, im Hinblick auf die kommende Götternähe'.
[11] For further discussion of the significance of the renaming of the gods see
Antoine Berman, 'Hölderlin, ou la traduction comme manifestation', in: Bernhard
Böschenstein and Jacques Le Rider (eds.), *Hölderlin vu de France* (Tübingen, 1987),
129–42 (especially 141–2).

Nor do the letters to Wilmans really treat of translation as such. In fact, though the remark in the letter of 28 September 1803 ('Ich hoffe...') is always taken as referring to Hölderlin's method of translating, its immediate context suggests it could be a foretaste of 'eine Einleitung zu den Tragödien' [an introduction to the tragedies] (vi/434) which Hölderlin intended to write but sadly never did. The hopes he has would then be fixed not on the effect of the translation alone but on his success in formulating the introduction, which he still has to write. This would also account for Hölderlin's rather abstractly alluding to 'die griechische Kunst' [Greek art] (vi/434) rather than simply to Sophocles; perhaps the introduction would have developed the ideas in the 'Anmerkungen' into larger theories about Greek art as a whole. Of course, if this is what Hölderlin was saying to Wilmans, it still has a relevance for the translations themselves. But it indicates how far Hölderlin seems to be from reflecting on translation as a distinct process in itself. The method he invokes, bringing out 'das Orientalische', is in theory at least something that could be performed within the Greek, without the auxiliary of translation. He speaks more as if he were about to re-edit the text than translate it. It is writing he talks about, and translation is soundly embedded in that activity, not to be separated off into a different zone. This contrasts absolutely with the earlier remarks in letters to Neuffer, in which translation is the 'means' to a (higher) 'end' (vi/125). In the course of about ten years, translation has shifted from a subsidiary, peripheral position, only slightly more dignified than copying out key passages, to the centre of Hölderlin's poetic life.

Between those two points where Hölderlin's thinking about translation comes up onto the surface, between 1794–6 and 1803–4, falls nearly all the actual translating he did; reflection on translation is confined to practice. But much of Hölderlin's thought on other subjects, which he did give expression to, is also closely related to the dynamics of his translations.

CHAPTER 3

Homburg:
Hölderlin's Poetic Thinking

Denn unter dem Maaße
Des Rohen brauchet es auch
Damit das Reine sich kenne.

('Die Titanen', ll. 64–6)

Novalis and Friedrich Schlegel, to a lesser extent Herder as well, were always willing to look beyond the specific activity of translating a foreign work and out towards the related and analogous preoccupations which translation can usefully be a figure of, and which themselves lend translation a wider significance. The prime motive for examining Hölderlin and translation is obviously what he did with Pindar and Sophocles, but these translations must be understood as a coherent part of all Hölderlin's work. To do this it is necessary to try and enter into Hölderlin's poetic thinking—the way he thought about poetry and the way his preoccupation with poetological problems coloured and structured his thinking on all other matters. In all its permutations, Hölderlin's thought, which was strongly analogical, operated according to a certain pattern and returned again and again to the same concerns.[1] The pattern could be characterized as dialectical and the concerns as revolving around the problem of representation (and further, both pattern and concerns might be called Heraclitean). Translation, and specifically Hölderlin's method of translation, is immediately important because it combines both the pattern and the concern, and shows them to be intimately linked.

---

[1] Cf. Beissner, 35 for one understanding of this pattern.

This third chapter looks at Hölderlin's thought at the point where it is most evident, in the writings of the time he spent in Homburg from 1798 to 1800.[2] The move to Homburg prompted Hölderlin to a reassessment of his whole position. The forced separation from Susette Gontard had as one of its results a renewed application to his work: he began again. Without a job it was harder than ever to stave off the claims of the *Konsistorium* and his mother's own desire to see him safely ensconced in a living in Württemberg. In his letters home he presents his new situation in Homburg as a final urgent attempt to prove himself as a writer, to follow his 'eigenstes Geschäfft' [the occupation most his own] (vi/297). There is a strange alliance of utter conviction as to the nature of the 'höhern und reinern Beschäfftigungen [...] zu denen mich Gott vorzüglich bestimmt hat' [higher and purer undertakings for which God has particularly destined me] (vi/297) and the sense that (even though he has by now finished *Hyperion*) he has hardly begun to get off the ground. He had saved enough money from his time in Frankfurt to live, he hoped, for a year, and, bar illness, he was able to write day after day. He worked very intensely; in spite of protestations that he would find the opportunity to make 'einen Gang ins Wirtembergische' [a journey into Württemberg] (vi/289) and visit his family shortly, he did not do so until Easter 1800 at the earliest, having not been home since the end of 1795.

During the period in Homburg Hölderlin's main endeavours were directed towards his play, *Der Tod des Empedokles*, and towards his project of editing a literary magazine and thereby continuing his independent existence near Susette. It was to be called *Iduna*, but came to nothing. But he did write, or begin, a number of essays which were to appear in the journal, as well as others, probably never intended for publication, in which he attempted to determine his poetic position and think through ideas about the workings of poetry. Some of these were directly connected with the work in hand, the tragedy. Others were more general, but they all derived out of the

---

[2] I follow the dating established by Beissner. This may be wrong, but the alternative chronology proposed by Sattler in the *FA* retains the sequence: first the essays, then Pindar, which is essential to my reading. Whichever dating one adopts, Hölderlin wrote most of his essays in Homburg. Sattler and his co-editors have redated much of Hölderlin's work, not always very convincingly; but they have made it clear that Beissner's dates are questionable. In many cases accurate dating is simply impossible.

growing awareness, heightened by translating Sophocles and Pindar, of 'den sichern, durch und durch bestimmten und überdachten Gang der alten Kunstwerke' [the thoroughly considered and purposeful course of ancient works of art] (vi/380) and of the comparative aporia of modern writers, their lack of any 'kalkulables Gesez' [calculable law] (v/195) by which they might proceed. This intense reflection on the nature of poetry and the poet's vocation accompanied or provoked a turning-point in Hölderlin's writing. In the last months of his stay in Homburg he did his translation of Pindar. As I understand it, the translation amalgamates and concentrates the things Hölderlin had been dwelling on, as well as developing them and putting them to the test. In so far as Hölderlin's concerns in Homburg between 1798 and 1800 as laid out in the following pages are related to his practice as a translator, it is thus more the Pindar I have in mind than the translations of Sophocles.

I

In November 1798, not long after his removal to Homburg, Hölderlin wrote to Neuffer that: 'Das Lebendige in der Poësie ist jezt dasjenige, was am meisten meine Gedanken und Sinne beschäfftiget' [Life in poetry is what now occupies my thoughts and feelings more than anything else] (vi/289). He is writing out of a sense of dissatisfaction with his poetry so far, addressing his 'poëtische Hauptmängel und wie ihnen abzuhelfen ist' [main poetic faults and what can be done about them] (vi/291). This in spite of the fact that he had written 'Da ich ein Knabe war...' and the Diotima poems.

What does Hölderlin mean by 'das Lebendige in der Poësie'? The rest of the letter, as it details his failings, and points to a remedy, gives an indication. His remarks centre round the problem of how something can be represented in poetry, specifically 'das Reine' [purity], which we could equate with an idea or ideal:

Das Reine kan sich nur darstellen im Unreinen und versuchst Du, das Edle zu geben ohne Gemeines, so wird es als das Allerunnatürlichste, Ungereimteste dastehn, und zwar darum, weil das Edle selber, so wie es zur Äußerung kömmt, die Farbe des Schiksaals trägt, unter dem es entstand, weil das Schöne, so wie es sich in der Wirklichkeit darstellt, von den Umständen unter denen es hervorgeht, nothwendig eine Form annimmt, die ihm nicht natürlich ist, und die nur dadurch zur natürlichen Form wird, daß man eben die Umstände, die ihm nothwendig diese Form gaben, hinzunimmt. (vi/290)

[Purity can only be represented in impurity and if you try to render fineness
without coarseness it will appear entirely unnatural and incongruous, and
this for the good reason that fineness itself, when it occurs, bears the colour
of the fate in which it arose; and beauty, when it appears in reality, necessarily
assumes a form from the circumstances under which it emerges which is not
natural to it and which only becomes its natural form when it is taken
together with precisely the conditions which of necessity gave it the form it
has.]

And again: 'ohne Gemeines kann nichts Edles dargestellt werden'
[nothing fine can be represented without coarseness] (vi/290).
Hölderlin is writing against abstraction: just as in reality ('in der
Wirklichkeit') nothing occurs pure, but only exists in relation to other
things and necessarily bears 'die Farbe des Schiksaals [...], unter dem
es entstand', so also in the poem ('sich [...] darstellen'). 'Das Reine',
'das Edle' should appear not absolute, but in relation to, even in
conflict with, the impure, as something which, within the poem, has
to work for its expression. Then it is actually realized as a process,
rendered 'fühlbar und gefühlt' [feelable and felt] (iv/243) through
tension and opposition rather than being talked *of* in terms which
easily lead to stereotype.

Hölderlin, in a letter which looks back and sees 'wie es meinen
Darstellungen an einem und dem andern fehlt' [how my works are
lacking in various respects] (vi/289), has come to this insight via
poems of his own which attempt to present absolutes directly, such as
the Tübingen hymns ('Hymne an die Freiheit', 'Hymne an die
Schönheit', etc.), which in the main are only *about* freedom, beauty
and so on, and through seeking to isolate them as ideals inevitably fall
short. As Hölderlin said himself in a letter to Schiller, they suffer from
'Scheue vor dem Stoffe' [being shy of experience] (vi/249), they shirk
the necessary bodying forth of metaphor. 'Das Lebendige' is absent
from them because they are too monumental, trying to state things—
'Nein, Unsterblichkeit, du bist, du bist!' [No, immortality, you are,
you are!] (i/117)—rather than incorporating them. Hölderlin's self-
criticism seems to be mainly directed against these early poems,
against their bloodless abstraction and hyperbole. A poem's being
'lebendig' means that it is closer to the forms of life itself, inheriting
the structures of reality. Thus, in 'lebendiges Verhältniß' [living
proportion] (vi/426), true representation is possible, where uniform,
'monotonous' portrayal is rejected, and a dynamic, varied form, in
which sense evolves through being endlessly checked and prompted,

proffered and withdrawn, is articulated. Then, life will manifest itself in the poem, 'der Gesang [...] glükt' [the poem works] (ii/119). 'Das Lebendige', which in one form or another recurs throughout Hölderlin, can be put in relation with two other words that name the poles of Hölderlin's thinking. It is a mid-way between 'das Positive' [fixity] (iv/221) and 'das Ungebundene' [abandon] (ii/197), the two extremes by which life is threatened. In the 'Anmerkungen zur Antigonä' Hölderlin calls them 'das allzuförmliche' [the all-too-formal] and 'das unförmliche' [the formless] (v/271); 'das Lebendige' is at a point where form is sustained by and perfectly controls what would otherwise have no form. Formality starts dominating if form endures *qua* form and not as a response defined by the energies it contains. Formlessness, where everything is swept away, comes if the form can no longer give this definition to what flows through it. Hölderlin's favourite image for 'das Lebendige' is a river: its banks channel energy that would otherwise lose itself and seep away. In holding the water to a course, the banks convert potential into actual energy; but it is the action of the water that shapes the banks. Hölderlin reflects on this in what may be one of the last things he wrote before his 'change of personality', 'Das Belebende' (the final *Pindar-Fragment*).[3]

Hölderlin relates his perceived failure to attain 'das Lebendige' to his own character. In the course of the letter he shifts seamlessly from talking about poetry to talking about himself and back again, using the same terms, the same basic divisions, for both. His early poems were reluctant to include 'Gemeines' [coarseness] (vi/291) in the same way as he has avoided 'die eiskalte Geschichte des Tages' [the ice-cold happenings of everyday life] (vi/290):

Es fehlt mir weniger an Kraft, als an Leichtigkeit, weniger an Ideen, als an Nüancen, weniger an einem Haupton, als an mannigfaltig geordneten Tönen, weniger an Licht, wie an Schatten, und das alles aus Einem Grunde; ich scheue das Gemeine und Gewöhnliche im wirklichen Leben zu sehr. (vi/289)

[I lack not so much strength as lightness, not so much ideas as nuances, not so much a main tone as a spectrum of diverse tones, not so much light as shadow, and all this for one reason: I shun the common and ordinary aspects of real life too much.]

---

[3] The phrase 'change of personality' is Michael Hamburger's: Friedrich Hölderlin, *Poems and Fragments*, tr. Michael Hamburger, 3rd edn. (London, 1994), xxxviii.

If his early poems tried to put things in too abstract a manner, focusing on intellectual concepts and merely furnishing them with extraneous embellishment, that came from his own shying away from the texture of the real world, which has resulted in a similar abstraction on a personal level. For a lack of interaction between the inner subject and the world outside leads on the one hand to stasis, and on the other to a situation where whenever the inner does try and impinge on the outer, whenever it attempts to *communicate*, it appears hopelessly shrill and incongruous and in fact fails to communicate effectively, remaining isolated. The intended solution, to both the poetic and the personal dilemma (but the personal is only viewed in so far as it affects the poetic), is a receptivity to a wider range of experience (not a turning away from ideas, but the understanding of them within the specifics of time and locality), and thus to a wider range of tone in the poems. Through this mixing of elements, in a particular constellation, the truth can appear. For it is in the end the question of how to say the truth that Hölderlin is getting at:

Ich muß [die Dinge, die auf mich zerstörend wirken] wo ich sie finde, schon zum voraus als unentbehrlichen Stoff nehmen, ohne den mein Innigstes sich niemals völlig darstellen wird. Ich muß sie in mich aufnehmen, um sie gelegenheitlich (als Künstler, wenn ich einmal Künstler seyn will und seyn soll) als Schatten zu meinem Lichte aufzustellen, um sie als untergeordnete Töne wiederzugeben, unter denen der Ton meiner Seele um so lebendiger hervorspringt. (vi/290)

[When I come across them I must make it a principle to take the things that have a harmful effect on me as indispensable material, without which my innermost will never come to full expression. I must take them up into myself so that when the opportunity arises (as an artist, if that's what I want and am one day to become) I can use them as shadow to my light, reproduce them as subordinate tones among which the tone of my soul will project itself with all the more life.]

So through a greater openness the uncongeniality of the world will translate into a sort of *fond* to the poem against which what the poet truly wishes to express, 'der Ton meiner Seele', will come into relief. Ideally, there is a symbiosis between the development of the poet and the poem.[4] Yeats's choice: 'perfection of the life or of the work' is not entertained. The ultimate criterion for the success of this chiaroscuro

---

[4] At one point Hölderlin talks of himself as if he were a poem: 'ich muß [die Dinge, die auf mich zerstörend wirken] nicht an sich, ich muß sie nur insofern

is the degree to which 'der Ton [der] Seele' is 'lebendig' [alive], is truly manifest. A poem which is not 'lebendig' does not function as a poem at all, the poem will have failed in its task of rendering manifest.

Hölderlin must have felt the Tübingen hymns to be untruthful because what he wanted to express came across monolithic, lifeless. The search for a form commensurate with and expressive of the impulse of the poem, which can translate the impulse, not unaffected, but modulated into an object of sensuous apprehension, into a form in which it is realized fully for the first time and thus only then really exists at all, the search for this form is the search to express the truth. Hölderlin is making the discovery Hegel summarized in the words Brecht painted on the beam of his study: 'Die Wahrheit ist konkret' [Truth is concrete].[5] Attempts to speak a truth outright will always be flawed, because, belonging to reality, that truth is too various and complex to accept a single, stark definition. And in so far as the truth relates to an absolute, there can be no direct bridge between that and the limits of everyday reality, the shortfall of words. So Homer (*Iliad*, iii 146–61), to give a sense of Helen's beauty, does not try and describe her, or abide by abstract claims, but shows instead other characters' reactions when they see her. And through this he avoids 'das Allerunnatürlichste, Ungereimteste' [the entirely unnatural and incongruous] (vi/290). Homer's old men are a metaphor, a vehicle, of the beauty of Helen; they are the means by which it could be properly conveyed. They bring into play a *relation*, and the truth resides in that relation, which is dynamic, something to be entered into, a dialectic, which avoids the false simplicities and imposition of statement. That seems to be what Hölderlin means by 'das Lebendige in der Poësie'; but 'das Lebendige' is a vague term, and so a wide one. It refers just as much to the precise interaction of words in a poem, the way certain words in juxtaposition, energized by the sinew of syntax and the motion of rhythm, enliven each other and make each other speak again, as it does to the larger difference between the abstraction of Hölderlin's old poems and his sense of what his new ones must become, opening up to the historical. 'Das Lebendige in der Poësie' (vi/289) remained Hölderlin's chief preoccupation while in Homburg. By the end of his time there more and more of it had

nehmen, als sie meinem wahrsten Leben dienlich sind' (vi/290). Cf. iv/244–5, and vi/284, ll. 54–5.

    [5] Benjamin, vi 526 (noted in a journal entry). All other references to Benjamin's *Schriften* are to his essay 'Die Aufgabe des Übersetzers'.

found its way into his poetry, as in the opening lines of 'Der Archipelagus':

> Kehren die Kraniche wieder zu dir, und suchen zu deinen
> Ufern wieder die Schiffe den Lauf? umathmen erwünschte
> Lüfte dir die beruhigte Fluth, und sonnet der Delphin,
> Aus der Tiefe gelokt, am neuen Lichte den Rüken?
> Blüht Ionien? ists die Zeit? ...

> [Are the cranes seeking you out again, and are the boats all
> Heading again for your shores? do longed-for breezes
> Blow on your quietened waters, and the dolphin, does he,
> Lured to the surface by spring, warm his back in the sunlight?
> Is Ionia in flower? Has the time come? ...]

II

Der Tod des Empedokles was what Hölderlin devoted most of his energies to while in Homburg. It was accompanied by a good deal of reflection on the form he was using, tragedy (he was also translating Sophocles at the time); and in the hierarchy of genres he set up, tragedy took the highest position (as it does traditionally). In it, the absolute could appear most fully, with a semblance of immediacy. In another letter to Neuffer, of 3 July 1799, he defines the tragic form thus:

die strengste aller poëtischen Formen, *die ganz dahin eingerichtet ist, um, ohne irgend einen Schmuk fast in lauter großen Tönen, wo jeder ein eignes Ganze ist, harmonisch wechselnd fortzuschreiten*, und in dieser stolzen Verläugnung alles Accidentellen das Ideal eines lebendigen Ganzen, so kurz und zugleich so vollständig und gehaltreich wie möglich, deswegen deutlicher aber auch ernster als alle andre bekannte poëtische Formen darstellt. (vi/339)

[the strictest of all poetic forms, *whose whole purpose is to proceed through a series of harmonious changes without any ornament in almost exclusively major tones each of which is an independent whole*; and in this proud renunciation of all accidentals it presents the ideal of a living whole as briefly and at the same time as completely and meaningfully as possible, and thus more clearly but also more seriously than any other known poetic form.]

It thus demands strict renunciation of anything extraneous to the main line of the action, everything must be stripped down to essentials, commensurate with the aim of representing the ideal at its most untrammelled. In its changing conception *Empedokles* did become more and more focused, so much so perhaps that it became impossible to complete, so much was cut away that even the bones of dramatic structure could find no place in it. But 'Verläugnung alles Accidentellen' is also something which is to occur within the action: the ultimate denial is the death of the hero; it is this death which endows tragedy with its special significance, because the normal restraints of representation can be transcended. Hölderlin explains the mechanics of this in a lapidary note, 'Die Bedeutung der Tragödien', which also provides the philosophical premisses underlying the disquisitions on manifestation in the letter to Neuffer of 12 November 1798.

In this note, Hölderlin starts off by saying that tragedy can best be understood through a paradox. This is the paradox that the absolute, which Hölderlin identifies here with nature, can only ever appear mediated through something else, that is, it appears 'in seiner Schwäche' [in its weakness], and not 'in ursprünglicher Stärke' [in primal strength] (iv/274); we experience not the thing itself but a faint equivalent, its 'Erscheinung' [appearance or phenomenon] (iv/274), a sign.[6] 'Im Tragischen nun ist das Zeichen an sich selbst unbedeutend, wirkungslos, aber das Ursprüngliche ist gerade heraus' [In tragedy the sign is insignificant in itself, without effect, but the primal is right there] (iv/274). So by making the medium of the absolute as weak as possible, to the point of extinction, when the hero dies, a wondrous inversion can take place whereby 'alles Ursprüngliche' [all that is primal] (iv/274) is 'gerade heraus', immediately there. Hölderlin expresses this in the terms of mathematical formulae, and actually seems to have something such in mind: as one side diminishes the other augments in inverse proportion.[7] Tragedy thus permits direct apprehension of 'der verborgene Grund jeder Natur' [the hidden ground of every nature] (iv/274), or at least an approximation to that, so much closer than any other mode that it is what Hölderlin calls elsewhere 'ein furchtbarer aber göttlicher Traum' [a terrible but divine dream] (iv/283). Tragedy seems then to permit the impossible—unmediated presence: what cannot have presence in the real world

---

[6] Cf. Hölderlin later: 'Das Unmittelbare, streng genommen, ist für die Sterblichen unmöglich, wie für die Unsterblichen' (from 'Das Höchste', one of the *Pindar-Fragmente*).

[7] Hölderlin was interested in mathematics, for its purity. See the letter to his brother, 10 Jan. 1797 (vi/230–1); also vi/242, lines 25–30.

can become immanent in the workings of tragic drama. But we need to pay close attention to Hölderlin's formulation:

Eigentlich nemlich kann das Ursprüngliche nur in seiner Schwäche erscheinen, insofern aber das Zeichen an sich selbst als unbedeutend =0 gesezt wird, kann auch das Ursprüngliche, der verborgene Grund jeder Natur *sich darstellen.* (iv/274)[8]

[In the normal course of things the primal can only appear in its weakness, but in as far as the actual sign is posited as insignificant (=0), the primal, the hidden ground of every nature, can represent itself.]

He is still talking about a representation, which of course tragedy is. But it is a privileged one because the process of metaphor can as it were fall away, recede, giving the appearance and feeling of direct revelation. There is still the essential vehicle—a tragedy is not a play with no hero, but one where the hero dies. At one level Hölderlin may well have believed in the direct access of tragedy to the absolute: he will have had in mind the religious significance of Greek tragedy, which was of documentary importance to him as a record of divine presence. But 'Die Bedeutung der Tragödien' is anyway only a theoretical statement, a particular notation.

There is something unsettling about this view of the tragic hero, as a mere sign which only signifies once it is removed. But through the different versions of *Empedokles* the role of the hero does lessen, till he becomes a victim only. This despite a clear interest in the personage, not to say an identification with him; and perhaps this discrepancy, between the theoretical reduction of Empedokles to a token and Hölderlin's involvement with him, is one of the many possible reasons for the eventual abandonment of the play.

But before abandoning the *Empedokles* tragedy Hölderlin worked very hard indeed at finding a way of dramatizing his hero's predicament. This was difficult, because the main story, even as the emphasis changed throughout the three versions, remained that of the ode 'Empedokles', written in Frankfurt: Empedokles hurls himself into 'des Aetna Flammen' [Etna's flames] (l. 4) to regain the full life of union with the gods he had once experienced, then lost. All the motivation is thus internal and practically not susceptible to dramatic exposition. In the first two versions at least, the final suicide can only be understood at all if Empedokles can give us a sense of what he has

---

[8]   My italics.

lost and of what there is to gain, and *Empedokles* turns round this problem of adequately representing the quality of the fulfilment that once was. But such a condition means in Empedokles' terms (and Hölderlin's) divine presence, life 'voll göttlichen Sinns' [full of the sense of God] (ii/111), and the poetry must thus be commensurate with it and body it forth in words. The tragedy stands or falls on the success of this; only if the language is 'lively' enough can the fulfilment be made manifest and so Empedokles' death comprehensible. The recasting of the blank verse of the first version into the shorter, irregular lines of the second, where the iambic beat still predominates but becomes quicker, more nervous, should be seen in this light. In those passages Hölderlin is trying to energize the language, forcing it into a new form as his needs become more urgent:

> Wo seid ihr, meine Götter? weh ihr laßt
> Wie einen Bettler mich und diese Brust
> Die liebend euch geahndet, stießt ihr mir
> Hinab und schloßt in schmählichenge Bande
> Die Freigeborne, die aus sich allein
> Und keines andern ist? Und dulden sollt ichs
> Wie die Schwächlinge, die im scheuen Tartarus
> Geschmiedet sind ans alte Tagewerk?
> Ich habe mich erkannt; ich will es! Luft will ich
> Mir schaffen, ha! und tagen solls! hinweg!
>
> (iv/15)

> [Where are you now, my gods? oh you've left
> Me like a beggar and you cast me down,
> This heart of mine which used through love to sense you
> Is now confined in narrow bonds of shame
> Though born in freedom and of itself alone,
> Belonging to no one. Am I supposed to bear it
> Like those weaklings fettered to their work
> Day after day in guilty Tartarus?
> I know myself and who I am. I want that!
> I want air to breathe and light around me. Away!]

becomes

> Wo seid ihr, meine Götter?
> Weh! laßt ihr nun
> Wie einen Bettler mich
> Und diese Brust
> Die liebend euch geahndet,

Was stoßt ihr sie hinab
Und schließt sie mir in schmählichenge Bande
Die Freigeborene, die aus sich
Und keines andern ist?
. . . . . .
Unduldbares duldend gleich den Schwächlingen, die
Ans Tagewerk im scheuen Tartarus
Geschmiedet sind.
. . . . . .
                              täusche nun die Kraft
Demüthiger! dir nimmer aus dem Busen!
Weit will ichs um mich machen, tagen solls
Von eigner Flamme mir!

                                                    (iv/102–3)

[Where are you now, my gods!
Oh! you've left me
Like a beggar now
And this heart of mine
Which used through love to sense you,
Why do you cast it down
And confine it in narrow bonds of shame
Though born in freedom and of itself,
Belonging to no one?
. . . . . .
Bear the unbearable like the weaklings
In guilty Tartarus, fettered
To their work.
. . . . . .
                              don't deceive yourself
Too humbly, about the strength that dwells in you.
I want open space around me, light
Thrown by my own flame!]

In these last lines, though he returns to the pentameter (as he does in
the last version), the drastic heightening of the language attests to
Hölderlin's impulse towards a continual trumping of what has gone
before. The language is intensified into a more extreme idiom in a
manner which anticipates the later rewriting of poems, such as 'Der
gefesselte Strom' into 'Ganymed', or of parts of the Sophocles
translations. The manuscripts of Empedokles actually contain marginal
notes in which Hölderlin is spurring himself on to a more lively
execution: 'wo möglich, noch lyrischer!' [if possible even more

lyrical] (iv/511); 'stärker! stolzer! lezter höchster Aufflug' [more power! more pride! the last and greatest upsurge of all] (iv/554); 'der Stoff ist richtig, aber linkisch geordnet!' [the material is right, but in the wrong order] (iv/570). There is an interesting note on Empedokles: 'Seine Sünde ist die Ursünde, deßwegen nichts weniger, als ein Abstractum, so wenig, als höchste Freude ein Abstractum ist, nur <muß> sie genetisch lebendig dargestellt werden' [His sin is original sin and therefore anything but abstract, no more abstract than total joy, it's just got to be depicted organically, with life] (iv/464). Here it is put expressly that 'das Lebendige in der Poësie' (vi/289) counters the danger of abstraction; 'genetisch' here means much the same as 'concrete' and, as in the letter to Neuffer, Hölderlin is pursuing the mechanics of making intangibles (if original sin is not abstract it is at least more tractable to abstract definition than to concrete representation) tangible in poetry.

'Leben' [life] and its derivatives, and compound forms containing it, must be the key word in the play.[9] Whereas in the letter to Neuffer 'das Lebendige' seems to indicate the state of the poetry when something is successfully realized in a (living) relation with the other elements of the poem, in *Empedokles* it is sometimes used for the absolute *tout court*:

> Nicht gegenwärtig werden
> Darf Göttliches vor ihnen.
> Es darf ihr Herz
> Lebendiges nicht finden.
>   (iv/91)

> [The gods must not become
> Present to them.
> Their hearts
> Must not find life.]

Or perhaps, in line with the letter, we should take these words to mean that 'Lebendiges' will arise out of *interaction* between 'Göttliches', when it appears, and the receivers of it, the people.[10] They are the words of Hermokrates, the high priest, talking of the people of Agrigent. He sees his job as protecting them from divine

---

[9] Cf. David Constantine, *Friedrich Hölderlin* (Munich, 1992), 86. He points out that such words are particularly common in the drafts.

[10] But cf. iv/109, l. 504 where 'das Lebendige' seems to include 'die Götter und ihr Geist' (l. 515).

presence and so is opposed diametrically to Empedokles, who was once 'vertraut/Mit Göttern' [familiar/With gods (iv/92)] and has attempted to convey this communion to others. Hermokrates confronts Empedokles with a religious anger, conscious of the total opposition ('Er oder wir!' [Him or us!] iv/96). He believes the people need to be spared, not enlightened, afraid of their fragility: 'wie dürres Gras/Entzünden sich die Menschen' [like dry grass/People catch fire] (iv/91). As a religious leader, he seems to hold that only a few can contain the divine without damage, and he is presumably one of them, though there is no proof of this. This is obviously not the only way we can understand his character—he is guarding vested interests as well as divine secrets, and Empedokles is challenging his authority, encouraging the Agrigentians to throw off every convention and adopt the ideals of the French Revolution (iv/65–6)—but it is the way at least partially endorsed by the play itself and by the fate of its subject, Empedokles.

For the play was to relate the *death* of Empedocles, and his death is precisely linked to the revelation of the divine within him. He has acted as a vehicle, and he knows his abandonment must be total. There is a sense in which Empedokles is actually conscious that his own desire for life through death is a kind of strategy employed by the Spirit to allow it to pass on fully to a new form:[11]

> Es muß
> Bei Zeiten weg, durch wen der Geist geredet.
> Es offenbart die göttliche Natur
> Sich göttlich oft durch Menschen, so erkennt
> Das vielversuchende Geschlecht sie wieder.
> Doch hat der Sterbliche, dem sie das Herz
> Mit ihrer Wonne füllte, sie verkündet,
> O laßt sie dann zerbrechen das Gefäß,
> Damit es nicht zu andrem Brauche dien',
> Und Göttliches zum Menschenwerke werde.
>
> (iv/73)
>
> [Whoever
> The Spirit has spoken through must quickly die.
> Divine nature often manifests

---

[11] Perhaps Hermokrates is also privy to the exigencies of the Spirit. The ambivalence of 'muß' in 'Untergehen muß/Er doch!' (iv/96) reflects his private desire *and* his grasp of what must come to Empedokles.

Itself through man divinely: they perceive
It then among their many attempts at knowledge.
But once the mortal whose heart has been filled
With nature's joy announces it to them
O let the vessel be destroyed, so that
It cannot serve for other purposes and
Being godly come into the use of man.]

The passage of the Spirit is deadly, and thus Hermokrates' attitude is quite justifiable and is in accord with the misgivings Delia has about Pausanias' affirmation of Empedokles' death (iv/115). The containment of the Spirit, its manifestation, can only be temporary.

> Ist doch
> Das Bleiben, gleich dem Strome den der Frost
> Gefesselt. Thöricht Wesen! schläft und hält
> Der heilge Lebensgeist denn irgendwo,
> Daß du ihn binden möchtest, du den Reinen?
> Es ängstiget der Immerfreudige
> Dir niemals in Gefängnissen sich ab,
> Und zaudert hoffnungslos auf seiner Stelle,
> Frägst du, wohin? Die Wonnen einer Welt
> Muß er durchwandern, und er endet nicht
>
> (iv/79)

[Its staying is only like a river fastened
By the frost. Fool. Does the holy spirit
Of life sleep or linger anywhere
That you might hold it in its purity, you?
It is always full of joy, why should it fret
Itself to death for you in captivity
And give up hope by staying where it is?
Do you ask where it goes? It travels through
A whole world of delights, and never ends]

is Empedokles' riposte to Pausanias' refusing to accept he intends to die.

There is a closer-than-usual relationship between the concerns of the play and the demands these concerns make on the poetry: Empedokles serves as a vessel for the Spirit (iv/73); that is, he is its metaphor, that by which it can be grasped and without which it would be unknown. In the terms of the letter to Neuffer, he is the 'Gemeines' without which 'Edles' cannot be represented (vi/290). Through that conjunction he becomes 'der Lebendige' [full of life] (iv/112), just as 'das Lebendige in der Poësie' (vi/289) springs from the dialectical resolution of the problem of representation. Hölderlin also saw the poet, and following a famous opening of Pindar's (to *Olympian* 7),[12] the poem, as a vessel, as his poem 'Buonaparte' states most straightforwardly: 'Heilige Gefäße sind die Dichter' [The poets are holy vessels] (i/239). In 'Buonaparte' the vessel is broken while it is still being filled:

> Er kann im Gedichte nicht leben und bleiben,
>   Er lebt und bleibt in der Welt.
>
>   (ll. 9–10)
> [He cannot live and remain in the poem
>   He lives and belongs in the world.]

It thus never takes full form (the poem is unfinished and assumes no regular metrical pattern, its lines merely laid out typographically as if they were part of an ode). But even 'finished' forms must be undone. There is a correlation in *Empedokles* between Empedokles' plenitude and emptying and the constant undercutting of those moments in the play when the language conjures up images of fulfilment; time after time Hölderlin will galvanize words into intense manifestation and then reveal the fulfilment they depict as either past or illusory:

> Da rausch' es anders, denn zuvor, im Hain,
> Und zärtlich tönen ihrer Berge Quellen—
> All deine Freuden, *Erde!* wahr, wie sie,
> Und warm und voll, aus Müh' und Liebe reifen,
> Sie alle gabst du mir.
> . . . . . .
> Und, wie Gewölk der Flamme, löseten
> Im hohen Blau die Sorgen mir sich auf.
>
>   **Pausanias**
> O Sohn des Himmels!
>
>   **Empedokles**
> Ich war es!
>
>   (iv/106–7)[13]

---

[12] Not translated by Hölderlin, but he was very struck by it. See Albrecht Seifert, *Untersuchungen zu Hölderlins Pindar-Rezeption* (Munich, 1982), 149.

[13] Cf. the passage reported by Mekades, ending 'So sprach der Übermüthige' (iv/94–6).

[The wind rushed through the trees in another way,
And the sound of streams in the hills became more urgent—
The joys of all the earth were true, as warm
And full they ripen out of toil and love:
You gave them all to me.
. . . . . .
As cloud gives way to lightning or the sun
In the upper blue my cares dissolved to air.

Pausanias
O son of heaven!

Empedocles
I once was.]

This is followed by another rising wave which also comes crashing down ('ich bin heraus geworfen' [I have been cast out], iv/107). The movement points forward to Hölderlin's mature style in the elegies and hymns, where again moments of fulfilment are set resolutely in the past, as no more than encouraging images. In *Empedokles* the defining moment, when he was loved by the gods (iv/11), has occurred before the action of the play. We then get evocations of it which in turn are undermined. This distancing I see as part of the response to the tenet: 'ohne Gemeines kann nichts Edles dargestellt werden' (vi/290). Hölderlin accepts language's ability to create illusions, and works that recognition into the body of poems, with great honesty. By presenting, in a dialectical fashion, both poles of language, in which, as he says, 'von einer Seite weniger oder nichts lebendig Bestehendes, von der anderen Seite alles zu liegen scheint' [on one hand there seems to be little or nothing that has life, but on the other hand everything has] (iv/282), he can articulate a greater truth. This corresponds with a more general assertion made in 'Reflexion': 'Nur das ist die wahrste Wahrheit, in der auch der Irrtum, weil sie ihn im ganzen ihres Systems, in seine Zeit und seine Stelle sezt, zur Wahrheit wird' [The only real truth is that in which even error becomes truth, through being given a time and a location in its total economy]. But here as well, Hölderlin is thinking first of all of poetry; there is an immediate corollary: 'Diß ist auch die höchste Poësie, in der auch das unpoëtische, weil es zu rechter Zeit und am rechten Orte im Ganzen des Kunstwerks gesagt ist, poëtisch wird' [The greatest poetry, too, is that in which even the unpoetic becomes poetic through being said at the right time and in the right place within the economy of the work] (iv/234–5).

III

Empedocles' philosophy, especially those parts of it which appear to come from Heraclitus, seems to have had an influence on the play. Empedocles understood the world to be alternately dominated by Love (Φιλότης) and Strife (Νεῖκος); both were always at work, but in variant proportion:

Double is the birth of mortal things and double their failing; for the one is brought to birth and destroyed by the coming together of all things, the other is nurtured and flies apart as they grow apart again. And these things never cease their continual interchange, now through Love all coming together into one, now again each carried apart by the hatred of Strife.[14]

The action of *Empedokles* is set in a period of strife.[15] All three versions locate the opposite state before the play, and Empedokles can only look back to it from a position of loss, from the present. The present time of the play is thus like our present as it is depicted in Hölderlin's poems: a period of transition defined by absence, in which the look back into the past is the source of the strength and hope necessary to effect the move into a better future. It is the pattern outlined most clearly in 'Brod und Wein', the triadic base of thinking which informs the whole of Hölderlin's undertaking. Now, 'indessen' [meanwhile] (ii/94), the mid-point, is the time of perpetual transition, when infinite possibilities are constantly forming and dissolving, and there is thus no end to the 'Dissonanzen der Welt' [dissonances of the world] (iii/160) these different potentialities engender. But the comprehension of conflict and contradiction as part of a larger pattern, encouraged by Heraclitus and Empedocles, enables it to be seen as a creative force, equally creative in fact as the opposite principle of harmony. Hölderlin combines and compresses Empedocles' cycle into the concept of 'liebender Streit' [loving strife]

---

[14] As handed down by Simplicius; in G. S. Kirk, J. E. Raven and M. Schofield, *The Presocratic Philosophers*, 2nd edn. (Cambridge, 1990), 287. For the Heraclitean origins, see 193.

[15] Cf. Jeremy Adler, 'Friedrich Hölderlin on Tragedy. Part II: "The Ground of the Empedocles" and "On the Process of Becoming and Passing Away"', *Comparative Criticism* 7 (1985), 147–73 (149).

(i/210; ii/96), so conflict is drawn even more surely into the total process of life. It provides *in nuce* Hölderlin's poetics[16] and, spanning out from it, what amounts to the dynamic underlying his understanding of the ways of virtually every sphere of human existence. Within the span of a poem, 'Heimkunft' presents 'liebender Streit' as a principle which can be celebrated (l. 6), the principle of creation itself—as dawn in the Alps is evoked in analogue to the beginning of the world. It was a notion peculiarly congenial to Romantic writers. Blake wrote: 'Without Contraries is no Progression. Attraction and Repulsion, Reason and Energy, Love and Hate, are necessary to Human existence'.[17]

The essays in which Hölderlin worked out his poetics were written at the same time as *Empedokles* and bear on it at many points.[18] Two essays in particular, 'Grund zum Empedokles' and 'Das Werden im Vergehen', proceed directly from work on the tragedy, clarify and extend and reorient what was going on there, but at the same time form part of the larger theoretical deliberations of essays like 'Über die Verfahrungsweise des poëtischen Geistes'. A sense of how the different modes of writing Hölderlin adopted are intertwined and continually in response one to the other, so that poems, tragedy, essays, letters and translations are the different manifestations of a congruity of thought and preoccupation which is their grounding, is vital to understand what was happening to Hölderlin while in Homburg.[19] As in the letter to Neuffer of 12 November 1798, the new poetics arrived at in Homburg arose out of a stringent critique of earlier work, and the theories were both applied to and derived from work in progress. The letter, as Beck notes (vi/896), contains the germ of Hölderlin's poetic theory, with its insight into the need for 'mannigfaltig geordnete Töne' [a spectrum of diverse tones] as part of the way towards 'das Lebendige in der Poësie' (vi/289). In the Homburg essays, continuing this idea, Hölderlin describes and

---

[16] Cf. Constantine, *Hölderlin*, 125

[17] William Blake, *Poetry and Prose*, ed. Geoffrey Keynes (London, 1941), 181.

[18] But cf. note 2 above.

[19] See Wolfgang Binder, 'Hölderlins Dichtung Homburg 1799', in: *Friedrich Hölderlin: Studien von Wolfgang Binder*, ed. Elisabeth Binder and Klaus Weimar (Frankfurt am Main, 1987), 157–77, which relates Hölderlin's development in Homburg to the defining experience of that time, the separation from Susette Gontard.

discovers very precisely what must go into a poem if it is to work, and in particular tries to find the 'modulation in tones' that lies behind each type of poem, each genre.

Hölderlin's poetics are very complex, and the complexity is compounded by their largely unfinished state and by the opacity of their idiom. The main essays do not seem to have been meant for publication; they were, like the Pindar translation, a private experiment, turning the essay form back into the ongoing means of investigation it had been originally (Johnson calls an essay 'an irregular undigested piece'). At one point Hölderlin has a good word for them: 'Denkversuche' [experiments in thinking] (iv/256). They pursue the belief that poetry has 'a logic of its own, as severe as that of science; and more difficult, because more subtle, more complex, and dependent on more, and more fugitive causes'.[20]

They are the sedimentation of Hölderlin's thinking but the process is not complete. Their provisional character is specially apparent in the abundance of terms used for what must be the same concepts; Hölderlin has made no attempt to normalize the usage. Thus in 'Über den Unterschied der Dichtarten' (iv/266–72) 'Schein' [appearance], 'äußerer Schein' [outward appearance], 'Kunstkarakter' [art-character], 'uneigentlicher Ton' [unactual tone], 'Ausführung' [execution], 'metaphorischer [Ton]' [metaphorical tone], 'Ausdruk' [expression] and 'Sprache' [language] all mean the same thing; in other essays there are yet more terms. On top of this, familiar words are often used in very private, unconventional senses (for example 'Bedeutung' [meaning], iv/245), and the meaning of many has to be relearnt before the essays can start to open up. In this, parts of the essays operate as Hölderlin, in 'Über die Verfahrungsweise des poëtischen Geistes', says poems do. Hölderlin seems to proceed with words, the matter in which his thoughts come into being, much as the 'poëtischer Geist' [poetic Spirit] (iv/244) does, using any material at its disposal that is 'receptive' (iv/243) in order to manifest itself, pulling it into its sphere as it needs it and then abandoning it. The effect is that the greater context is only relevant to a limited degree. At one point in the 'Verfahrungsweise' this context is called the 'Wirkungskreis' [sphere of influence]:

Er ist das, worinn und woran das jedesmalige poëtische Geschäfft und Verfahren sich realisirt, das Vehikel des Geistes, wodurch er sich in sich selbst

[20] Coleridge, *Biographia Literaria*, i 4.

und in andern reproducirt. *An* sich ist der Wirkungskreis größer als der poëtische Geist, aber nicht *für* sich selber. Insofern er im Zusammenhange der Welt betrachtet wird, ist er größer; insofern er vom Dichter vestgehalten, und zugeeignet ist, ist er subordinirt. (iv/244–5)

[It is that in and against which the current poetic task and process realizes itself, the vehicle of the Spirit, through which it reproduces itself within itself and in others. *In* itself the sphere of influence is greater than the poetic Spirit, but not *for* itself. In so far as it is considered in the context of the world, it is greater; in so far as it is held fast by the poet, and apportioned, it is subordinate.]

Hölderlin effects a similar subordination of words in his essays, but in the medium of prose they do not naturally dislocate themselves out of their usual sphere of reference. One thing the essays perhaps do, inadvertently, is illustrate concretely the differences between prose and poetry. But there are passages where the pitch and rhythm of the prose virtually elides these differences, and it is certain they need to be read otherwise than most essays, with some of the expectations and suspensions we bring to poetry.[21]

That does not mean the essays do not render a prose logic, only that such a logic does not exhaust their meaning. And though they have been the subject of much exegesis and commentary, they cannot be said to have been exhausted. The poetics they contain occupies a strange and ill-defined position: neither generally entertained as a serious theory of poetry (whatever that might be) nor immediately applicable to Hölderlin's own poems.[22] I cannot give a full account of the poetics; instead I mean to focus on those parts which are particularly germane to translation, though the whole import of that relation will not be apparent until later chapters, especially the next. But as translation is so close to the core of Hölderlin's thinking, the analogy between poetic composition and translation so complete, a simple version of the poetics will emerge, and in some respects translation may be a help to understanding them. Those facets which the light of translation picks out are all crucial to the poetics, even if other aspects, not quite so crucial, are neglected.

---

[21] For one such rhythmical passage, see iv/261, ll. 30–4.

[22] Lawrence Ryan attempts to use the essays as a grid through which to view the composition of the poems, but he stresses that this is fraught with difficulties: *Hölderlins Lehre vom Wechsel der Töne* (Stuttgart, 1960), 4.

Hölderlin's poetics is based on a conception of metaphor, in its whole scale of senses: as a figure, and as carrying over, transition, *translatio*. In his writings, as I said, 'Metapher' and 'Übergang' are mostly interchangeable expressions. And he makes no distinction in his theory between a particular metaphor (in the usual sense) and the whole poem seen as a place and act of transition and interchange, as when he defines the lyric poem as 'eine fortgehende Metapher Eines Gefühls' [a continuous metaphor of one feeling] (iv/266). It is the ability of the poem to body something forth, to make manifest, through metaphor, that is placed at the centre of attention then, which in itself is not unusual. What is unusual is the close anatomy of that ability as a dynamic process, as if the awareness of the movement in the etymology of metaphor had influenced Hölderlin's understanding of how it worked.

The terms in which Hölderlin describes the process of a poem in 'Über die Verfahrungsweise des poëtischen Geistes' are extremely abstract. It is helpful to come at them via the 'Grund zum Empedokles', which, having given up the second version of his play, Hölderlin wrote as a means of taking stock and reorienting the drama. There, because he has a particular work (or at least a particular genre—tragedy) in mind, he writes in a more graspable idiom. These remarks on tragedy apply with variations to all the genres.[23] As 'die strengste aller poëtischen Formen' [the strictest of all poetic forms] (vi/339), tragedy is the test case.

In the 'Grund zum Empedokles' Hölderlin outlines the important paradox that while the poem must issue 'aus des Dichters eigener Welt und Seele [...], weil sonst überall die rechte Wahrheit fehlt, und überhaupt nichts verstanden und belebt werden kan' [from the poet's own world and soul, because otherwise the required truth will everywhere be lacking, and nothing at all can be understood and brought to life] (iv/150), the poet's experience must not appear as such, but alienate itself, translate itself into an 'objective correlative': 'das eigene Gemüth und die eigene Erfahrung in einen fremden analogischen Stoff übertragen' [translate one's own feelings and experience into foreign, analogous material] (iv/150). This is not unlike Eliot's comparison of 'the mind of the poet' with a catalyst— essential, but strangely uninvolved itself.[24] The contrasting qualities of

[23]   As Hölderlin demonstrates: iv/151, ll. 19–22.
[24]   In 'Tradition and the Individual Talent', in: *The Sacred Wood*, 4th edn. (London, 1934), 47–59 (54).

likeness ('analogisch') and foreignness ('fremd') are equally important, but the effectiveness of the metaphor is increased as it becomes more distant from, other than, the poet's personality, which must be renounced:

> Die fremden Formen müssen um so lebendiger seyn, je fremder sie sind, und je weniger der sichtbare Stoff des Gedichts dem Stoffe der zum Grunde liegt, dem Gemüth und der Welt des Dichters gleicht, um so weniger darf sich der Geist, das Göttliche, wie es der Dichter in seiner Welt empfand, in dem künstlichen fremden Stoffe verläugnen. (iv/151)

> [The more foreign the foreign forms are the more lively they must be, and the less the visible material of the poem resembles the material which it is based on, the feelings and the world of the poet, the more imperative it becomes that the Spirit, the divine as the poet has apprehended it in his world, be present in the artificial foreign material.]

This brings something new: as worked out more fully in 'Über die Verfahrungsweise des poëtischen Geistes', the poem's overriding objective is the realization of the 'Geist'.[25] A poem that is 'lebendig' is one filled with the Spirit ('das Göttliche' for Hölderlin). These lines are saying that as the personality of the poet is excluded from 'the visible material of the poem' it becomes all the more important that the Spirit should manifest itself there. They seem to be addressing the danger in the principle of estrangement: the distancing from the poet's experience could lead to the desertion of 'das Lebendige' (vi/289) from the poem, so that 'überall die rechte Wahrheit fehlt' [the required truth is everywhere lacking] (iv/150). But what the passage suggests is that the limitation of the personality, or the cultivation of impersonality, actually creates more space in the poem for the 'Geist' to express itself freely. The measure of a successful poem, then, is the extent to which it can alienate its metaphor, depersonalize it, while still retaining that vital 'analogisch' connexion which secures its truth; the poem is thus left uncluttered for the Spirit to enter into it.

But the deliberate exaggeration of the disparity between the metaphor and that to which it is analogous, is, on a more purely poetological level, a further response to the questions of manifestation, of how a thing may be represented in a poem, considered by Hölderlin in the 1798 letter to Neuffer I have already referred to several times. If the essential problem is: how does a poem

---

[25] Cf. the passage from the 'Verfahrungsweise' quoted above, pp. 88–9.

relate to reality? the answer is: by analogy, by equivalent.[26] There can be no more immediate relation between them, there is no getting round the difference, or, if you like, the 'untruth', of words and images. What the poem has to do is negotiate its own truth. When Hölderlin affirms the possibility of the poet's translating his 'Totalempfindung' [total emotion] into something else, 'und zwar um so sicherer, je fremder bei der Analogie dieser Stoff ist' [and all the more certainly, the more foreign the material is in its analogy] (iv/151), he is pointing out that by accentuating this 'foreignness' he draws attention to it, admitting the discrepancy between reality and imagination, and amalgamating this discrepancy into the processes of the poem. It is thus more truthful, because it embodies the relation of art to life, and singles out the particular status of art. Seen from another angle, this means that a poem will admit its illusory nature, something we have seen in relation to *Empedokles* and which Hölderlin finds ever more subtle and convincing ways of revealing, through to his hymns.

If this seems rather abstract, the ultimate effect is actually one of concreteness in the poems themselves. The singularity of words, their structure and the way they are put together, become the focus, their importance lies less in what they refer to, than in the particular combinations they adopt, their texture and interaction. For Hölderlin, at least if we take his poetics *à la lettre*, neither the subject–matter nor the quiddity of a poem is the important thing, but that it should be a place of passage of the Spirit. His poetics is ultimately religious in import.[27] But what this means for a secular understanding can best be thought of as a rendering concrete. 'Über die Verfahrungsweise des poëtischen Geistes' details the process by which the Spirit enters into the poem, but what is important is that it should be 'fühlbar und gefühlt' [feelable and felt] (iv/243) and the moment of greatest enspiritedness is thus also the moment of greatest concreteness, when 'Stoff' is permeated by 'Geist' (iv/243) and 'das Lebendige' (vi/289) results in the 'Begründung und Bedeutung' [grounding and meaning] (iv/245) of the poem.

---

[26] Cf. Seamus Heaney, *The Redress of Poetry* (Oxford, 1990), 2–3: 'If our given experience is a labyrinth, then its impassability is countered by the poet's imagining some equivalent of the labyrinth and bringing himself and us through it'.

[27] Cf. 'So wäre alle Religion ihrem Wesen nach poëtisch' (iv/281). See Constantine, *Hölderlin*, 125.

Some of the terms of the 'Verfahrungsweise' have thus been anticipated. I have also borrowed the term 'das Lebendige' from the letter to Neuffer to denote the interpenetration of 'Geist' and 'Stoff', as there it denoted the interaction of 'purity' and 'impurity'. Hölderlin no longer uses the term itself in quite that sense, but he has a profusion of other expressions. I retain it in order to construct a certain uniformity within my own remarks, but also to connect with Hölderlin later when he talks about 'der lebendige Sinn, der nicht berechnet werden kann' [the living sense, that cannot be calculated] (v/195) or finds the language of his *Antigone* translation 'nicht lebendig genug' [not lively enough] (vi/435). Hölderlin's letters in the Homburg period are full of the qualifying use of 'lebendig' in a sense very close to that suggested in the letter to Neuffer and isolated here: 'ein lebendiges Wort' [a living word] (vi/293), 'lebendige Kraft' [live strength] (vi/297), 'die lebendige Ruhe' [lively calm] (vi/305), 'ein lebendiges Bild' [a living image] (vi/329), 'lebendige Kunst' [living art] (vi/346), 'die lebendige Seele' [the living soul] (vi/374). Poetry should both be and make of its readers 'ein lebendiges tausendfach gegliedertes inniges Ganzes' [a live, intricately articulated, intense whole] (vi/306). But Hölderlin also uses the term, as well as the noun 'Leben', in a varying sense, especially in 'Über die Verfahrungsweise des poëtischen Geistes' and the 'Grund zum Empedokles'. In this last 'Leben' sometimes stands for 'Natur' [nature] and sometimes for the successful blending of 'Natur' and 'Kunst' [art]; similarly, in the 'Verfahrungsweise' Hölderlin sometimes puts 'das Lebendige' in opposition to 'das Geistige' (iv/262), so it means much the same as 'Stoff' ('Leben' seems to indicate the particular sphere of 'Stoff' in which one individual moves, his or her total experience).[28]

'Über die Verfahrungsweise des poëtischen Geistes' centres on the precise workings of the interaction between 'Geist' and 'Stoff' that constitutes a poem. The interaction occurs as a necessary process of conflict—'ein nothwendiger Widerstreit' (iv/241)—necessary because

---

[28] One could understand this passage, where Hölderlin talks of 'die höchste Entgegensezung und Vereinigung des Lebendigen und Geistigen' (iv/262), to refer to a moment when 'Stoff' is already imbued with 'Geist' (and 'Leben' is thus fully 'lebendig') and 'Geist' has taken on concrete form in interaction with the 'Stoff' of reality ('das Geistige' as expressing greater substantiality than 'Geist'). 'Das Lebendige' and 'das Geistige' would then mean the same thing, or different aspects of the same thing, the point 'wo Geist und Leben auf beiden Seiten gleich ist' (iv/262). 'Das Lebendige' perhaps then does have the potent sense after all.

only through it, in its dialectical warring, can the Spirit be felt, as it merges with the sensuousness of matter and breaks out of its pure unfeelable form. The Spirit must 'go out of itself' ('aus sich heraus [...] gehen', iv/241), become specific, just as experience, the world, must accept the straitening of the poem and be 'subordinate' (iv/245).[29] The straitening is in fact the transition, the metaphor, in which 'Geist' and 'Stoff' meet and appear in 'Wechselwirkung' [interaction] (iv/245) and 'Entgegensezung' [opposition] (iv/249), brought into relation with one another by the 'Begründung und Bedeutung des Gedichts' [grounding and meaning of the poem] (iv/245).[30] This 'Begründung und Bedeutung' is the movement of the poem, its total course; it develops the conflict between Spirit and matter to a point of 'höchster Gegensaz' [supreme antithesis] (iv/250)—'das Berühren der Extreme' [where extremes meet] (iv/246)—which is at once a moment of balance, symbiosis, where 'Entgegensezung' is also 'Vereinigung' [union] (iv/249). Conflict is thus resolved, it becomes 'harmonious'; or, conflict is simply reappraised, seen as 'möglich und als Nothwendig' [possible and necessary] (iv/249),[31] and:

in diesem Puncte [ist] *der Geist in seiner Unendlichkeit fühlbar* [...], der durch die Entgegensezung als Endliches erschien, [...] das Reine, das dem Organ an sich widerstritt, [ist] in eben diesem Organ *selber gegenwärtig* und so erst *ein Lebendiges.* (iv/249–50)[32]

[*at this point the Spirit*, which through opposition appeared as finite, is *feelable in its infinity*; the pure, which was in conflict with the organ [= vehicle] in itself, is in precisely this organ *conscious of itself* and so only then *a living thing*.]

The Spirit thus needs matter, the encounter with matter not only

---

[29] See pp. 88–9 above.

[30] Hölderlin goes into the precise nature of this 'Wechsel' in 'Über den Unterschied der Dichtarten' and 'Wechsel der Töne'.

[31] This moment of reversal, at the point of greatest opposition, is the key moment of a poem, like the caesura of the Sophocles notes (v/196). From its vantage-point the course of the poem so far is thrown into a new perspective. The essay 'Das Werden im Vergehen' is Hölderlin's fullest analysis of the moment of transition (both in history and in the poem), which he sees as a process of conflict holding both dissolution of the old and formation of the new; the latter can only be perceived when the dissolution is recapitulated in the memory, as 'idealische Auflösung' (iv/283). There is thus a similar alteration of perspective. This essay is discussed in relation to the Pindar translation in Ch. 4.

[32] 'Das Reine' here is a synonym of 'Geist' (Ryan, 47).

allows it to appear, but also to reach consciousness of itself, and this is the privilege of poetry.[33]

'Über die Verfahrungsweise des poëtischen Geistes' is founded on an analogy which will make it easier to understand what Hölderlin means by this: 'wenn diß der Gang und die Bestimmung des Menschen überhaupt zu seyn scheint, so ist ebendasselbe der Gang und die Bestimmung aller und jeder Poësie' [if this seems to be the course and destiny of man in general, it is also the course and destiny of all poetry] (iv/263). The 'Gang und die Bestimmung des Menschen überhaupt' he describes as the passage out of the 'ursprüngliche Einfalt' [original simplicity] (iv/262) of childhood, through a period of 'entgegengesezte Versuche' [opposed attempts] to a 'Stuffe der Bildung' [stage of development] where the promise of childhood is at last fulfilled—'reiner Wiederklang des ersten Lebens' [the first life sounding purely again] (iv/263)—and man enters life fully for the first time, in consciousness of the limited nature of his childhood and able to reconstitute an analogous state freely. The 'high point' thus comprises the uniqueness of childhood and is able to look back at it *'conscious of itself'*. (iv/250)[34]

The course of the poem is linked to this in two ways: it recapitulates the 'Gang und die Bestimmung des Menschen überhaupt' (iv/263), which is a necessary passage for the poet himself; and the recreation of the poet's original 'Stimmungen' [moods] (iv/248) has the same structure as the successfully realized life:

wie der Mensch auf dieser Stuffe der Bildung erst eigentlich das Leben antritt und sein Wirken und seine Bestimmung ahndet, so ahndet der Dichter, auf jener Stuffe, wo er auch aus einer ursprünglichen Empfindung, durch entgegengesezte Versuche, sich zum Ton, zur höchsten reinen Form derselben Empfindung emporgerungen hat und ganz in seinem ganzen inneren und äußeren Leben mit jenem Tone sich begriffen sieht, auf dieser

---

[33] Cf. Fred Lönker, *Welt in der Welt: Eine Untersuchung zu Hölderlins 'Verfahrungsweise des poëtischen Geistes'* (Göttingen, 1989), 57–8: 'So ist der Geist zwar immer schon in einem Darstellungsprozeß begriffen, aber er ist sich nach Hölderlins Theorie nicht selbst gegenwärtig. Dafür bedarf es seiner Reproduktion in der Dichtung. Erst in ihr gewinnt der Geist, dem dieses Streben nach Materialität oder Realität ursprünglich zukommt, Beziehung auf sich.'

[34] This development is the 'exzentrische Bahn' from a 'Zustand der höchsten Einfalt' given by '*die bloße Organisation der Natur*' to a 'Zustand der höchsten Bildung', a recovery of the former '*durch die Organisation, die wir uns selbst zu geben im Stande sind*' (*Fragment vom Hyperion*, iii/163).

Stuffe ahndet er seine Sprache, und mit ihr die eigentliche Vollendung für die jezige und zugleich für alle Poësie. (iv/263)

[just as man at this stage in his development enters fully into life and divines his role and his destiny for the first time, so the poet, at the stage when he has also worked his way up from an original emotion, through opposed attempts, to the tone, to the highest pure form of that emotion, and finds himself in the whole of his inner and outer life quite taken up with this tone, at this stage the poet divines his language, and with it actual fulfilment for the poem and at the same time for all poetry.]

Such a moment, when language is felt and found, is 'eine neue Reflexion' [a new reflection] (iv/263):

sie giebt dem Herzen alles wieder, was sie ihm nahm, sie ist belebende Kunst [...], und mit einem Zauberschlage um den andern ruft sie das verlorene Leben schöner hervor, bis es wieder so ganz sich fühlt, wie es sich ursprünglich fühlte. (iv/261)

[which returns to the heart all it had taken, it is enlivening art [...] and with one magic stroke after another it conjures up the lost life in greater beauty until it feels itself once again as whole as it was at first.]

It is this capacity language has (galvanized in the context of a poem) of reflexion and recovery that enables the Spirit, when urged into the poem, to be conscious of itself. Language is consciousness, and in poetry it is charged to the full. The Spirit 'reproduces itself' freely in history, but only in the nexus of the poem does the representation of that 'Reproduction' (iv/242) allow it the heightened condition of self-consciousness.

Self-knowledge, the sense of being conscious of your exact position in history and being able to formulate it, is the focus of those parts of the 'Verfahrungsweise' which deal with the 'Mittelzustand' [mid-state] between childhood and 'reife Humanität' [mature humanity] (iv/255). (The conflict there, at the mid-point, is structured similarly to the conflict at the heart of a poem.) Passage out of this 'Alleinseyn [...] diesem Leben mit sich selbst, diesem widersprechenden Mittelzustande' [solitude, this life with oneself, this contradictory mid-state] (iv/255) is to be made through encounter with something outside oneself. This is the rule:

Seze dich mit freier Wahl in harmonische Entgegensezung mit einer äußeren Sphäre, so wie du in dir selber in harmonischer Entgegensezung bist, von Natur, aber unerkennbarer weise so lange du in dir selbst bleibst. (iv/255–6)

[Put yourself *through your own choice* in harmonious opposition with an outer sphere, just as you are in *harmonious* opposition in yourself, by nature, but unrecognizably as long as you remain within yourself.]

What is important is the self-exposure to something beyond one's own experience, a kind of disencumberment of the self through distancing. This could take place through the encounter with art, and in this sense the analogy Hölderlin draws between 'der Gang und die Bestimmung des Menschen überhaupt' and 'der Gang und Bestimmung aller und jeder Poësie' (iv/263) is more than a mere analogy: the first is reached through the agency of the second, and the second is the result of the first.[35] The 'poëtischer Geist' had to step out of itself to realize itself fully (iv/241); the individual must take the same course:

eben weil er mit dieser [einer äußern Sphäre] *nicht so innig verbunden ist, von dieser abstrahiren und von sich, in so fern er in ihr gesezt ist, und auf sich reflectiren* kann, in so fern er nicht in ihr gesezt ist, diß ist der Grund, warum er aus sich herausgeht, diß die Regel für seine Verfahrungsart in der äußern Welt. Auf dieser Art erreicht er seine Bestimmung [...]. Diß ist die wahre Freiheit seines Wesens. (iv/257)

[*precisely because he is not so closely connected with this external sphere, can abstract from it and from himself in as far as he is placed within it, and can reflect on himself in as far as he is not placed within it, this is the reason why he goes out of himself, this is the rule for his manner of proceeding in the world outside. In this way he attains his destiny [...]. This is the true freedom of his being.*]

The freedom consists in being able to expose one's being to a sphere where its real essence and potential come to light; it is an instance of freedom because it is a step outside the delineations of one's own self as defined by its historical situation. Simultaneously, this 'manner of proceeding' represents the only way of letting the 'outer sphere' enter into and express itself in the present time; it is in that transaction and conflict that the true meaning of both becomes apparent. What in the 'Verfahrungsweise' is set out as a philosophical injunction appears elsewhere as the response, or one possible response, to a specific problem: the nature of our relationship with antiquity, of how to negotiate independence and nourishment from it, of how to make of it a vital tradition and not a deadening absence. The Greeks

---

[35] Cf. Ryan, 102: 'die Dichtung wiederholt formal die Bewegung des zu sich kommenden Geistes, aber gleichzeitig führt sie das geistige Leben einer neuen, sonst nicht erreichbaren Vollendung entgegen'.

were for Hölderlin, as a writer, the 'äußere Sphäre' with which interaction was most decisive and delicate and desirable.

IV

In 'Der Gesichtspunct aus dem wir das Altertum anzusehen haben' Hölderlin begins an investigation of the relationship between antiquity and modernity. The train of thought is very like that in a letter to Schiller of 20 June 1797 on the difficulty of writing in a period when great practitioners are already at work (vi/241–2). The problem is the sheer weight of the ancient example, its absolute influence—this must be acknowledged and understood, since to ignore it will simply bring greater domination by it; but at the same time we must avoid a slavish attitude, because that will lead (and has led) to a situation where only a forked choice appears possible, a choice between two undialectical roads:

> Es scheint wirklich fast keine andere Wahl offen zu seyn, erdrükt zu werden von Angenommenem, und Positivem, oder, mit gewaltsamer Anmaßung, sich gegen alles erlernte, gegebene, positive, als lebendige Kraft entgegenzusezen. (iv/221)[36]
>
> [There really seems to be no option open between being crushed by received ideas in their 'positivity' and, with violent presumption, setting oneself as a living force against everything learnt and given, anything merely acquired.]

That is, submission or revolt. Unfortunately Hölderlin did not finish the essay. But its last words, a footnote, indicate the way lying in between 'erdrükt [...] werden' and 'gewaltsame Anmaßung', which are both 'einseitig schief' [one-sided, wrong-headed] (iv/235). It is an attitude developed in 'Über die Verfahrungsweise des poëtischen Geistes' and tested in the Pindar translations: 'Reaction gegen positives Beleben des Todten durch *reelle Wechselvereinigung* desselben' [reaction against positive animation of what is dead by *real symbiotic union* with it] (iv/222).[37] Instead of giving past achievements an absolute, formal status and trying to reinstate something no longer

---

[36] By 'das Positive' Hölderlin means what has become fixed and formal ('allzuförmliches', v/271), with no life. Cf. Mark Ogden, *The Problem of Christ in the Work of Friedrich Hölderlin* (London, 1991), 100, where he quotes Hegel's definition of a 'positive religion'.

[37] The phrase is written down the margin in very short lines, 'positives' coming at the end of a line. The *FA* (xiv/96) places a full stop after the word, though there is no trace of one in the manuscript.

applicable to our situation ('positives Beleben des Todten'), we must engage with that achievement and use it to give force to our essential differences from it, so that it has its proper value as an enlivening influence and not a deadening one. Only then, in fact, are we responding to it rightly or really understanding it in a true sense at all, by letting the precise relations between past and present operate dialectically, in creative encounter.[38]

For this to happen, a thorough, knowledgeable discovery of antiquity needs to be made. The more we learn, the more we become aware of 'eine fast gränzenlose Vorwelt' [a virtually boundless anterior world] (iv/221) and the danger of succumbing under the welter of 'positive Formen' [positive forms] (iv/221) becomes more and more real, the need for 'reelle Wechselvereinigung' more and more pressing. For if something is 'positiv', especially a work of art, that comes from our attitude to it, and is not an intrinsic property of the thing itself. The achieved works of the past can be helpful to us simply because there is so much to be learnt. Hölderlin looks at this from the perspective of the 'Bildungstrieb' (iv/221) which he identifies in the ancients as in us and which consists of the desire 'das Ungebildete zu bilden' [to give form to what has no form] (iv/221). Though the Greeks seem to have left us so little raw material, the exact knowledge of how they gave form to what they found, of their successes and false turnings, will contribute to our own modern direction from the 'gemeinschaftlichen ursprünglichen Grunde' [common original ground] (iv/222) which lies at the source of both Greek art and existence and ours.[39] Classical works of art provide us with a wealth

---

[38] A more recent version of Hölderlin's insistence on interaction between the old and the new is Eliot's idea of 'conformity': 'The necessity that [the poet] shall conform, that he shall cohere, is not one-sided; what happens when a new work of art is created is something that happens simultaneously to all the works of art that preceded it. The existing monuments form an ideal order among themselves, which is modified by the introduction of the new (the really new) work of art among them. The existing order is complete before the new work arrives; for order to persist after the supervention of novelty, the *whole* existing order must be, if ever so slightly, altered; and so the relations, proportions, values of each work of art toward the whole are readjusted; and this is conformity between the old and the new' ('Tradition and the Individual Talent', 49–50).

[39] This view later changes, or is at least refined, so that in the letter to Böhlendorff (4 Dec. 1801) Hölderlin says that 'außer dem, was bei den Griechen und uns das höchste seyn muß, nemlich dem lebendigen Verhältniß und Geschik, wir nicht wohl etwas *gleich* mit ihnen haben dürfen' (vi/426).

of attempts at the manifestation of this ground, and we can feel our way among them, get to know the means of manifestation, gain a sense of 'lebendiges Verhältniß und Geschik' (vi/426), while 'aus Einsicht' (iv/222)—insight, that is, into our different historical situation—never repeating those same ways. This is like a programme for Hölderlin's dealings with Pindar.

At about the same time as this essay was written, in June 1799, Hölderlin gave beautiful expression to the possibilities of 'reelle Wechselvereinigung' in the draft of a letter to Susette Gontard. The tone is deeply pessimistic, but the letter is a testimony to the rightness of Hölderlin's belief that light appears best among shadows.

Täglich muß ich die verschwundene Gottheit wieder rufen. Wenn ich an große Männer denke, in großen Zeiten, wie sie, ein heilig Feuer, um sich griffen, und alles Todte, Hölzerne, das Stroh der Welt in Flamme verwandelten, die mit ihnen aufflog zum Himmel, und dann an mich, wie ich oft, ein glimmend Lämpchen umhergehe, und betteln möchte um einen Tropfen Öl, um eine Weile noch die Nacht hindurch zu scheinen—siehe! da geht ein wunderbarer Schauer mir durch alle Glieder, und leise ruf' ich mir das Schrekenswort zu: lebendig Todter!

Weist Du, woran es liegt, die Menschen fürchten sich voreinander, daß der Genius des einen den andern verzehre, und darum gönnen sie sich wohl Speise und Trank, aber nichts, was die Seele nährt, und können es nicht leiden, wenn etwas, was sie sagen und thun, im andern einmal geistig aufgefaßt, in Flamme verwandelt wird. Die Thörigen! Wie wenn irgend etwas, was die Menschen einander sagen könnten, mehr wäre, als Brennholz, das erst, wenn es vom geistigen Feuer ergriffen wird, wieder zu Feuer wird, so wie es aus Leben und Feuer hervorgieng. Und gönnen sie die Nahrung nur gegenseitig einander, so leben und leuchten ja beide, und keiner verzehrt den andern. (vi/336–7)

[Every day I have to invoke the absent god again. When I think of great men at the great moments of history, how they caught at the things around them like holy fire and transformed everything dead and wooden, the world's straw, into flame which flew up with them to the heavens; and then of myself, how I often go about like a poor glimmering lamp, ready to beg a drop of oil to shine into the night a bit longer—then, I tell you, a curious shudder goes through my whole body, and softly I call out to myself the terrible words: more dead than alive.

Do you know the reason for all this? People are frightened of one another, they are afraid that one's genius will consume another's, and so they are willing to grant each other food and drink, but no nourishment for the soul, and they cannot bear it when anything they say or do is taken up in someone else's mind and transformed into flame. The fools! As if anything that people could say to each other were more than firewood, which only becomes fire again when it is caught by the fire of the spirit, just as it issued from life and from fire. And if only they will not begrudge each other mutual nourishment they will both have life and light, and neither will consume the other.]

This is a manifold lament: a lament for the lack of mutually enlivening exchange between writers, and between the present and the past, behind which lies the knowledge of the exchange possible in love. It is an attempt to summon up contact across a distance of absence; the space between Homburg (where Hölderlin was) and Frankfurt (where Susette Gontard was) becomes figurative. It is the lament of the poet 'in dürftiger Zeit' [in a barren time] (ii/94), working in the absence of divinity, of an existence infused with the Spirit, and feeling hopelessly disabled: to be a 'lebendig Todter' is the correlate to 'positives Beleben des Todten' (iv/222)—false appropriation of antiquity ('große Männer [...] in großen Zeiten'), when it is rendered wooden and meaningless, negates the transforming power it can provide and leaves the modern age cold. But given the fit interaction between the two which the second paragraph envisages, 'so leben und leuchten ja beide, und keiner verzehrt den andern', firewood becomes living flame.

Behind Hölderlin's firewood there lies the Greek ὕλη, which means wood, firewood, but also matter. The interaction held in that image is the one worked out between 'Geist' und 'Stoff' in 'Über die Verfahrungsweise des poëtischen Geistes'. Both need the other, and only in combination can they come to anything. In isolation they remain dead, imperceptible. This draft also seems to refer to Hölderlin's relations with other writers and his plan to found a journal, for which he was largely dependent on the goodwill of people of reputation. But the most important thing about it is the vitality with which it identifies a general problem of relation without referring specifically to any one instance. It is as if the resolution of it, the attainment of the proper relation between things, will work like magic. It is the search for 'das Lebendige in der Poësie' (vi/289) extended and generalized. But of course it is only in particular concrete events that the ideal, dialectical interaction, 'reelle Wechselvereinigung' (iv/222), can occur.

Perhaps a year later, or less, Hölderlin took these conclusions literally, or very specifically, and applied them in his translation of

Pindar. It was the continuation not just of the preoccupations of the letter to Susette Gontard, but of virtually all the ways and objects of thinking I have been trying to bring into the perspective of this chapter. Hölderlin was, in a sense, translating Pindar, Pindar's poems were the matter on which he worked; but there was the hope that this might force 'das Lebendige' into his poems, set fire to *his* 'Brennholz' (vi/337).

CHAPTER 4

The Pindar Translation

> wohl nemlich mag
> Den Harnisch dehnen
>   ein Halbgott, dem Höchsten aber
> Ist fast zu wenig
> Das Wirken

> ('Kolomb', ll. 129–33)

I

Hölderlin's poems had to wait a long time before they were heard. And though the Pindar translation was first published before the hymns and fragments appeared in Hellingrath's edition in 1916, it has had to wait even longer to be properly received. In part, Hellingrath's edition and study of the translations paved the way for the impact the new Hölderlin poems then made (just as within Hölderlin's work the translations led to the hymns). But whereas these poems, and with them the rest of the *oeuvre*, immediately became classics, altering the understanding of the shape and potential of German poetry, the translations, after Hellingrath's enthusiasm, did not seem to benefit from this. In 1928 Günther Zuntz refused to countenance them except as a document, though he was perfectly happy with the poems.[1]

Now, under the tutorship of Hölderlin's poetry, we have perhaps begun to learn how to read them. Hellingrath notes that Pindar was more accessible to an age under the influence of Klopstock.[2] Perhaps Celan has changed the climate again. But the strangeness of these

---

[1] Günther Zuntz, *Über Hölderlins Pindar-Übersetzung* (Kassel, 1928), 84.
[2] Hellingrath, *Pindarübertragungen von Hölderlin*, 25.

translations, their new way with words, should not, just because we have grown more tolerant of it, be glossed over.

The extremity of what Hölderlin was undertaking when he made his Pindar translation needs to be kept in mind. He had a basic method which he applied pretty much unflinchingly: to translate the Greek word for word, that is, attending not only to where the Greek word appears in the sentence, but to its position in the line.[3] To do this, translate according to one overarching principle, is an odd procedure, and not at all obvious. More normally translation consists of an intricate web of considered compromises and approximations. Hölderlin's way, on the face of it, is every bit as wilful as some of Celia and Louis Zukofsky's translations of Catullus, which are also based on a single principle, copying the sounds of the original Latin.[4] But Hölderlin had his reasons, and his method did not arise entirely *in vacuo*. What promise might such an extreme technique have held? But first, how might Hölderlin have arrived at it at all? As was suggested in the first chapter, there are certain precedents, which Hölderlin seems to have evolved radically.

The most important of these is Voss's Homer. Voss had shown what exact attention to the form and position of the Greek words within their lines could do: not only did his translations give a better insight into the Greek original, but they furnished a new language. That does not seem to have been Voss's primary intention in adopting the technique he did, but it was the most obvious result: the suggestion of a productive equation between self-restriction and the finding of new poetic possibilities. Hölderlin simply pushed one side of the equation to its logical extreme, with apparent readiness to accept a substantial amount of failure in return, but in the hope that he could thereby release potentials of poetic language previously undreamt of. It is a simple step, but a radical one, made with the same logic that marks the extraordinary thought-processes of the poetological essays.

---

[3] The importance of word-order does not seem to be sufficiently recognized. See the discussion of Hölderlin's version of the opening line of O2 by Dieter Bremer and Christiane Lehle, 'Zu Hölderlins Pindar-Übersetzung: Kritischer Rückblick und mögliche Perspektiven', in: Uwe Beyer (ed.), *Neue Wege zu Hölderlin* (Würzburg, 1994), 71–111 (104), where it is ignored.

[4] See Catullus, (*Gai Valerii Catulli Veronensis Liber*), tr. by Celia and Louis Zukofsky (London, 1969). The Preface reads: 'This translation of Catullus follows the sound, rhythm, and syntax of his Latin—tries, as is said, to breathe the "literal" meaning with him'.

Although Hölderlin was aware of Voss's reputation and achievement, he only read his Homer translations, or at least took proper cognizance of them, at a relatively late stage. We know this from one of his Homburg essays, 'Über die verschiednen Arten, zu dichten', which clearly belongs to those short pieces intended for *Iduna* and so was probably written in late summer 1799.[5] If we accept Beissner's dating of the Pindar translation (early 1800), it followed closely on this encounter with Voss; but the tone of respect and recognition in Hölderlin's reference to Voss is unmistakable, and even if with Sattler (FA, xv/26) we think of the Pindar translation's having been done in December 1800, well over a year after the *Iduna* essay, it seems certain that Voss is the chief stimulus. Quoting *Iliad* ix 485–98 to demonstrate the 'natürlicher Ton, der vorzüglich dem epischen Gedichte eigen' [natural tone which belongs especially to the epic poem], Hölderlin adds the footnote: 'Ich brauche wohl wenigen zu sagen, daß diß Vossische Übersezung ist, und denen, die sie noch nicht kennen, gestehe ich, daß auch ich zu meinem Bedauern erst seit kurzem damit bekannter geworden bin' [I hardly need to say that this is Voss's translation, and to those who are as yet unfamiliar with it I admit that to my regret I too have only recently got to know it properly] (iv/229). To confine ourselves to the passage quoted in the essay, Hölderlin will have been impressed by 'Weder zum Gastmahl gehn, noch daheim in den Wohnungen essen' [Neither going to the feast, nor eating at home in the dwellings] which maps onto the Greek (οὔτ' ἐς δαῖτ' ἰέναι οὔτ' ἐν μεγάροισι πάσασθαι, 1. 487) exactly. Correspondences like these will have corroborated the then much-circulated idea that German and Greek were akin, that there was some kind of inherent affinity between the two languages.[6] Talking to Coleridge, Klopstock said 'he had often translated parts of Homer and Virgil, line by line, and a German line proved always sufficient for a Greek or Latin one. In English you cannot do this.' Coleridge then adds: 'the German possessing the same unlimited privilege of forming compounds, both with prepositions and with epithets, as the Greek, it can express the richest single Greek word in a single German one, and is thus freed from the necessity of weak or ungraceful paraphrases'.[7] Hölderlin's translation of Pindar can be

---

[5] *FA*, xiv/97. An earlier reference to Voss as a translator: vi/152.

[6] Cf. Beissner, 33. Beissner suggests that Hölderlin's belief in this was shaken by translating Pindar.

[7] Coleridge, *Biographia Literaria*, ii 171–2.

understood as an attempt to push this perceived affinity to the utmost, to test it and force it to reveal its part of truth.

But there may have been other models or memories at work. Hölderlin had already read some Pindar, and written about him in his dissertation 'Geschichte der schönen Künste unter den Griechen' (on Pindar: iv/202–3); Seifert shows that he almost certainly used a 1697 edition of Pindar published in Oxford to help him, and this edition contains a facing Latin translation which reproduces the line-divisions of the Greek exactly.[8] As a schoolboy too, learning the elements of Greek and Latin, Hölderlin will have had to parse sentences and translate them word for word.[9]

Voss is unavoidable, as he was to any serious translator of the time. But there is a translation even more compelling in its sharing of some of the main traits of Hölderlin's Pindar: Junckherrott's New Testament. Its attention to word-order and etymology, to a point where normal German articulation dissolves, prefigures much of what Hölderlin does with Pindar. Even now, it is one of the few things to match Hölderlin's Pindar in extremity of purpose and result. I shall say more about the complexion of the Pindar translation later on, but one aspect which brings it into close relation with Junckherrott could be singled out now: the probing of the primary sense of words in their etymology. I quoted Junckherrott's justification of his practice of working the Greek for every last trace of meaning its words might yield. An extreme example is his translation of ἀποκάλυψις Ἰωάννου as 'Abhindeckung Johannis da von der gedecktwerdung da abhin'. Hölderlin is not so pedantic, but he concentrates on the original (or presumptively original) sense of a word with equal intensity. The Greek πλοῦτον, meaning 'wealth', becomes 'Vielheit' [muchness] at P3 195, translated according to the root πολύ ('much'). Similarly αἴθων is given as 'brennend': 'der brennende Fuchs' [the burning fox] (O11 20), which translates its root meaning but ignores its common application to animals (to their colour). Composite words sometimes receive the same treatment: 'Vorverkündigung' [pre-announcement] (P4 56) stems from πρόφασις ('pretext'); εὐκλέας ('glorious') is broken down into 'wohllautend' [well-sounding] (O2 163).[10]

In this last case Hölderlin is continuing a process initiated in Pindar. Pindar uses the word in a passage on his own poetry, comparing his

---

[8] Seifert, *Untersuchungen zu Hölderlins Pindar-Rezeption*, 41–5.
[9] Cf. Senger, 86.   [10] Cf. Zuntz, 18–19.

poems to arrows: they are εὐκλέας ὀϊστοὺς, 'glorious arrows', but as they stand metaphorically for poems the literal meaning of εὐκλέας shines through, distancing the word from its conventional sense. (This is encouraged a few lines before, where Pindar's arrows are φωνᾶντα, translated by Hölderlin straightforwardly as 'tönend' [sounding] (O2 152)). Hölderlin then completes the movement in his translation, where the sense of 'glorious, famous' disappears altogether and the arrows become euphonious ('wohllautend').[11]

This tendency cannot be described as a principle. There are several occasions on which Hölderlin resists any temptation to bring out the root meaning of a Greek word and gives instead the figurative meaning. This is most surprising in his translations of γᾶς ὀμφαλός, which Pindar used for Delphi ('navel of the earth'). It occurs three times in the odes Hölderlin translated (once in a varied form: ὀμφαλὸν εὐ-/δένδροιο [...] μάτερος—'navel of the well-wooded mother'), and ὀμφαλός is always rendered as 'Mittelpunct' [mid-point] (P4 131; P8 85; P11 17).[12] In the poems though, the expression is taken up three times.[13] It seems to find its way in through a form of translation. In the rewriting of 'Der gefesselte Strom' into 'Ganymed' the expression 'Busen der Erde' [bosom of the earth] (ii/67) becomes 'Nabel der Erde' [navel of the earth] (ii/68), as part of the intensification the poem undergoes (the change is roughly equivalent to the shift from 'Fesseln' [shackles] to 'Schlaken' [slag] in l. 13). Given the method of pushing words into the extreme, the change is almost one Hölderlin could have arrived at himself, without Pindar's example: to have gone from 'Busen' to 'Nabel' would have been exactly the passage out of the conventional Hölderlin was aiming at. But once he had found Pindar's expression ('Nabel der Erde') by his own means, within the logic of his own poetry, he seems to have been able and free to use it again, acknowledging and integrating the Pindaric origin by making it refer to a place, Frankfurt, as it had first referred to Delphi (ii/250, ll. 15–16).

The treatment of ὀμφαλός is unusual within the Pindar translation but not unique. It shows how dangerous it is to make any general

---

[11] At P1 20 Hölderlin translates κῆλα ('arrows') as 'Zaubersänge'; see below.

[12] Once, in P8, Beissner shows that Hölderlin first wrote 'Nabel' (v/397). The *FA* merely has slips of the pen, and the facsimile seems to uphold this view.

[13] In 'Ganymed', 'Vom Abgrund nemlich...' and 'Griechenland' (Beissner's third version). At *Oedipus*, l. 488, Hölderlin translates: 'Mitte der Erd', but at l. 915 (*FA*, l. 920): 'der Erde Nabel'.

statements about the character of the translation as a whole. As with the *Oedipus* and the *Antigonä* it is the result of several approaches to the original which was never brought into total consistency. Still, most critics identify a striving for compressed, shocking expression, which actually seems to outdo Pindar as it cuts through meanings which for his audience would have been beyond question, the only apparent ones.[14]

This probing after an 'original meaning' is not so much a search for meaning 'behind' the words as a concentration on the words themselves, an insistence on their substance as text, as scripture, as something infinitely rich. No other translator I have come across gets closer to it than Junckherrott. One would very much like to know whether Hölderlin ever came across his New Testament; or whether the forces and influences which provoked Junckherrott's translation could also have been operative in the theological tradition Hölderlin came into contact with at the Tübingen *Stift*.[15] As it was withdrawn soon after publication (in 1787 it was rare[16]), the chance is small; but the link with Pietism, and the time Hölderlin spent in Frankfurt, not far from Offenbach, where Junckherrott had published his New Testament, make it a possibility. It is an attractive one because it would provide a biographical instance of the undoubted influence of Biblical on literary translation at this juncture in its history.

Whether there is a direct connexion or not, Hölderlin's translations certainly issue from this perspective, in which literary works are given the same attention as Scripture, following on from a shift that left its most obvious mark on the translations of Voss.[17] But for Hölderlin, this shift is almost irrelevant, because the works of Pindar and Sophocles were in a real and pressing sense holy texts just as the Bible was, 'bestehendes' [what is left] (ii/172) that recorded the presence of the divine on earth. It was not just that literary texts had been endowed with the same status as holy ones; for Hölderlin they had documentary value, they were vital evidence. In the 'Anmerkungen zur Antigonä' Hölderlin compares the manner in which the god is revealed in tragedy with the manner in which he appears in in the Gospels: 'der Gott eines Apostels ist mittelbarer, ist höchster Verstand im höchstem Geiste' [the God of an apostle is more mediated, is

---

[14]   Cf. Zuntz, 16.
[15]   The book is not in the *Stift*'s library, as the librarian has kindly informed me.
[16]   Senger, 81 (the footnote).   [17]   Cf. pp. 21–2 above.

supreme reason in supreme spirit], more mediated, that is, than 'der unmittelbare Gott, ganz Eines mit dem Menschen' [the immediate God, wholly one with man] of tragedy (v/269). And Pindar's odes are yet another preservation of the divine, they represent the festivals in which the presence of the god was manifest, and they recount the myths which themselves hold the archetypal accounts of the gods' interaction with the world of men and women.[18]

This is not to say that the religious significance of Pindar exceeded the literary for Hölderlin. From the beginning Pindar represented the absolute standard of lyrical poetry. But since at bottom poetry was for Hölderlin a religious undertaking, the distinction between religious and literary significance is not quite valid. Hölderlin applied the deepest scrutiny to the structure and movement of the Pindar ode, among other things his translation was that, an intense study; but it was precisely as the fabric and workings of revelation that it claimed his attention. Here were the means by which the presence of the gods had been conserved and made 'fühlbar und gefühlt' (iv/243). The precise form demanded for that reason the utmost respect. But although Hölderlin was studying technique, searching as in Sophocles for the 'kalkulables Gesez' [calculable law] (v/195), that part of poetry which he believed could be learnt, he was also translating a religious text, where the transfer was of theological import, and in practice the different procedures we may discern at work in the Pindar translation cannot be separated out. They are joined by a more modest intention. Although Zuntz thought there were hardly any traces of the Pindar translation's having influenced Hölderlin's own poems, it was obviously instrumental to Hölderlin's development into his mature poetry.[19] Hölderlin seems to have gone to Pindar's Greek with a mind to directly inflecting his own language by putting it through the paces of a foreign one. This is an extension of the common idea of improving and exercising one's language through translation, a practice recommended as an apprenticeship since classical times.[20] As often, Hölderlin takes it to an extreme: rather than seeing translation as a challenge to test the resources of the writer and develop his skill with words, he forces the language itself to adopt the syntax and

[18] Cf. Maurice Benn, *Hölderlin and Pindar* (The Hague, 1962), 66; R. B. Harrison, *Hölderlin and Greek Literature* (Oxford, 1975), 282.
[19] Zuntz, 74; Beissner at v/376; David Constantine, 'Hölderlin's Pindar: The Language of Translation', *MLR* 73 (1978), 825–34 (834); Sattler, *FA*, xv/12.
[20] See p. 10 above.

constructions of the original tongue in a consciously artificial manner by imposing his word-for-word method upon it. In theory Hölderlin himself hardly intervenes, the language is systematically refracted and the elements of a new diction emerge. In practice though, there are, even within the technique, numerous small decisions to be made; and then Hölderlin will sometimes override the strict word-for-word principle altogether.[21]

The word-for-word transcription makes intrinsic sense as religious transfer, as technical inquiry, and as the means to a new lexis; but at the same time it is more than all these things.

II

Hölderlin translated seven of Pindar's Olympian and ten of his Pythian odes; or if he translated more they have not been transmitted to us.[22] Like the greater part of the poetological essays, the translation was private, not only in the sense that it seems not to have been intended for publication and makes no concession to a potential reader, but in the sense that he makes only very scant use of the help available in the form of books and commentaries. He was translating from the most recent edition, Heyne's of 1798, but he made many mistakes which Heyne's Latin translation could have prevented. Similarly, although Hölderlin owned Gedike's prose version of the Olympian odes, it does not appear to have much influenced his own translation. Hölderlin deliberately narrowed the focus to an intensely personal, unmediated encounter with Pindar.[23] The privacy is important, since it goes against most assumptions about the translator's role and so about the nature of translation itself. Schleiermacher for example, in his translation lecture, sees the job of the 'true translator' as bringing

---

[21] See below. Zuntz (9–16) lists instances where 'der Geist der deutschen Sprache' makes departure from the Greek inevitable.

[22] Of O9 we have only the title and first line, and several of the others are incomplete.

[23] For the private character of the Pindar, see Hellingrath, *Pindarübertragungen von Hölderlin*, 22; on 74–5 he says he found no influence of other translations. Hölderlin owned those by Gedike and, on Pindar: J. G. Schneider, *Versuch über Pindars Leben und Schriften* (Strasburg, 1774); both these books are in the *Nürtinger Bücherliste* printed in vii,3/388–91. The assumption that Hölderlin did not use Heyne's *interpretatio latina* is questioned by Bremer and Lehle, 81. In a separate volume, the *interpretatio latina* is set out as prose (and thus does not break its words like the Greek), is very literal and stays very close to Pindar's word-order, though not as close as Hölderlin's German.

together 'diese beiden ganz getrennten Personen, seinen Schriftsteller und seinen Leser' [those two quite separate people, his author and his reader], and the rest of his essay is really based on this perceived contract (Störig, p. 47). There are several points where Schleiermacher's remarks show how strange Hölderlin's Pindar was to the time; but of his general conclusion that the only true translation is one that communicates the foreignness of the original by having the receiving language bend to it the Pindar translation appears as an extreme example, going beyond anything Schleiermacher envisaged.

Hölderlin's word-for-word, line-by-line technique followed Heyne's text very exactly. He must have known that Heyne's arrangement was arbitrary, based on his new understanding of Pindar's metres but in no way ordained by the sources. Still he chose to adhere to it as if it were part of the given form Pindar had employed, in an elected blindness to contingency. Heyne's text was in very short lines, and he broke the words without regard for etymology and word-formation in order to carry through his conception of the metre. In O2 for example, Heyne splits the word ἄν-/θεμα (l. 130), where the root word ἄνθος is all one element. As a result Hölderlin often fractures his words too, though usually less radically.[24] Otherwise he disposes the words according to where their main body lies in the Greek, or sometimes he ignores Heyne's editing, on the occasions when his own poetic judgement asserts itself.[25] But this occurs comparatively rarely; in the main, and sometimes for long stretches of text, Hölderlin proceeds 'mechanically', letting himself be guided by each Greek word as it comes, in a remarkable attitude of submission.[26]

It is that, submission, 'der wunderbarste Stand der Erniedrigung' [the most curious state of abasement] in Schleiermacher's phrase. The attitude of passive receptivity, where the German bends to the Greek, is clearly sought after, and it may be programmatic, an applying of the poetics of the essays. A denial of the claims of personality, like that required of the poet: 'der tragische Dichter [verläugnet], weil er die tiefste Innigkeit ausdrükt, seine Person, seine Subjectivität ganz, so auch das ihm gegenwärtige Object, er trägt sie in fremde Personalität, in fremde Objectivität über' [the tragic poet, because he is expressing

---

[24]   But cf. O8 62 'wohlbe-/ritten', where the Greek is divided more naturally: εὐ-/ίππους.

[25]   See Constantine, 'Hölderlin's Pindar', 828, with examples.

[26]   The word 'mechanical' is used by Constantine in 'Hölderlin's Pindar' (e.g. at 827).

the deepest intensity, renounces his person, his subjectivity, entirely, as well as the object before him, he translates them into foreign personality and foreign objectivity] (iv/151). That belongs in the context of *Empedokles*, and there it is easy to see how the strategy of translating the 'ground' of feeling into the 'sign' of another, foreign situation is followed through. But it is also revealing for the Pindar: the 'sie' ('er trägt *sie* in fremde Personalität [...] über') refers back to both objects—not only the poet's subjectivity has to be renounced, but also 'das ihm gegenwärtige Object'. And that is in fact what happens in the Pindar translation. Both German and Greek are annulled so that they can meet in 'fremde Objectivität'. What appears at first as total subordination is really 'mit Demuth und Glauben getheilt' [shared between humility and faith] (vi/408); violence is done to the Greek, to the wholeness of Pindar, as it is brought across to a middle ground.

The result of this practice is a kind of *Unding*, neither Greek nor German:

> Es empfieng aber die silberfüßige Aphrodita
> Den Dalischen Gastfreund die göttlichgebauten Wagen
> Berührend mit der Hand der leichten.
> Und sie auf süßen
> Betten, die liebenswürdige legte, die Schaam,
> Gemeinsame vereinend dem Gott
> Hochzeit gemischt mit dem Mädchen   22
> Hypseus des weitgewaltgen,
> Der der Lapithen, der waffenerhabnen
> Damals war König,
> Von des Ozeans Stamm der Heros
> Der zweite, welchen dereinst in des   27
>   Pindos berühmten Gewölben
> Die Nais die fröhliche in des Pe-
> neus Bette Kreusa geboren,
>
> Der Erde Tochter.
>
>   (P9 16–31)

> [But the silver-footed Aphrodite received
> The Delian guest, touching the god-built chariots
> With her gentle hand.
> And on sweet
> Beds she laid the charming, the shame,
> In common joining to the god

> Wedding mingled with the girl
> Of Hypseus the far-powerful,
> Who of the Lapiths, the sublimely armed
> At that time was king,
> From the ocean's tribe the hero
> The second, whom once in
>   Pindos's famous vaults
> The Naiad, the happy one, in Pe-
> neus's bed, Kreusa, bore,
>
> The earth's daughter.]

Apart from very small points—the connecting τε ... τε is omitted in line 22 and 'in' (l. 27) is set a line earlier than the corresponding Greek ἐν—Hölderlin has retained the Greek word-order precisely. The line-divisions are also respected, except in the line into which 'in' is brought forward: it pushes 'Pindos', which in Greek is broken over the line-ending (Πίν-/δου), wholly into the next line. There are no lexical errors, the strangeness of the German comes entirely from the way it is obliged to conform to Greek syntax, but from this unnatural deployment of German words results a curiously loose-knit language: particularly in lines 19–22 the relations between the words seem to float and offer themselves in various combinations; without recourse to the Greek, it is impossible to say, for example, whether 'die liebenswürdige' refers back to Aphrodite, forward to 'Schaam' or even further forward to 'Hochzeit'. This uncertainty is compounded by Hölderlin's translating σφιν (l. 19) as 'sie', thus concealing the dative (= '*their* beds'). There are many such passages, and often the difficulties are increased by the fact that Hölderlin introduces lexical and grammatical errors, or by the corruptness of his text, so that the German really is incomprehensible as such. It is obviously true, as Hellingrath said, that the prose sense of the Greek was not a chief concern of Hölderlin's as he translated, but this does not mean that Pindar's stories, the matter of the poems, did not interest him; only that he was not here seeking to communicate that aspect.[27] The translations are none the less founded, ultimately, on the capacity of words to mean something, as translation must be, even if that meaning is not the object of their intention. When I speak of word-order as

---

[27]   Norbert von Hellingrath (ed.), *Hölderlins Pindar-Übertragungen* (Berlin, 1910), 5. Seifert has made it clear in his book that the content of the poems concerned Hölderlin deeply.

the prime mover of Hölderlin's Pindar translations it is always with this proviso, namely that the common ground of meaning of the two languages underpins the whole translation.[28] And as we read them, things other than the meanings of words may play on our minds, particularly rhythm, but we necessarily proceed by attempting to piece together the diverse elements before us, and what both enables and prompts us to do this is meaning, the way words signify.

Hölderlin was conducting an experiment, to determine the exact nature of the relationship between German and Greek, to see what would issue when they were run together. The ideal, the dream, would be the seamless, utter amalgamation of the two, a revelation of the habitation of the German by the Greek. 'Allda' [*there*] (ii/250) he would be then. And though the translations tended to give the lie to this, the undertaking itself was part of the project to gather Hesperia and Hellas together in the imagination. And sometimes Greek and German seem to fuse into a language unheard before which partakes equally of Pindar and Hölderlin. Even on their own these moments justify the whole enterprise. Here is such a moment, from the same poem as the last quotation:

> Des
> Mädchens aber, woher, das Geschlecht
> Du erfragst, o König? das herrschende
> Der du von allem das Ende
> Weist und alle Pfade;
> Und welche die Erde im Frühlinge Blätter
> Ausschikt, und wie viel
> Im Meere und den Flüssen Sand
> Von den Wellen und den Stößen der Winde gewälzt wird,
> Und was aufkömmt, und was
> Einst seyn wird, wohl du siehst.
>
> (P9 77–87)

> [But
> Of the girl, whence, the family
> You ask, o king? you who the controlling
> End of everything
> Know and all the paths;
> And which of the leaves the earth in the spring
> Sends out, and how much

---

[28]   Cf. Benjamin, iv 12.

In the sea and the rivers sand
By the waves and the pounding of winds is rolled
And what is approaching, and
What one day will be, that you see.]

These lines may tempt us back to the Greek to determine what is Hölderlin's and what Pindar's, but we are not forced back; the German, though quite unconventional, is self-sufficient, and though in its origins tightly strictured, it appears to move freely. The effect is of a perfect lateral transition from one language to the other, even if in reality it is more accurate to think of it as a fusion. Such moments are very rare, there is hardly anything continuous as successful as this in the whole translation. They shine out as revelations amid a context which demonstrates how on the whole the urging of German and Greek to coalesce is an impossibility.[29]

III

I have already drawn one possible link between the character of the Pindar translation and Hölderlin's poetological thought, relating his insistence on the diminution of the poet's personality to the submissive mode of translation. And, as I said, I understand the translation to be of a piece with his other preoccupations in Homburg, continuing them and concentrating them into actual practice. This means thinking of it as a transition, leading towards Hölderlin's greatest poems, particularly the most Pindaric, the hymns. But transition was really the essence, for Hölderlin, of the business of living in his time, and all his works could be described as a meditation on transition, on the night that has to be gone through, the 'zaudernde Weile' [hesitant time] (ii/91), and on the *means*, the 'Zeichen und Worte' [signs and words] (vi/420) of making the crossing into daylight. The vital thought is that the present holds the source of the future. In 1793 Hölderlin wrote to his brother: 'Diß ist das heilige Ziel meiner Wünsche, und meiner Tätigkeit—diß, daß ich in unserm Zeitalter die Keime weke, die in einem künftigen reifen werden' [This is the sacred goal of my desires and of all my actions— to germinate in our time the seeds which will ripen in a future age] (vi/93); this desire never changed, though it became more urgent.

---

[29] Constantine also singles out this passage from P9 ('Hölderlin's Pindar', 830, and *Hölderlin*, 239).

Hölderlin in his theory saw a poem as an 'Übergang', a place and an agent of transition. And a poem was a manifestation. The truth is that we are always in transition, that stasis exists only in death, and a manifestation can occur at any time and always within transition, not after it. The manifestation may momentarily transfigure the present, but not stop it, and the condition of transition will continue even then. Transition is itself the site of manifestation for Hölderlin, and therefore to speak of the Pindar translation as transitional is not to reduce it to a mere link. And though the passage to the hymns went via the Pindar, Hölderlin was writing some of his finest poems at about the same time as the translation.[30] Hölderlin's most elaborated thoughts on transition come in the essay 'Das Werden im Vergehen'.[31] It belongs with the other essays, particularly the 'Grund zum Empedokles'. It treats of the present in history seen as a point of flux, and the way one period passes into the next. The complex dynamics described can be understood to structure the Pindar translation too. Both emerge as separate manifestations of a fundamental pattern of thought, which in its perhaps simplest and certainly best-known form appears as the triadic system expounded in 'Brod und Wein'. It is obviously dangerous to want to draw all these different patterns of movement—historical, poetological and philosophical—too closely together, for they *are* different. A triadic pattern evolves naturally from the basic divisions past, present and future; it could even be said to be at the heart of our conception of things, the three dimensions in which we live and imagine; and it was particularly common in the thinking of Hölderlin's time—take the thesis, antithesis, synthesis triangle, or the teleological scheme underlying Kleist's 'Über das Marionettentheater'. A basis of three, even a particular dynamic implicating three things, is not enough to found any kind of meaningful analogy on. But the degree to which the Pindar translation can be understood in the terms of 'Das Werden im Vergehen' suggests a relationship close enough to be intrinsically important. That such a relationship exists points to an underlying constancy in Hölderlin's mode of operating, of thinking and writing. To draw the analogy is to draw attention to archetypes of Hölderlin's work—but not to claim he was conscious of them. Hölderlin

---

[30] Exactly which depends on dating. But at least 'Wie wenn am Feiertage...' and 'Der Archipelagus'.

[31] In the *FA* 'Das untergehende Vaterland...' (the opening words) because the essay is unfinished and left untitled by Hölderlin.

expanded and experimented with the medium of exploratory prose, and with the potential of translation, within a short space of time (even combining Beissner's and Sattler's datings, there cannot be more than a year between them, and they could overlap); and if like movements are at work in both, that should not be surprising. On the contrary, it confirms the coherence, the single-mindedness, of Hölderlin's project at this time. The transposition out of theory into practice comes through the middle ground of the Pindar translation, which functions precisely as a place where poetological thinking can be combined with the particulars of composition: 'das Lebendige in der Poësie' not just as a principle, but in the workings of poems.

'Das Werden im Vergehen' treats of a turning-point in history, when the transition is made from the old world to the new, and the relation to it of tragedy.[32] That turning-point is the present, we are in a constant flux of change, and different constellations are continually dissolving and assembling, the present is always a period both of growth and of decay. But the essay focuses on a particular instance as an exceptional event, when an old world is ending—'*dieser Untergang oder Übergang des Vaterlandes*' (iv/282)—and a new one struggling to take shape. Hölderlin concentrates on interpreting this decline ('Untergang') as a transition ('Übergang'), and thus as a renewal.

As with much, Hölderlin describes these historical shifts for their potential for revelation. The points of transition are vital because in them is manifested what otherwise only exists as an abstract 'in aller Zeit' [in all of time]: 'die Welt aller Welten, das Alles in Allen, welches immer *ist*' [the world of all worlds, the all in all, which always *is*] (iv/282), the divine ground to existence. A world which has become fixed no longer expresses this; the 'Welt aller Welten' only appears among dissolution or becoming, dissolution *and* becoming, for what Hölderlin insists on is that the two are the same process, seen from different perspectives. They are a period of transition, and only in transition, not in stasis, can the 'Welt aller Welten' appear. An old world dissolves (must dissolve) in order that an epiphany can occur. This is transition, *Über-gang*, as metaphor, a process in which a showing forth takes place. Hölderlin understands the poem as a place of transition into which the Spirit can enter; and here the movements

---

[32] Recently it has been argued that the whole essay describes the action of *Empedokles* and is not intended as an interpretation of history outside the drama: Ernst Mögel, *Natur als Revolution: Hölderlins Empedokles-Tragödie* (Stuttgart, 1994), 58–122.

of history, like a poem, are seen as a metaphor. Hölderlin's thinking continues along the path of his earlier reflections on the manifestation of the pure in the impure:

Dieser Untergang oder Übergang des Vaterlandes (in diesem Sinne) fühlt sich in den Gliedern der bestehenden Welt so, daß in eben dem Momente und Grade, worinn sich das Bestehende auflöst, auch das Neueintretende, Jugendliche, Mögliche sich fühlt. (iv/282)

[*This decline or transition of the country* (in this sense) is felt in the limbs of the existing world such that at precisely the moment at which what already exists dissolves, what replaces it, the new, the youthful, the possible, is also felt, and to the same degree.]

The transition, the translation from past to future, and thus the absolute which is bodied forth 'im werden' [in the becoming] (iv/282) of this moment, is felt as a contrast, the new is felt against and through the old. The principle of representation through dialectical relations, the search for 'das Lebendige' which preoccupies Hölderlin without remit, is now extended into historical processes. 'Wie die Sprache' [like language], they also signify, they are the 'Ausdruk Zeichen Darstellung eines lebendigen aber besondern Ganzen' [expression sign representation of a living but particular whole] (iv/282), and the efficacy of their signifying depends on the same laws: it is the warring of opposed elements, their cohabitation, that brings about realized expression.

What starts off in the guise of an analogy ('*wie* die Sprache') reveals itself later in the essay to be more than that; and the comparison with language thus appears not as an illustration but as the amalgamation of a further aspect of the same process: language in the form of poetry (of tragedy) is part of the transition and the means by which it is most fully realized and so completed. Its role is not subsidiary, but cardinal. Hölderlin introduces the term memory—'Erinnerung'—, and with it that of 'idealische Auflösung' [ideal dissolution] (iv/283) as opposed to the dissolution which is the premiss for the essay, and which Hölderlin also calls 'wirklich' [actual] (iv/284). Memory is the action of tragedy, in which the end of the old world is represented and so becomes ideal. The representation, or act of memory, means a detached retrospect on the turmoil of transition in which destruction is understood as part of change and as existing simultaneously and intrinsically alongside the construction of the new. This recapitulation overcomes the 'gap' ('Lüke') between past and future, and in it the transition is made, because what before was perceived as a decline can now be seen to be a new beginning. The dissolution was not only a dissolution; or as Hölderlin says, it was necessary:

Die Auflösung also als Nothwendige, auf dem Gesichtpuncte der idealischen Erinnerung, wird als solche idealisches Object des neuentwikelten Lebens, ein Rükblik auf den Weg, der zurükgelegt werden mußte, vom Anfang der Auflösung bis dahin, wo aus dem neuen Leben eine Erinnerung des Aufgelösten, und daraus, als Erklärung und Vereinigung der Lüke und des Contrasts, der zwischen dem Neuen und dem Vergangenen stattfindet, die Erinnerung der Auflösung erfolgen kann. (iv/283)

[The dissolution therefore, as necessary from the point of view of ideal memory, becomes as such the ideal object of the newly evolved life, a backward look down the path that had to be travelled from the beginning of the dissolution up to the point when out of the new life a memory of the dissolved, and out of this, in turn, as an explanation and reconciliation of the gap and the contrast which occurs between the new and the past, the memory of the dissolution can result.]

From the vantage-point of memory the dissolution appears 'als das was sie eigentlich ist, als ein reproductiver Act' [as what it actually is: a reproductive act] (iv/284). It is a question of rethinking something in its true terms, in the realization which controls 'Über die Verfahrungsweise des poëtischen Geistes': that the Spirit never rests, that it is always seeking new forms and destroying the old ones: 'das Leben [durchläuft] alle seine Puncte [...], und um die ganze Summe zu gewinnen, auf keinem verweilt, auf jedem sich auflöst, um in dem nächsten sich herzustellen' [life runs through all its points and, in order to gain the total sum, dwells on none of them but dissolves each time to reconstitute itself in the next] (iv/284). Again, the laws of life and those of poetry are interdependent.

In analogy with the course of 'Das Werden im Vergehen' we can read the Pindar translation. Its very form is a function of the same underlying ways of thought and understanding. The transitional point, reflected upon as the present in which we are under way in the essay, is subjected to a meditative analysis in the Pindar. It is a translation in which the crossing over, the intermediary stage which a conventional translator will skip over or repress, becomes uncomfortably apparent. The gap is translated. If we think of a translation as a modulation (as in music) out of the original, then the Pindar translation is an unresolved chord, with the modulation in progress. But the unresolvedness is exactly its rich potential, the potential to be found in moments of transition underlined in 'Das Werden im Vergehen': 'im übergehenden ist die Möglichkeit aller Beziehungen vorherrschend' [in the moment of transition there is the possibility of all relations] (iv/282). It is because of this vast expansion of possibility that the passage from one world to the next is so important and a locus of manifestation. Fixed forms are particular, one constellation of possibilities, and as such mask other forms. Their dissolution, the traverse into in-betweenness, makes for a creative condition where all forms are in play, but none dominant; where certain combinations present themselves and then recede in general flux. Hölderlin thought as Novalis did: 'Nichts ist *poëtischer*, als alle *Übergänge* und heterogène Mischungen' [Nothing is more *poetic* than all *transitions* and heterogeneous mixtures].[33]

Pindar's Greek was also an established, transmitted form, and Hölderlin seems to have approached it with the intention to break it, guided by the belief in the transience of all forms, in the necessity of their yielding to new ones. Translation, as Benjamin asserts, is itself a particular form, 'ein ganz eigentümlicher Darstellungsmodus' [a mode of representation *sui generis*], and to translate is to assist the passage into a new manifestation.[34] The movement out of the old and into the new, to use the essay's terms, is anatomized in the translation, and the focus on precisely what happens as Pindar is made to shift into Hölderlin's German is intensified by Hölderlin's translational method, which in its severity tends to make the languages clash together, so that, at a kind of mid-point or no-man's-land between the two there results a double language where the transformation from Greek to German is crystallized or not quite completed. The Pindar translation can be thought of as lying between the original Greek and an imaginary, fully translated, self-sufficient German. From the middle text one must look back to the Greek nearly always to understand properly (or at least to understand something approaching the original), but at the same time the German contains the seeds of its own modulation into independence, where it can stand and work as poetry on its own. And in fact this third, right-hand text is not all imaginary, there are moments when the transition seems to be complete, such as P9 77–87 (quoted above), any number of short phrases throughout, the later retranslation of P4 180–9 in the first

---

[33] Novalis, iii 587.   [34] Benjamin, iv 12.

Pindar-Fragment ('Untreue der Weisheit') or of bits of P1 (v/291–2; FA, xv/365–72), or this:

> Tagwesen. Was aber ist einer? was aber ist einer nicht?
> Der Schatten Traum, sind Menschen. Aber wenn der Glanz
> Der gottgegebene kommt,
> Leuchtend Licht ist bei den Männern
> Und liebliches Leben.   (P8 135–9)

> [Beings of a day. But what is a man? But what is he not?
> The shadows' dream, are humans. But when the brightness
> The god-given, comes,
> Shining light is with the men
> And lovely life.]

Giving the Pindar translation a past, present and future like this allows the analogy with 'Das Werden im Vergehen' to be pursued into its particulars. The old world, as a specific arrangement of Nature and human beings (iv/282), or as Greek text, passes from its one 'Beziehungsart' [kind of relation] (iv/282) into a process of apparent disintegration. This interim stage, while it is being lived through, is terrible and bewildering because all established relations are upset and undone, there are no landmarks. Hölderlin says it has 'einen eigentümlichen Karakter zwischen Seyn und Nichtseyn' [a peculiar character between being and not-being] (iv/283), and this is also a good description of the Pindar translation: to read it is to be set in a region which is almost pre- or non-lingual or before the ordering of consciousness, because it is an unresolved mixture of different systems where the very articulation of sense seems to be both impeded and enacted.[35] The Greek is dismantled into German words, and its structure cannot signify in them; German is given a foreign structure in which its words cannot properly operate.[36] But this region is also extremely fertile—the translations are rich in exciting juxtapositions and sequences of syntax that startle into a new awareness of the possibilities of language. There is the sense of a resource not quite tapped. The effect the translations produce is a wavering between the two languages, a fluctuation which occurs as we read between those

---

[35] Heinrich Lützeler talked of the translation as being 'vorgrammatikalisch oder übergrammatikalisch bestimmt': 'Hölderlin als Übersetzer', *Neue Jahrbücher für Wissenschaft und Jugendbildung* 2 (1926), 687–700 (698).

[36] Pierre Bertaux called it 'non pas [...] allemand [...] mais [...] un langage compréhensible aux Allemands': *Hölderlin: Essai de biographie intérieure* (Paris, 1936), 370.

moments when the language rejects us and those when it captivates us:

> Wie nemlich die Meerslast
> Tragend tief des andern Gefäßes,
> Ununtergetaucht bin ich, wie das Korkholz,
> Über der Mauer der See.
>
> (P2 143–6)[37]
>
> [For like the sea's burden
> Bearing deep of the other vessel,
> Unsubmerged I am, like cork,
> Above the wall of the sea.]

The connexion between the potential released at points of historical change and the meaning for writing of unfixity is made by Hölderlin himself in the essay: 'Im Zustande zwischen Seyn und Nichtseyn wird aber überall das Mögliche real, und das wirkliche ideal, und diß ist in der freien Kunstnachahmung ein furchtbarer aber göttlicher Traum' [But in the state between being and not-being the possible becomes real, and the actual becomes ideal, at all points, and this, in the free imitation of art, is a terrible but divine dream] (iv/283). This openness of circumstance, this infinite possibility, provides the conditions in which art becomes possible; but also, paradoxically, in which it is most needed to effect the transition and overcome the middle confusion. It makes a sense of precisely the non-sense that fosters it, and works towards its own superfluity, towards the effacing of its own premisses. Art enters into the flux surrounding it and takes its rise from the uncertainty, borrowing from it. That the poet must be in a fully undetermined, open state at the point of composition is something Hölderlin insists on in 'Über die Verfahrungsweise des poëtischen Geistes'. Of the poet he says (it reminds one of Keats's 'negative capability'):

die Summe aller seiner Erfahrungen, seines Wissens, seines Anschauens, seines Denkens, Kunst und Natur wie sie in ihm und außer ihm sich darstellt, alles ist wie zum erstenmale, eben deßwegen unbegriffen, unbestimmt, in lauter Stoff und Leben aufgelöst, ihm gegenwärtig, und es ist vorzüglich wichtig, daß er in diesem Augenblicke nichts als gegeben annehme, von nichts positivem ausgehe, daß die Natur und Kunst, so wie er sie kennen gelernt hat und sieht, nicht eher *spreche*, ehe *für ihn* eine Sprache da ist. (iv/263–4)

---

[37] In *FA* lines 144–7.

[the sum of all his experiences, his knowledge, his intuition, his thinking, art and nature as manifested within him and without him, everything is present to him as if for the first time, and for that very reason is unfixed, undetermined, dissolved into sheer material and life, and it is of the utmost importance that at this moment he take nothing for granted and make no positive assumptions; that nature and art as he sees them and has come to know them do not *speak* until a language is there *for him*.]

But out of this there must issue a 'Gebild' [form] (iv/265), a new world, a particular combination of the possibilities liberated by the transitional decline. And from the new constellation the whole process appears to make sense, what before could only be felt, or read, as disintegration, becomes recognizable as growth and articulation. It is an act of recovery. Those passages of the Pindar which make a wholly successful crossing illumine and validate the 'middle' text as a 'schöpferischer Act' [creative act] (iv/286), just as tragedy, in the scheme of 'Das Werden im Vergehen', completes the process of transition by representing the dissolution (by 'remembering' it): fully comprehended it becomes 'furchtlos' [without fear] (iv/283). It is a pattern that recurs throughout Hölderlin. 'Friedensfeier' works on the same dynamic: in the 'andere Klarheit' [other clarity] spread by the god's appearance, all the confusion up to that point is revealed as the ripening of history: 'sie hören das Werk,/Längst vorbereitend, von Morgen nach Abend, jezt erst' [only now do they hear,/Long in preparation, from morning to evening, the work] (ll. 29–30).

The achieved parts of the translation by their own success enhance the rest and give the whole a rationale. Knowing its character of transition we can read it again for the many beginnings it holds and learn to see there 'im ersten Zeichen Vollendetes schon' [in the first sign the thing perfected] (ii/13). And reading it thus, aware of its *potential*, its richness becomes more and more evident, and the readiness of the reader to let notions of normal German syntax and grammar stretch, to become an adept at following German down Greek constructions, grows alarmingly rapidly. The language demands a 'suspension of disbelief' and convinces again and again by its concrete potency and strangeness. (It is almost certain, and certainly unavoidable, that for an English reader the infringements of German grammar and usage jar less than they would for someone with German as their mother-tongue.) Part of its attraction must come from its exotic quality and from the 'fascination of what's difficult'. We have to engage in a mental wrestle as we read, one that has at least a semblance of retracing Hölderlin's own wrestle with Pindar, though in fact it is a different encounter.

IV

Similar congruities and analogies to those between the Pindar translation and 'Das Werden im Vergehen' exist between the translation and other aspects of Hölderlin's reflections on poetry. The figure I have argued is common to both translation and essay, in which the look backwards recapitulates all that has come before and thereby enables the comprehension of the whole, also informs 'der Gang und die Bestimmung aller und jeder Poësie' (iv/263).[38] It is a recurrent movement in Hölderlin's work. True, the account of Hölderlin's poetic thinking I gave in the last chapter was deliberately shaped to the theme of translation, but it was not, I think, falsified by being given that bias, and its essentials come through.

The Pindar translation can be seen as a study in transition, and is itself the transit from theory to practice, a kind of theory *in* practice, a more concrete application of the ideas thought out in prose. The main terms of Hölderlin's poetics bear a strong resemblance to the dynamics of translation, particularly as they are engaged in the form of the Pindar translation, which even seems to be partly determined by the structure of the poetics. I am thinking particularly of the way Hölderlin builds a maximum degree of conflict into the translation, the way he forces the languages to meet head on. The poetics hold that it is at the point of greatest conflict—'höchste Entgegensezung' (iv/262), 'Zwist' (iv/149)—that the Spirit is felt (that the poem works). According to Hölderlin's delineation of the course of the 'tragische Ode' (that is, a Pindaric ode) at the start of 'Grund zum Empedokles', the poem actually contrives this opposition: 'der Zwist [...], den die tragische Ode gleich zu Anfang *fingirt*, um das Reine darzustellen' [the quarrel which the tragic ode *fakes* at the very start, in order to represent the pure] (iv/149).[39] Something analogous is engineered in the encounter of the Pindar translation, the languages are encouraged to quarrel.

It is tempting to think that Hölderlin may have had translation in the back of his mind as a paradigm for some of the operations he was

---

[38] Cf. above, pp. 95–6.   [39] My italics.

exploring. Though he never touches on it explicitly in the essays, he was translating throughout his time in Homburg: before the Pindar, he did (at least) a first version of O1, part of the eighteenth of Ovid's *Heroides*, the first stasimon of *Antigone* and the opening of the *Bacchae*. Certainly the Pindar translation makes good sense as an extension of Hölderlin's poetological preoccupations into a practice, as an enactment of the poetics. And in this it functions in a very particular way, because of its peculiar position: at the mid-point between theory (for which it is a testing-ground) and original composition (of which it is an analogy), and at a remove from both, it allows the realization of the poetics and the foreshadowing of actual poems.

It is important to fathom what Pindar meant for Hölderlin. In one of his dissertations he called his poetry 'das *Summum* der Dichtkunst' [the *summum* of the poetic art] because it combines 'in dieser gedrängten Kürze die Darstellung des Epos und die Leidenschaft des Trauerspiels' [within its compact brevity the narrative depiction of epic and the passion of tragedy] (iv/202–3). That is, it represents an abstract or essence of the whole of Greek literature. Pindar thus comes to be an emblem for the Greek achievement (much as tragedy is commonly seen to be), and so to translate him is to engage with the problem of the modern relationship to antiquity, always at the centre of Hölderlin's attention, directly.

So Pindar was a poet with something like absolute status, and on top of this, or as another aspect of the same phenomenon, there is the religious significance of his poetry I mentioned in relation to Hölderlin's method of translation, its value as document. Ancient Greece was principally important to Hölderlin as a time and place of divine immanence. Pindar's poetry had both recorded and itself been a manifestation of the immanent Spirit. Hölderlin wanted the same immanence in his own time, he wanted his poetry to be able to provoke the passage of the Spirit, to be inspired, as he saw Pindar's to have been. Pindar provided the traces of the Spirit, one of its best and most expressive forms. We can suspect that Pindar's poetry, as an epitome of Greece, in whose terms Hölderlin almost exclusively understood the meaning of the Spirit, but even more so as the sacred fragments of perhaps the Spirit's most perfect epiphany, came to be a vital analogy, an analogy of the very highest quality and authority, of the *Geist*. Pindar is not the presence Hölderlin wants to urge into his poetry, but an analogy so close that it tends towards identification. But it is firmly as analogue that we must see it, as compelling precisely because there is the final ineluctable dividing-line. Difference is as essential as similarity for the functioning of analogy.

In Hölderlin's poetics a poem works to bring the Spirit into its dynamics, but the poems themselves inevitably fail to do so and what they voice is its absence, a sense of what it would be like through the almost unbearable desire for it to be there. Now in a sense with translation it is the same: the Greek poem can never be fully reconstituted in the German, a lack or discrepancy is always implied. But whereas in the poetry the absence, however strongly the need and the longing be realized, must always remain an absence and as such only definable in negative terms, in the translations what cannot be fully conveyed is quite specific and actual: the Greek text. By making the analogical transposition from poetic Spirit to Pindar's Greek, the poetics, at their most extreme, can be turned into a form of practice. The idea of conflict as a creative force is trusted to even in the particulars of a translation, and verified. To attempt the manifesting of Pindar in the *Stoff* of the German language, driving the two together in a deliberately contrived process of conflict, is to create *in nuce* the conditions under which at the zenith of its ideal the poetic theory would have the poem express the Spirit. What of Pindar can be brought into German in the measure of success or failure underwrites or invalidates the poetics. The translation, structured according to the principles of the poetics, enacts them, and by going through and working out their tensions and motors, provides a proof of their possible value and effectiveness. Because of the distance afforded by this analogical status a freedom from the deep seriousness of the full-blown poetics can be attained: were the poetics truthful they could when transposed a step further, into the mechanics of an original poem, body forth the Spirit itself. That is the (utopian) hope. Analogy, as a way of thinking, thus permits the translation of Pindar to represent the ideal poem, which is something in the end accessible *only* via analogy.

Translation presents an especially encouraging and enticing counterpart to the workings of a poem because it does relate; something of Pindar passes into a new form, however imperfectly. The issue of the clear, successful moments of the translation out of the confused knot is a luminous betokening of similarly realized moments in the poetry, of moments when the Spirit would find a new manifestation; just as the epiphanies in the poems would shadow forth the real coming of fulfilled life in the world. But both of these relations are themselves only analogies. What the poems would most like to believe but are forced to negate is that their images could be directly related to the real world by expressing the Spirit into it and so affecting it fundamentally. As it is, they can only function as counter-images, of what the world is not like, and remain empty, though beautifully and empoweringly so.

And, though Hölderlin may sometimes have wished to believe it, the translation of Pindar was not a passage of the Spirit itself either. Pindar is not the Spirit but a past manifestation of it, an old form, and to translate him is to convey that old metaphor, that particular form of the Spirit which was proper to a specific time and place. It is a transference of the holy, the sacred vessels, fragments, traces, but can only hopefully symbolize what is really needed: the vessels of a new manifestation. The traces are preserved in and meditated upon as memory, as proof that the full life was once reality; and studied for an understanding of the mechanics of revelation. But these activities are very much of the interim, they hold only promise. Those points of 'leuchtend Licht' (P8 138), of full reignition of Pindar in German, are not a return of the Spirit but only the reanimation of its former housing, the restoration of a relic. As such they are precious tokens of something more. But the *method* by which the transition is effected is the same as that by which the Spirit might be made to fill the poem; its worth as a dynamic of manifestation is proven. Whereas there is an analogy between the Pindar translation and the ideal poem imagined in Hölderlin's poetics, the workings and movements that inform these two are not, in the end, analogous merely, but at bottom identical. They have been transferred from the poetics to the translations.

v

Hölderlin saw a poem as a bringing-into-relation of disparate spheres, and his poetics is the search for the exact nature of a just relation. Out of things justly related 'das Lebendige' may spring, in poetry, but not only in poetry. Translation is entirely a matter of relation: the nature of the relation between original and version determines the type of translation in question. There must always be a recognizable relation between the original and the translation for the translation to be so called at all, but this relation can be various and is never straightforward. In some sense a translation is always a mutilation, but more importantly it is a mutation, a transformation into something different and particular. The original has to change (and sometimes this change may be felt to be a loss) as it comes across into the new language; the question for the translator is how that change should be managed, and whether it should be elided (concealed), or accented.

Hölderlin's technique draws attention to the process of translation and emphasizes the transformation Pindar must undergo; nothing is smoothed over. His translation reveals the insufficiency and obfuscation of conventional translations, though according to the expectations attaching to these it is clearly at fault itself. It does nothing to hide the foreignness of the original, makes no attempt to naturalize it or fit it anywhere in our understanding. It is aligned with nothing modern apart from the German language, and that only reluctantly. Bertaux comments that Hölderlin does not seem to be aiming at 'un équivalent à ce qu'un Grec pouvait comprendre à la lecture de Pindare, mais à provoquer une émotion comparable à celle d'un Allemand, de Hölderlin lui-même lisant ce texte grec' [an equivalent of what a Greek might gather from a reading of Pindar, but at provoking an emotion comparable to that of a German, of Hölderlin himself, reading the Greek text].[40] But often, reading the translation, the sense is less of one man's comprehension than of a virtually impersonal encounter between the two *languages*, of German's response to the Greek (and as Beissner and Seifert have indicated, Hölderlin's understanding went far beyond what can be gleaned from the translation, it cannot be read as evidence for his reading of Pindar). With a passage such as:

> Der Götter aber das Angesicht, das unverderbliche bitt ich
> Das freundlichhelfende, für eure
> Begegnisse. Wenn nemlich einer Trefliches erreicht hat,
> Nicht mit weiter Arbeit, vielen weise
> Scheint er mit unnachdenkenden
>
> Das Leben zu waffnen mit rechtrathschlagenden
> Künsten. Das aber nicht an Menschen liegt;
> Ein Dämon aber giebt es
> Anderswoher andere von oben herunter treffend,
> Einen andern aber unter der Hände
> Maas läßt er hernieder.
>
> (P8 101–11)

---

[40] *Essai*, 365.

[The gods' though, their countenance unperishable, I ask,
Amiably helpful, for your
Encounters. If namely someone has achieved great things,
Not with long work, to many wise
He seems with unthoughtful ones

To arm life with well-counselled
Arts. That though does not lie with humans;
A demon though there is
Striking from elsewhere others from above,
But another under the hands'
Measure he leaves down here.]

with such a passage, it is not Hölderlin and not Pindar we get but the attempt to make Pindar's meaning and form pass into German. There is a staging of the interaction of Greek and German, of their mutual untractability and occasional meshing, a kind of conflict on the page. Much of the time, what is conveyed is the impossibility of conveying the Greek. This 'liebender Streit' [loving strife] (ii/96) is embodied in Hölderlin's text so that it becomes an index of the relationship between the two languages: the interaction is rendered palpable, the actual *process* whereby Greek does or does not enter the German, whereby German receives or does not receive the Greek, is realized. The difference between the languages is the main factor in the language of the translation. How the two systems *meet* is at the focal point, and what issues is a dialectical result which crystallizes the circumstances of the meeting. It is a true relation in that none of the difficulties of the transaction are shunned, but woven into the texture of the whole. Most translations are heavily biased on the side of the language of arrival and fabricate an easy reception of the foreign. Well-known receptacles are filled with disparate matter, a particular convention of transition is instated and the foreignness of the original is denied. With this denial the possibility of actual encounter is done away with. Real encounter means engaging with the form of the Greek as the only embodiment of its meaning, and not purporting to give access to something behind the words. If Hölderlin's Pindar does seem to reach into deep structures of the Greek, revealing something unexpected, that is only in relation to the prejudices about the nature of classical works we have acquired from our familiarity with conventional translations.

The possibility which the search for a true dialectical relation opens up is that of a fusion, when the elements of both languages coincide and as it were complement each other. The Greek forces the German into a constellation which it had never quite adopted before but which releases a potential, something it always had. I am thinking of those moments previously considered as perfect transitions through the process of conflict into clarity, the paradigmatic moment being P8 135–9 because it contains an image of epiphany that illustrates exactly its effect within the translation as a whole. In these moments, there seems to be a sort of complicity between Pindar and Hölderlin. Here are the lines from the end of P8 again, along with the Greek:

> Tagwesen. Was aber ist einer? was aber ist einer nicht?
> Der Schatten Traum, sind Menschen. Aber wenn der Glanz
> Der gottgegebene kommt,
> Leuchtend Licht ist bei den Männern
> Und liebliches Leben.[41]

> Ἐπάμεροι. τί δέ τις; τί δ᾽ οὔ τις;
> Σκιᾶς ὄναρ, ἄνθρωποι. ἀλλ᾽, ὅταν αἴγλα
> Διόσδοτος ἔλθῃ,
> Λαμπρὸν φέγγος ἔπεστιν ἀνδρῶν
> Καὶ μείλιχος αἰών.

Hölderlin cleaves very close to the vocabulary, line-division and general shape of the Greek, so the correspondences seem mirror-perfect, but the lines are inflected by minute divergences: the copula in the first two lines is added, the singular σκιᾶς is rendered by the plural 'der Schatten', the necessary articles and preposition ('bei') are supplied. In line 135 comes the only departure from Pindar's word-order: 'nicht' is put at the end of the line giving it a strong ending (the Greek οὔ is penultimate). There is no reinterpretation or revision of the Pindar involved, but these variations are so placed as to free the German entirely from its original. There is a poise where the foreign pressure exerted on the language, threatening it, is precisely countered by the new articulation it has found, and what is normally felt as a conflict between the two languages is transcended. This fusion has its parallel in the poetics, where the apex of the poem is attained as the quarrel between its parts resolves into 'harmonische Entgegensezung' (iv/255).

That such moments of balance seldom occur suggests how precarious they are and the background of incompatibility and discord they come

---

[41] For translation see p. 121 above.

from. The stringent search for these isolated patches of common ground entails much failure, but perhaps the failure is important too, for what it shows to be unreachable by German and unmitigatedly different between the languages. The degree to which they conjoin or divide reveals something of the relation between two authors, languages, cultures and epochs, and the moments of mutual illumination, of coherence, open a possible passage back and forward between them. It seems that these moments could only be found via a violence, a terrible battering at the source text; but coupled with a readiness to incorporate those opportunities of fusion that makes them seem like beautiful gifts.

The problem of how to achieve a proper relation with the past, especially the past of classical Greece of which Pindar is an emblem, is perhaps Hölderlin's obsession: in it he sees the key to the happy development of the present. It is a question of remembering what is essential, of creating a true tradition and above all of ensuring that the influence of the Greek past is enlivening and not deadening. The Pindar translation needs to be seen in this light, perhaps above all in this light. Its method as I have just considered it, as a means of precise relation, seems to convert the precept of '*reelle Wechselvereinigung*' (iv/222) arrived at in the essay where Hölderlin begins to deal with the difficulties of tradition and influence, 'Der Gesichtspunct aus dem wir das Altertum anzusehen haben'.

Hölderlin understood the danger and necessity of influence. He also had a pretty good idea, from the start, of the direction he wanted to go and of the people who could point the way. One of his earliest poems (1787/8) identifies his two main models:

> Ists schwacher Schwung nach Pindars Flug? ists
> Kämpfendes Streben nach Klopstoksgröße?
> ('Mein Vorsaz', ll. 11–12)

> [Is it a feeble attempt to fly like Pindar?
> A competitive striving after the greatness of Klopstock?]

Of these, Pindar affected Hölderlin's poetry most directly and radically, though Klopstock probably provided the means for that to be possible, a language into which Pindar could come.[42] But an overpowering influence on Hölderlin's young person and poetry was

[42]   On Pindar's influence on Hölderlin, see the whole of Seifert, *Untersuchungen zu Hölderlins Pindar-Rezeption*.

Schiller. For a while Hölderlin wrote poems wholly in the Schillerian mode. The letters he sent him are ample evidence of the ravaging that influence can inflict. 'Ich gehöre ja—wenigstens als res nullius—Ihnen an' [I belong to you—at least as a *res nullius*], Hölderlin wrote after fleeing from him and Jena. He was emptied by a sense of insufficiency and barrenness: 'Ich friere und starre in dem Winter, der mich umgiebt. So eisern mein Himmel ist, so steinern bin ich' [I'm going stiff with cold in the winter that surrounds me. The sky is made of iron, and I am made of stone] (vi/181). Coming under Pindar's influence, though spared the tensions of personal contact, he was also subject to the total historical pressure of antiquity. He was as lucid about the reality of that pressure as about the painful dynamics of the relationship with Schiller, aware that even the desire for originality was only a reaction against an attitude of subordination to antiquity which had become the norm, and that there could be no simple evasion of its prerogative. Hölderlin saw that all civilizations had foundered because of their inability to assimilate and develop the achievements of their predecessors, and that predicament had become critical in his own time, unsettled by the French Revolution, and, in literary terms, dominated by classical Greece. The threat of losing one's 'eigene lebendige Natur' [own living nature] (iv/221) thus spans out far beyond the immediate dilemma of an author's dealing with a precursor, to the life of a nation engaged in the process of substantiating itself against and with the achievements of what had come before. And because language is always at the core of a nation, translation plays a vital role in anticipating and effecting that process. The main problems of finding an enabling relation between antiquity and the present, as Hölderlin addresses them in the 'Gesichtspunct' essay, transfer naturally to the co-ordinates of translation. And it is through translation that Hölderlin tried to resolve these problems: at first more for himself, with the Pindar; and then with the intention of working on his contemporaries, with the versions of *Oedipus the King* and *Antigone*.

The thing is to find a way of relating to antiquity, above all through its literature, in such a way that it sustains and stimulates rather than crushes. The consequences of the stifling of the creative instinct, which Hölderlin places at the centre of civilization, are terrible. '*Denn diß ist der einzige Fehler der Menschen*', says Hölderlin, '*daß ihr Bildungstrieb sich verirrt*' [*For this is the only mistake mankind can make: to lose its creative urge*] (iv/221). This implies the finding of a particular path, one which may start from the same place as a classical work but which traces its own way in correspondence with the specific constellation of the times to its 'eigentümliche Stelle' [very own place] (iv/222). The past becomes damaging if it is perceived to prescribe a path as the only possible one. In reality it itself consists of myriad paths, different courses issuing from a common foundation, and this insight alone goes a long way towards unsettling the attitude which leads to antiquity becoming 'Positives' (iv/221) and deadening. None of these paths can be taken again, but our path, the modern one, takes its direction from them, necessarily, since they are part of our past, and total 'originality', or freedom from origins, does not exist.[43] As our course is inevitably determined by precursors ('bestimt', iv/222), it will benefit from exact knowledge of that determining and a hand in shaping it, choosing which lines it deflects from, and so altering their own relation to other paths. This seems to be what Hölderlin means by 'reelle Wechselvereinigung', a dialectical movement which avoids letting antiquity become static and nominal and the kind of influence which numbs, and so destroys.

In translating Pindar, Hölderlin will undoubtedly have had the considerations of the essay in mind. The translation can be understood as a study of a high-road, perhaps the main passage, from the 'Urgrund aller Werke und Thaten der Menschen' [primal ground of all human works and deeds] (iv/222) to a manifestation. But it is also a study in self-preservation, a coming-to-terms with the force of Pindar's influence, a special channelling so that a direction may be taken from it. From the identification with Pindar in the early poem and the total admiration of the second Magister-Specimen there had to evolve a means of situating that presence and getting a grasp on it rather than being grasped. Not of negating it, but of so twisting it that it became manageable. Hölderlin fled from Schiller, but Pindar could not be fled from, he had to be met head-on, and Hölderlin had derived the necessary violence from the depth of his abasement before Schiller.

According to Harold Bloom, and as an idea it seems convincing, the way a poet has to cope with the influence of a precursor is deliberately to misinterpret him, an insight Bloom derives from psychological defence-mechanisms described by Freud.[44] In that light

---

[43] 'Originalität ist uns ja Neuheit; und mir ists nichts lieber, als was so alt ist, wie die Welt', says the 'Editor' in the penultimate version of Hyperion (iii/235).

[44] See Harold Bloom, The Anxiety of Influence, 2nd edn. (New York, 1997).

the Pindar translation appears as a paradigm of the process, though Bloom concentrates on relations between poem and poem, not on any other means of controlling an influence. Bloom calls poetry a 'disciplined perverseness' (p. 95), which fits the Pindar exactly. In P1, Hölderlin translates three words in the genitive, πολεμίων ἀνδρῶν καμόντων ('when the enemy was in distress'), which he must have been capable of recognizing as a genitive absolute construction, as 'Kriegrischer Männer kämpfender' (l. 151), keeping the three genitives. It is an appropriation, a deliberate forming of a particular, warped Pindar so as to create wilfully a precursor, an influence that is in fact an invention and can thus be called *own*. Having derived from Pindar something (necessarily, but pointedly) other than Pindar himself, in a move of misprision, Hölderlin can let the influence act, but in consciousness of his own hand in it free himself from the impediment of anxiety. Enough, at least, for Pindar to cause a productive tension and not a crippling.

Hölderlin's extreme, distorting method of translating thus has the extra purpose of contriving a personal Pindar, of displacing him. Whether that was Hölderlin's (conscious) intent or not, it is certainly the effect: he makes a space for himself. It is clear, reading the Pindar, to what extent Hölderlin has twisted the original. Bits of it have become incomprehensible, and bits of it luminous. As Zuntz says, he arrives at 'etwas Grundanderes [...] als den wirklichen Pindar' [something quite different from the real Pindar].[45] This through the severities of his method, but also through plain error and miscomprehension. But the error, when the translation is seen from this perspective, is an intrinsic part of the creative deviation. We can never really say, as we can with the Sophocles, where Hölderlin is forcefully imposing his own interpretation on the sense. Parts of the translation, though, have a coherence in themselves which is at odds with the Greek. A line in O14 Hölderlin gives as 'In Sorgen der Sänger' [in worries of singers] (l. 26). It is part of the sentence:

> Λυδίῳ γὰρ
> Ἀσώπιχον ἐν τρόπῳ
> Ἐν μελέταις τε ἀείδων
> Μόλον.

---

[45] Zuntz, 46.

C. M. Bowra translates:

> I have come with a song for Asopichos
> In the Lydian style with careful art.[46]

Ἐν μελέταις could mean 'in Sorgen' in the sense of preoccupations, Bowra's 'with careful art' is evasive; but ἀείδων means 'singing', 'singing of' ('with a song for Asopichos'), and is not the genitive plural of ἀοιδός ('a singer') Hölderlin takes it to be. But it sinks in, and surfaces again in the last couplet of 'Heimkunft':

> Sorgen, wie diese, muß, gern oder nicht, in der Seele
> Tragen ein Sänger und oft, aber die anderen nicht.

> [Worries like these a singer, gladly or not, must
> Bear in his soul, and often, but the other ones not.]

Seifert shows in detail how whole motifs and structures are taken over from Pindar and worked into the poems. His central thesis—that Hölderlin adapts the relation in Pindar between poetry and athletic contest to his own concerns about the transitional age—is an example of calculated misprision.[47]

Bloom sees the process of countering the anxiety of influence as entailing, inevitably, a lessening of the precursor. When the parameters are shifted to translation though, things can be different.[48] Hölderlin's translation of Pindar seems to enable both a benevolent influence (perhaps partly because it flows across languages) and an augmentation of the precursor Pindar. In the dialectic of the encounter between the two, the misprision is also a just relation, 'just' because it is an interaction that permits a flow of energy from the past to the present, a new manifestation of Pindar's poetry now. Of course it must change, and Hölderlin's exaggerated change corresponds with his idea that a metaphor is more effective if it differs radically from what it is expressing. There is a two-way relationship, a commerce— the one movement of the foreign into the proper, of Greek into German, brings with it an expansion of the language and experience of modernity as a new insight into antiquity is gained, but also an increase for Pindar, whose sphere grows. The interrelation is that

---

[46] Pindar, *The Odes*, translated by C. M. Bowra (Harmondsworth, 1969), 32.

[47] See Seifert, *Untersuchungen zu Hölderlins Pindar-Rezeption*, 89 et passim.

[48] Bloom's anxiety, which is mainly derived from the situation of the English Romantic poets, fits the German context as a whole perhaps less readily.

dreamt of and longed for in the letter to Susette Gontard I quoted from.[49] Its imagery, of firewood being consumed by flame, is apposite for the destructive-constructive mingling in which Hölderlin carried out his insights:

Wie wenn irgend etwas, was die Menschen einander sagen könnten, mehr wäre, als Brennholz, das erst, wenn es vom geistigen Feuer ergriffen wird, wieder zu Feuer wird, so wie es aus Leben und Feuer hervorgieng. Und gönnen sie die Nahrung nur gegenseitig einander, so leben und leuchten ja beide, und keiner verzehrt den andern. (vi/337)

That is the ideal Hölderlin sought in all relations, when 'reelle Wechselvereinigung' (iv/222), through disruption, forces an animating encounter, and both sides gain. He achieved it in his Pindar translation and the development from it into his own poetry. The benefit to Hölderlin is obvious, but he has also done more for Pindar than any other modern, by carrying him into contemporaneity. The translation is crucial not only for its place in Hölderlin's work, and its revision of what translation can mean, but also for what it gives us of Pindar: for all the twisting and fragmentation, he is penetrated and revealed as never before. In a way Hölderlin creates a more extreme version of Pindar, extending his 'harte Fügung' (Hellingrath's adaptation of the term from classical rhetoric ἁρμονία αὐστηρά, which connotes the abrupt, even abrasive, juxtaposition of words) into actual brokenness. His drastic incursion, which leads Pindar out beyond itself, is vital and corresponds to what the Romantics were discovering and exemplifying at the same time, the power of translation to heighten and reanimate.[50] Pindar has without doubt been read more, and more closely, as a result of Hölderlin's intervention. As Benjamin says: 'in völlig unmetaphorischer Sachlichkeit ist der Gedanke vom Leben und Fortleben der Kunstwerke zu erfassen' [the thought about the life and continuance of works of art is to be taken as a wholly unmetaphorical matter of fact].[51] Or as Steiner puts it: 'the classic wanes to the status of the academic or falls silent unless it is re-appropriated by translation, unless the living poet examines and affirms its relevance to the current idiom'.[52]

[49] Pp. 100–1 above; translation there.   [50] Cf. pp. 31–6 above.
[51] Benjamin, iv 11.
[52] George Steiner (ed.), *The Penguin Book of Modern Verse Translation* (Harmondsworth, 1966), 27.

vi *Pythian 1*

There is no particular reason for paying special attention to *Pythian 1*—in many respects any poem would, by being looked at on its own and in more detail, illuminate the Pindar translation as a whole. The intention is, by concentrating on a single poem, to give an indication of the frequency and admixture of certain features of Hölderlin's translational style. It is the texture of a Pindar poem as translated by Hölderlin that should emerge—Hölderlin's approach, and the extent of his total control of the text: how far he looked forward and back as he proceeded. It is less a question of Pindar's poem and how the translation relates to it than of the translation itself as we have it before us. In P1 at least, the attempt does not seem to be made to deliver the whole of Pindar's sense, a coherent meaning. But that Hölderlin's translation does not convey an elegant strand that could be extracted from the complex original is in itself as revealing of it as those versions which do. What concerns me here is the result of Hölderlin's method of translation, and the extent to which this result can be read. And I am trying to illustrate; to detail the form which provoked the sometimes abstract reflections that joined the translation to other aspects of Hölderlin's work; to be descriptive, not critical.

By saying that Hölderlin's poem (P1) lacks coherence I mean that it is very hard, if not impossible, to read it as a narrative. Pindar is already hard in this respect, but Hölderlin makes no elucidatory moves; in fact his translation is even more resistant to a linear reading with logical transitions. Yet Hölderlin does lend coherence to his poem as a structure. In Heyne's arrangement the Greek poem consists of five triads, each having twelve, twelve and fifteen lines (strophe, antistrophe and epode) and corresponding metrics. Hölderlin never reproduces this pattern of lines exactly, but his own arrangement yields a symmetry. All his epodes have fifteen lines as in the Greek. The strophes and antistrophes vary: in the first and last (fifth) triads they are both a line short of the Greek; and in the three middle triads the strophe is a line short, but not the antistrophe. The two symmetries could be represented: Pindar—aab, aab, aab, aab, aab; Hölderlin—ccb, cab, cab, cab, ccb. Hölderlin breaks up Pindar's order to institute one of his own. It matters little whether this is intentional or not—that the poem is shaped by a certain order is the thing—but the way the symmetry is arrived at suggests it was sought. The curtailing of the Greek begins, in the first three triads, by the overriding of Heyne's particularly severe lineation at the end of the strophes and antistrophes. The very short lines, which always entail amputation that pays no regard to word formation, are assembled into longer lines, and even in those antistrophes (the second, third and fourth) where the number of lines in the Greek is retained, there is never any division of words in German. Then in the fourth triad the strophe loses its line not at the end but at the beginning, when a similarly oddly cut phrase is reconstituted into one line:

> Τῷ πόλιν κείναν θεοδμά-
> τῳ σὺν ἐλευθερίᾳ

Dem jene Stadt mit göttlichschiklicher Freiheit (l. 114).

The fifth triad contains in the strophe the strongest refutation, and in the antistrophe the best proof, that the symmetrical pattern of the lineation was arrived at intentionally. The strophe has only eleven lines (that is, one short of the Greek) if a probably corrupt line Hölderlin left untranslated with dashes is not counted. But it could be the fact that he was forced to leave it which led him not to contract the last few lines, as he had done for all previous strophes apart from the fourth, where the first two lines were made one. The antistrophe appears simply to be wanting a line: Beissner notes that δόξας is not translated (v/418). He seems to take this to be an oversight, but with the overall symmetry in mind, which twelve lines here would have destroyed, one could take 'Prangen' [resplendence] (l. 174) to be a considered rendition of αὔ-/χημα δόξας ('acclaim of fame'), though to translate two words by one goes against the general technique. It does look as if Hölderlin has relaxed the strictness of his method so as to instate some metrical order in the poem. He does then, at least in this instance, translate with the poem as a whole in view. As in the majority of his hymns, line-count is the chief ordering principle employed. That Hölderlin obviously paid great attention to the number of lines he was using in his hymns and elegies suggests that the correspondence within Pi could well have been intended. But it stands whether or not that is so.

The counterpart to lineation in Pindar's poem is response—the metrical identity of the strophe and antistrophe with each other and with all other strophes and antistrophes, and that of the epodes among themselves. Hölderlin's technique does not allow him to reproduce this, his lines vary widely in length. Nor does he seem to have set much store by or spent much effort securing the few responsions within his reach; that is, either mirroring Pindar or setting up his own responsion in the translation. The first line, 'Goldne Leier Apollons', has seven syllables, and with no infringement of the word-for-word technique Hölderlin could have given it one more by including the elided *e* in 'goldne'. It would then, with eight syllables, have corresponded to the Greek Χρυσέα φόρμιγξ, Ἀπόλλω- *and* have matched the first line of the next strophe 'Aus welchem ausgespien werden' (l. 38). Hölderlin passed this opportunity up. The only notable responsion in P1 is between the last lines of the fourth and fifth strophes: 'Blühte der Lanze' (l. 124) and 'Stähle die Zunge' (l. 163). No attempt seems to have been made to set up echoes at key positions, such as the end of the epodes. Hölderlin was obviously much more interested in the rhythm of a line in its more immediate context. The best indications of attention to rhythm are the changes and corrections in the manuscript. Of those which affect the rhythm, only one makes the German fit the Greek, but syntactical and idiomatic factors seem at least as pressing (l. 74). There is another change (to l. 66) which moves off parity with the Greek. All the others work at the rhythm without reference to the original, sometimes to get a movement which we now regard as particularly Hölderlinian. For instance line 44: 'In die tiefe trägt des Pontus Ebne mit Krachen', where Hölderlin first wrote 'Ebene'; the suppression of the *e* gives the last five words the same rhythm as 'Auf leichtgebaueten Brüken' ('Patmos', l. 12).

Heyne's editing of this poem is particularly extreme and gives a very fragmented text; but Hölderlin is far more willing than usual to reintegrate it in translating, splitting very few words. The recasting of the short lines at the stanza-ends is paradigmatic. There are also points where the translation of the sense is unusually explicative, Hölderlin seems to be unfolding Pindar, directing him towards a reader, against his normal practice of emphasizing Pindar's pregnancy:

> Den schiffegetragnen
> Aber den Männern die erste Freude
> Zur Fahrt ist, daß ihnen im Anfang
>   förderlich komme ein Wind; gewöhnlich nemlich ists
> Auch zu Ende eine bessere Rükkehr
> Werde sich schiken.   (ll. 61–6)

[For those borne in ships
Though, the men, the first joy
Of the journey is that to them at the start
    a favourable wind might come; usual then it is
That at the end too a better return
Will be given.]

Ναυσιφορήτοις
Δ' ἀνδράσι πρώτα χάρις
Ἐς πλόον, ἀρχομένοις πομ-
    παῖον ἐλθεῖν οὖρον· ἐοικότα γὰρ
Κἀν τελευτᾷ φερτέρου νό-
    στου τυχεῖν.

[But to men
Borne in ships the first joy
Of the journey [is that] to the beginning ones a fav-
    ourable wind come; for it seems
That at the end too a better re-
    turn will befall.]

Line 63 translates only three words of Greek; the infinitive τυχεῖν is expanded to 'werde sich schiken' (l. 66), which is also lexically free. The whole sentence is clear. Another very uncharacteristic translation is 'Zaubersänge' [enchanting songs] (l. 20) for κῆλα ('arrows'). Pindar is using the word metaphorically as in O2, for poems, and Hölderlin, in '-sänge' removes the metaphor. He also adds 'Zauber-'. This seems to come from θέλγει, translated as 'besänftigen' (l. 21) but whose main sense is to lull by magic, to enchant. This kind of adjustment is quite foreign to the bulk of the Pindar translation, it is more in the style of the translations of Sophocles.[53]

Zuntz notes that Hölderlin is particularly careful in his translation of Pindar's gnomes. Lines 61–6 are an example of this. Within a Pindar poem such moments function as a taking of breath, a pause in which the course of the poem gathers and then resurges. Seifert says the contemporary criticism understood Pindar's gnomes as transitions: Schneider, whose book on Pindar Hölderlin owned, held this view, and Jacobs called them the 'Brücke, auf welcher er [...] übergeht' [bridges he crosses over by].[54] So Hölderlin's concentration on them

---

[53] See also l. 135.
[54] Zuntz, 9; Seifert, *Untersuchungen zu Hölderlins Pindar-Rezeption*, 67–8. Seifert is quoting from Friedrich Jacobs, *Nachträge zu Sulzers allgemeiner Theorie der schönen Künste*, 2nd edn. (1792).

seems to evidence study of how Pindar made his shifts and how he combined the disparate strands of his stories. He examined the transitions within the larger transition of his translation.

To get the links clear should induce a greater coherence of the whole. But these tendencies towards clarification, towards lucid structure, where the sense is extended towards the reader, are elsewhere in the poem undermined by their direct opposites. Lines 76–9 are severely broken in imitation of the Greek. However, the first break, 'Ge-/schike', translates a word undivided: μαχαναί, and there is no obvious reason for Hölderlin's not having split the word corresponding to the Greek word that *is* divided: πᾶ-/σαι. Incoherence is thus introduced, without due influence from the Greek. This is also the effect of much of the translation: in spite of the moments of relative lucidity it cannot be said that Hölderlin was seeking an overall clarity, a followable sequence that could be read as a whole. P1 is in fact more accommodating to a whole reading than most of the poems, little strings of narrative hold, but still it contains passages which interrupt or obscure the general flow, which hinder a total grasp of the poem. There are other translations which convey the story better, and Pindar's Greek itself is easier to trace through than Hölderlin's translation. But it is probably not untrue to say that no other poet, no other Greek poet, is given such a multifaceted image by the various translations that exist. Pindar's ellipsis and abruptness, features at times emphasized and augmented by Hölderlin, can lend themselves in many different ways, and to elicit from them something acceptable to conventional taste demands a narrowing of the focus onto a particular facet. This Hölderlin's translation does not do; all the multiplicity of Pindar is reproduced, all that other translations suppress or 'explain away'. The ambivalence inherent in the Greek is increased as it comes across into a German less capable of expressing precise relations in its syntax and grammar.

Were that all, the Pindar translation would hardly be more than a basic interlinear version, blemished by lexical errors. But the translations seem to have some substance as poems in themselves, which immediately detaches them from the status of mere translations, or rather, carries them into the world of real, living poetry which some translations inhabit. They have a rhythm.[55] Though the rhythm is not all that makes them into poems, without it

[55] Cf. Bertaux, *Essai*, 369.

they would never exercise the same fascination. Hellingrath thought that not to read them aloud would be 'madness'.[56] We have seen how Hölderlin worked on particular lines, but it is less the rhythm in the line than the larger rhythm that grows out of it which makes itself felt if the poems are read aloud. Sometimes this runs through passages very nearly incomprehensible, it is the rhythm then that makes them readable. It is astonishing that such a mechanical technique could engender a rhythm. The relation between 'gesezlicher Kalkul' [calculable law] (v/195) and 'das Lebendige in der Poësie' (vi/289), 'der lebendige Sinn, der nicht berechnet werden kann' [the living sense, that cannot be calculated] (v/195), seems *a priori* impossible. In the case of the translation, it suggests that the technique, while having word-for-word as its point of departure, in fact allows a degree of freedom which, though small, is enough to alter radically the total action of a poem. It also suggests how small are the variations and adjustments necessary to transform a dead line into a live one, and how wrong it is to think of the Pindar translation as an objective exercise. The technique creates a certain distance, but it is exactly the distance that allows room for the placing of Hölderlin's own accent, within the tightest confines. The combination of the fraction of play the method itself comprises (from the spectrum offered by the Greek, which meaning should the German word single out?) and the divergence from it Hölderlin permits himself equals an element of freedom which is exploited to the full. But to try to describe the alchemy in which what makes the translation a poem forms, in which the words are quickened by a rhythm, is to touch on something not wholly accessible and finally mysterious: some of the most successful passages, rhythmically and otherwise, cleave to the Greek with the utmost precision, with little or no variation, or with only the variation of what we call Hölderlin's 'errors'. To get a sense of the rhythm a fairly long passage is necessary. P1 tells of Typhos under Etna:

> den vormals
> Die Kilikische nährte die viel-
> benahmete Grotte, nun aber   31
> Die über Kuma meerabwehrende Gestade,
> Und Sikelia ihm drükt
> Die Brüste die haarigen; die Säule

---

[56] 'Es wird niemand so toll sein die Pindarübertragung anders als laut zu lesen': *Pindarübertragungen*, 82.

Aber die himmlische zusammenhält,
Der schneeige Ätna, das ganze Jahr
Des Schnees des scharfen Ernährer.

Aus welchem ausgespien werden
Des reinen Feuers heiligste   39
Aus Kammern Quellen; die Flüsse
Aber an den Tagen einen Strom des Rauches glühend,
Aber in Nächten Felsen
Die purpurne gewälzte Flamme
In die tiefe trägt des Pontus Ebne mit Krachen.   44
Jenes aber des Hephästos Bäche das Kriechende
Gewaltigste aufsendet; ein Zeichen
    wunderbar zu sehen, ein Wunder auch
Von dortgewesnen zu hören,   48

Wie es an Aetnas schwarzgezweigten
Gefesselt ist den Gipfeln
Und am Feld; ein Bette aber grabend
Den ganzen Rüken hingeleget spornt.   (ll. 29–52)

                          [whom earlier
The Cilician nourished the many-
    named cave, but now
Above Cuma the coast-line fending away the sea,
And Sicily presses
His breasts, which are hairy; the pillar
Though of the sky holds together,
Snowy Etna, all year long
Of the sharp snow the provider.

From which are spewed out
The pure fire's most sacred
From chambers sources; the rivers
Though in the days a stream of smoke glowing,
But in the nights boulders
The purple rolling flame
Into the depths conveys of level Pontus with crashes.
That thing though, that crawling thing of Hephaestus's sends up
The mightiest springs; a sign
    wonderful to see, a wonder too
To hear from people who've been there,

How it to Etna's blackly branched
Tops is fettered and
To the field; but digging a bed
Spurs the whole back lying down.]

The rhythm in this seems to come effortlessly out of the word-for-word transcription. There is very little divergence from the method one can point to except in the last lines of the strophe (46–8), which is normal for this poem, and only involves lineation and the omission, as often, of the particles μέν and δέ. Otherwise there are two points (close to each other): in line 39 ἀπλά-/του ('unapproachable') is translated as 'pure'—'des reinen Feuers'. (Perhaps a train of thought like that at the beginning of 'Die Wanderung', the mountain as a source of purity, is active:

> wie [...]
> Aus silbernen Opferschaalen
> Der Quell rauscht, ausgeschüttet
> Von reinen Händen.   (ll. 9–12)
>
> [how
> From silvery bowls
> The spring tips out, dispensed
> By pure hands.]

The closeness to P1 38–40 is striking and suggests a transformation of them.) And in line 41 'glühend' is taken wholly from the following line of Greek, after προχέοντι ('pour out') is left untranslated (after 'Tagen').[57]

There remains the variation within the bounds of the technique of which it can safely be said that some deliberate attention is being applied: the elision or addition of an optional *e*. There are three words in which it is omitted as against normal usage, and two in which it is added ('benahm*e*te', l. 31; 'ausgespien', l. 38; 'Ebne', l. 44; 'dortgewesnen', l. 48; 'hingeleg*e*t', l. 52). But there are at least as many which could take an extra *e* whose absence we cannot assume to be intentional or not. It is interesting, though, that of the five positive examples four give the 'Auf leichtgebaueten Brüken' cadence. Line 44 I have already mentioned in this context. Line 48, at the end of the strophe, repeats the whole rhythm: 'Von dortgewesnen zu hören';

---

[57] This omission may have arisen while copying, rather than being deliberate. The manuscript of the Pindar translation is almost certainly a fair copy.

Hölderlin worked to get this—the manuscript shows he first wrote 'es' after 'dortgewesnen' but then deferred it to the next line. Line 38, with a slightly different accent, also yields the same rhythm, and line 31 contains it if combined with what after all belongs with it ('die viel-/benahmete Grotte'). Such indications hardly begin to explain what is happening in these lines, or how they may have been arrived at. The rhythm they contain is not imposed from outside by the translator, as when Hölderlin does Sophocles' trimeters into blank verse; it evolves against the Greek, its movement is like a ripple blown by the wind against the resistance of the water.

VII

The rhythm and tone present in the translation is at times closer to the movement of Hölderlin's hymns and elegies than anything else in Hölderlin up to that point. A new diction seems to be released, a new attitude of language even, a newfound capacity. By extending the workings of the poetics, the theory of how 'das Lebendige in der Poësie' might be reached, into the dynamics of translation, the *means* for 'das Lebendige', for combining words into the new expressiveness Hölderlin needed, emerged. The translation enabled a renewal of Hölderlin's poetic language. On the translation from Greek into German there followed a further translation into original poems. (It is no easier to define exactly the second translation than the first. A particular cadence or expression is achieved by refracting the Greek in translation, but how, apart from obvious cases of direct borrowing, is this then imitated or realized in the original poetry?) The Pindar thus occupies that middle position I spoke of earlier. It is quite its own structure: it can be seen as an extreme version not only of the original, but of the poems that come after or concurrently with it.

Hölderlin's poetics may be understood as a continual effort to determine 'das Lebendige', and this consists in finding a precise relation of language in which manifestation is possible. Translation provides an analogue of this process: a form has to be found in which the Greek poem can be conveyed. Part of what is conveyed is the incommensurability of Greek and German. But that revelation of incommensurability is itself a form of expression: the German's brokenness is witness to something beyond itself, to something it cannot sustain. In that sense the Pindar translation foreshadows the stance of Hölderlin's great poetry; not as its beginnings, but as a fully developed prior instance. Adorno's description of the way language works in Hölderlin's poems treats of a quality which in a mostly cruder form is present in the translation of Pindar too, and Hölderlin seems to have found his way to it by translating, by translating Pindar. Adorno writes of precisely Hölderlin's diction, of how he works to bring his words into juxtapositions where they can signify, where they unsettle the preconceptions put about by established expression:

Hölderlin ist auf Verbindung aus, welche die zur Abstraktion verurteilten Worte gleichwie ein zweites Mal zum Klingen bringt. Paradigmatisch dafür, und von außerordentlicher Wirkung, jene erste Elegie aus 'Brot und Wein'. Nicht restituiert sie die einfachen und allgemeinen Worte, mit denen sie haushält, sondern fügt sie aneinander auf eine Weise, welche ihre eigene Fremdheit, ihr Einfaches als bereits Abstraktes, umschafft zum Ausdruck von Entfremdung.[58]

[Hölderlin is after combinations which make the words, condemned as they are to abstraction, sound again, as it were, for a second time. The paradigm, extraordinary in its effect, is the first strophe of 'Brod und Wein'. It does not reinstate the simple, general words it deals with, but puts them together in such a way as to transform the foreignness they have, the simpleness that is a result of their abstraction, into an expression of alienation.]

The kind of concreteness on which poetry depends is found, Adorno thinks, above all in the particular constellation of words. The new constellations, which work by countering accepted usage, by putting things in unexpected relation, seem to have been sought in the Pindar translation and are present there in abundance. 'Das Lebendige in der Poësie' comes through a deliberate inflection of the German language into the foreign:

> Die Rede
> In diesem Falle die Hofnung trägt,
> Noch künftig werde sie seyn, mit Kronen
> Und Rossen berühmt,
> Und mit wohllautenden Gastmahlen genannt.
> (P1 66–70)

> [Speech
> In this case carries the hope,
> And in the future it will be, with crowns

---

[58] Theodor W. Adorno, 'Parataxis: Zur späten Lyrik Hölderlins', in: *Noten zur Literatur* (Frankfurt a. M., 1981), 447–91 (473).

And horses famous,
And named with well-sounding feasts.]

Read in this light, as a source, there is no page of the Pindar translation which fails to yield a startling combination, a new rhythm. It seems richer and richer each time it is read.

Adorno describes another (related) characteristic of Hölderlin's language:

die Hölderlinschen Abstrakta sind so wenig wie Leitworte Evokationen von Sein unmittelbar. Ihr Gebrauch wird determiniert von der Brechung der Namen. In diesen bleibt stets ein Überschuß dessen, was sie wollen und nicht erreichen. Kahl, in tödlicher Blässe verselbständigt er sich gegen sie. Die Dichtung des späten Hölderlin polarisiert sich in die Namen und Korrespondenzen hier, dort die Begriffe. Ihre allgemeinen Substantive sind Resultanten: sie bezeugen die Differenz des Namens und des beschworenen Sinnes. Ihre Fremdheit, die wiederum erst der Dichtung sie einverleibt, empfangen sie dadurch, daß sie von ihrem Widerpart, den Namen, gleichsam ausgehöhlt wurden. Sie sind Relikte, capita mortua dessen an der Idee, was nicht sich vergegenwärtigen läßt: noch in ihrer anscheinend zeitfernen Allgemeinheit Male eines Prozesses. [...] [Sie] haben [...] ihr eigenes Leben, und zwar kraft ihrer Entäußerung von der Unmittelbarkeit. (pp. 463–4)

[Hölderlin's abstract words are no more direct evocations of being than mottos are. Their use is determined by the refraction of names. Names always remain with a surplus of what they want and cannot attain. Bare, deathly pale, this becomes independent from them. Hölderlin's later poetry polarizes into names and correspondences on the one hand, and concepts on the other. Its general substantives are resultants: they witness to the difference between the name and the conjured meaning. They receive their foreignness, which makes them part of poetry, by being as it were hollowed out by their counterpart, by names. They are relicts, *capita mortua* of what of an idea cannot be realized: even in their apparently unhistorical generality signs of a process. [...] They have [...] their own life, and this thanks to their relinquishing of immediacy.]

Lightly transposed, this description is also one of the language of Hölderlin's Pindar. The work in which sense is formed in the course of a poem, the frictions and antitheses out of which a fit means of expression is produced, are the movers of the new idiom of the translation. It is found dialectically, in the confluence of foreign tongues, and the words there, the 'middle text' of which most of the translation consists, are also 'Male eines Prozesses'. It is as a process that they constitute meaning. 'Meaning' has a dual import: the total sense bodied forth by the individual movement of each poem of the translation, and what we perceive of the signification of the original Greek. The to and-fro, 'die Differenz des Namens und des beschworenen Sinnes' that makes words luminous and expressive, that frees them from 'das Positive' and makes them living and concrete, is in the translation also between the new and the old poem, the modern and the ancient language. The whole process of the finding of poetic speech is present in the concrete instance of the translation.[59] As I said, the workings of the transition that translation is are, in the Pindar open, apparent. And it is by exposing its workings (though not only thus) that a language becomes poetic; it sheds the semblance of transparency under which it is normally used, and becomes patent, like paint on a canvas. In the Pindar translation this sometimes degenerates into the grotesque or merely bizarre, though much of what Zuntz took exception to now seems much more acceptable and sometimes among the most successful parts—in P1: 'Mit kranker Haut zwar gehend' [and walking with a sick skin] (l. 103).[60] The German words mark a distance from the Greek and so create their own space which is at the same time more truthfully expressive of the Greek than seamless translation would be. The insufficiency of the language formed becomes its means of articulation and its power. The new poetic diction, inhabited by 'das Lebendige', stems from a particular attitude to old forms which reveals their flaws, their impossible claims of direct access; and so paradoxically, through a break with that false relation, it becomes a better locus of manifestation.

The translation, in which that same process is in operation, is an intrinsic critique and correction of virtually all other translation. But what dominates the Pindar translation almost to the point of crippling it is inherent in all translation of the Vossian type: Benjamin talks of the 'Gebrochenheit' [brokenness] of the language of translation (he has Hölderlin's Pindar in mind). It is estranged from itself, 'ihrem eigenen Gehalt gegenüber unangemessen, gewaltig und fremd'.[61] This is the quality that Hölderlin's poems then evince, a large part of

---

[59]   Cf. another account of the Pindar translation's role in Hölderlin's finding his poetic voice: Rainer Nägele, 'Vatertext und Muttersprache: Pindar und das lyrische Subjekt in Hölderlins späterer Dichtung', *LpH* 8 (1988), 39–52.

[60]   Cf. Zuntz, 29.   [61]   Benjamin, iv 15.

what lends them their precise concreteness. The effect of some of Hölderlin's late fragments could best be described as that of a translation, in that they seem to indicate a pressure on their language from outside, a sphere of extra meaning not usually associated with their words, as if something were lacking. And that is it, Hölderlin's poetic world, and his poetic word, his language, are founded on absence. Working away at Pindar, the absence became most apparent and pressing to Hölderlin; the language produced translating him voiced absence at every point, as it removed itself still further. But the translation of that idiom into the constituents of poems, the absence at once more compelling and heart-rending as it became radiant, made its overcoming more vital, and possible, at least in poetic terms.

CHAPTER 5

Translation and Rewriting

Und in die Tiefe greifet
Daß es lebendig werde
Der Allerschütterer...

('Die Titanen', ll. 68–70)

Towards the end of 1803 Hölderlin wrote to his publisher Wilmans apologizing for the delay in sending him the manuscript of his translation of *Oedipus the King* and *Antigone*: 'Ich wollte, da ich die Sache freier übersehen konnte, in der Übersezung und den Anmerkungen noch einiges ändern. Die Sprache in der Antigonä schien mir nicht lebendig genug' [Looking things over with the benefit of distance I wanted to make a few late changes in the translation and notes. The language in the *Antigonä* seemed to me not lively enough] (vi/435). The translations of Sophocles are part of an attempt to connect more directly with a potential readership which Hölderlin's letters and poems at this time also increasingly reflect. It is the first concerted attempt since the failure of the *Iduna* project. Unlike the Pindar, which no one apart from Hölderlin seems to have seen, the Sophocles translations were aimed at a 'Publikum' (vi/434), and Hölderlin even hoped to have the plays performed, through Schelling's agency, in Weimar.[1] When Wilmans had agreed to publish *Oedipus der Tyrann* and *Antigonä* Hölderlin had written to him in gratitude:

Ich werde Ihnen immer danken, daß Sie mit Ihrer gütigen Zuschrift so mich getroffen haben, weil Sie zur Äußerung mir eine Freiheit machen, jezt, da ich mehr aus dem Sinne der Natur und mehr des Vaterlandes schreiben kann als sonst. (vi/434)[2]

[1] See letters to Wilmans 28 Sept. 1803 and 8 Dec. 1803 (vi/434–5).
[2] The many misprints put an end to this gratitude. See vii,3/300.

[I shall always be grateful to you for sending me your kind letter when you did, because you provide me with the opportunity to make myself heard now that I am able to write more out of a sense of nature and of my country than before.]

Opening up to a public contained in it the hope of having an influence, of making his writings instrumental in the change he perceived society to be going through; of participating in the processes of history. Friedrich Schlegel's journal *Europa*, which was also published by Wilmans at this time, shows a similar widening of perspective and concern for the present. In the letter in which Hölderlin says he still has some work to do on the tragedies, he also announces what must be the hymns, 'einzelne lyrische größere Gedichte' [several lyrical poems of some length], whose content 'unmittelbar das Vaterland angehn soll oder die Zeit' [is meant to deal directly with the country or the times] (vi/435); he intends to have each poem printed separately, almost like handbills, or pamphlets. In the next letter, also written in December 1803, Hölderlin tells Wilmans that he is looking through some poems to send him in response to his request for contributions to his journal. Hölderlin adds, perhaps rather sardonically: 'Es ist eine Freude, sich dem Leser zu opfern, und sich mit ihm in die engen Schranken unserer noch kinderähnlichen Kultur zu begeben' [It is a joy to sacrifice oneself to the reader and to enter with him into the narrow limits of our still-childlike culture] (vi/436). This suggests he understands the nine poems he did then send to Wilmans (the 'Nachtgesänge') as being styled, at least to some extent, to the fashions of the day, making concessions to the readers of Wilmans's *Taschenbuch. Der Liebe und Freundschaft gewidmet* (Hölderlin appears to disparage these poems as 'Liebeslieder' [love poems] in the same letter). In contrast with them, Hölderlin again refers to his hymns, which he seems to call 'vaterländische Gesänge' [patriotic hymns] (vi/436), presumably in the sense just quoted: that they should relate directly to 'das Vaterland [...] oder die Zeit' (vi/435). In spite of interest on Wilmans's part, these poems were not published in Hölderlin's lifetime, nor for a long time after.[3] One of them, 'Friedensfeier', the manuscript of which is probably the fair copy Hölderlin meant for Wilmans, is prefaced by a

---

[3] For Wilmans's interest, see: vii,1/179. 'Die Wanderung', 'Der Rhein', 'Patmos' and 'Andenken' appeared in journals, sometimes peculiarly, and except 'Die Wanderung', probably without Hölderlin's knowledge. See ii/713, 722, 765–6, 800.

note asking his readers for understanding and lenience towards the poem's idiom, which he expects them to find 'zu wenig konventionell' [too unconventional] (iii/532). Hölderlin's desire to engage with his time, to write 'mehr aus dem Sinne [...] des Vaterlandes' (vi/434), and thus a form of poetry which could be called political in that it is poetry concerned, however obliquely, with change, does not try to realize itself by speaking for any particular group. These poems were not read, and the gesture of extending into a community which the mode of the hymns invokes took place in almost total vacuum. Had they been published accessibly, we would expect a reception similar to that the Sophocles translations had: mockery and incomprehension. But perhaps things could have been different. Part of Hölderlin at least seemed to think so, and the fact that Wilmans, an established publisher, took on the Sophocles, complete with its astonishing 'Anmerkungen', should prompt us to consider that under slightly different circumstances the plays might have met with more understanding (though Wilmans can't have been averse to taking risks). At least one person was aware of the new rhythm and expressiveness of language the translation released.[4] Among Hölderlin's friends, comprehension of the seriousness of the Sophocles was hindered by their knowledge of his deteriorating mental and physical condition.[5]

The main obstacle though was undoubtedly the language itself, its hard simplicity, the demands it made. The 'Anmerkungen' seem to imagine a mediation towards (German) readers, both in themselves, and in their details: Hölderlin writes 'Vater der Zeit' [Father of Time] instead of Zeus, 'um es unserer Vorstellungsart mehr zu nähern' [to bring it closer to our way of thinking] (v/268). But for all their explicative gestures ('daher' [thus], 'nemlich' [namely], 'deswegen' [therefore], 'weil' [because], 'und so' [and so]) the 'Anmerkungen' remain intractable, simultaneously illuminating and perplexing. A comparison of *Empedokles* and the Sophocles versions (it is not misleading to think of Hölderlin's Sophocles as a later attempt to write tragedy) makes the strange, anti-classical colour of the new language of the translations particularly apparent. The idiom is difficult, sometimes scarcely readable, or not without knowledge of the promptings from the Greek. *Empedokles* had also been written with an

---

[4] Bettina von Arnim. See vii,4/190–2.
[5] See Schelling to Hegel, vii,2/261–2.

audience in mind.[6] But, as with the essays begun for *Iduna*, it seems willing to enter into a sphere of discourse which might be shared, which meets expectations, at least to some degree. Parts of the Sophocles are more akin to Hölderlin's exploratory essays in their inwardness and privacy. Again, the project of inflecting change in a particular direction, of which the political interpretation of the Antigone story in the 'Anmerkungen' is a part, manifests itself in a retreat from an idiom in which Hölderlin's writings might have been more widely read at the time.

It is probably simplistic to expect them to adopt such an idiom: Hölderlin is not, or rarely, trying to instruct or persuade, certainly not in the poems, and despite pronouncements in the letters and the apparent tendency of the 'Anmerkungen', perhaps not in the Sophocles translations either. But everything he wrote after 1800, and much that he wrote before that, was in intrinsic opposition to the dominant shape of his time. It proposed new forms and moved in sympathy with the French Revolution. The shift from ode to hymn images the turning against fixity in poetic form; or rather, since there is no exact moment when Hölderlin deserts metre and adopts free verse, the movement is imaged by the absence of metred verse after the reworkings of the odes among the 'Nachtgesänge' and of the elegies 'Brod und Wein', 'Heimkunft' and 'Stutgard' which took place at about the same time.[7] This absence lasted until the latest poems, written in Tübingen. It would be wrong to *equate* the breaking of conventions of verse-form and diction with a political opposition to established structures in society, as though there were a distinct analogy to be drawn between a metrically regular verse-pattern and the status quo. At least, such an equation has nothing to do with intention: the poetry and poets of Anglo-American modernism tell us that. But in themselves poems may suggest alternatives and countering possibilities by taking up a stance outside the mainstream, and free verse ('freie Rhythmen') can be part of that because, at least at the beginning of the nineteenth century, it represents a deflection from rather than a gravitation towards the norm. Experimentation with form helps free poetry from a complacency about itself which is also a political complacency.

---

[6] Cf. Pierre Bertaux, *Hölderlin und die Französische Revolution* (Frankfurt a.M., 1969), 110.
[7] 'Der Archipelagus' and a few other poems in metre were also reworked.

Hölderlin's hymns are in fact tightly, rigorously structured—to read 'Hälfte des Lebens' is to have a sense of a unit in strict control—, and most of his odes and elegies exceed the expectations their forms may raise. Still the hymns are a peculiar kind of challenge, working against the grain, and this is emphasized by their position within Hölderlin's oeuvre. Later, Hölderlin moved away from the triadic base of most of the hymns and into strophic hymns with no triadic structure, like 'Andenken' and 'Der Ister', and from them to short poems and fragments which intentionally or not so outstep convention as to question conceptions of what a poem is and how it should be read.[8] To extend and disorient expectation in this way is to have an effect that widens the view, and thus creates the premiss on which any hopes of change have to be founded. It is not only within form that experimental inquiry is important and a narrowness of experience may be opened out, and Hölderlin's formal innovations are not the only road he took in this direction. They are not even the most important, but indicate concisely the political intent of his work. Hölderlin derived them from Pindar, and Klopstock had made free verse unexceptional; none the less they differ from the metrical and strophic observances in Weimar and elsewhere. To focus on them makes it clear that this intent, although it needs contact with readers, does not aim at making an easy connexion.

All the same, Hölderlin was definitely in search of some sort of connexion. It is true, as the preface to 'Friedensfeier' suggests, that a great part of his hopes were projected onto a future age, an age that would be fit and understand him. But that future could have been quite close, and in fact the hopes never disentangled themselves from the present altogether. The continual striving after 'das Lebendige in der Poësie' (vi/289) seems in the Sophocles translations to be realized in the direction towards an audience, an immediate body of readers for whom the books are to be published. In his first letter to Wilmans, already quoted in Chapter 2, Hölderlin states his vision of the twist his translations would perform:

Ich hoffe, die griechische Kunst, die uns fremd ist, durch Nationalkonvenienz und Fehler, mit denen sie sich immer herum beholfen hat, dadurch lebendiger, als gewöhnlich dem Publikum darzustellen, daß ich

---

[8] Cf. Dieter Burdorf, 'Der Text als Landschaft: Eine topographische Lektüre der Seiten 73 bis 76 des Homburger Folioheftes', in: Uwe Beyer (ed.), *Neue Wege zu Hölderlin* (Würzburg, 1994), 113–41.

das Orientalische, das sie verläugnet hat, mehr heraushebe, und ihren Kunstfehler, wo er vorkommt, verbessere. (vi/434)

The fundamental tendency of the translation, as Hölderlin sees it, is in closest relation to its intention on the public. When, three months later, he writes that the language in the *Antigonä* seems 'nicht lebendig genug' (vi/435) he may partly mean that it does not bear strongly enough on, does not demand enough of, the reader. Not itself 'lively enough', it would be unlikely to make the reader so. The two letters reflect upon each other: to make the language more 'lively', Hölderlin will tap more exactingly the 'oriental' sources the Greek has obscured. So there is one complex movement involved: a movement towards the reader, but which also goes 'back' towards a ground on which the Greek reposes, hiding it. It is the same gesture of giving and withholding, of opening and closing, observable in the hymns, whose dynamics want an audience, a community, but go against the demands of the prevailing one.

   This chapter will examine more closely the period 1803–4, when the last touches were put to the Sophocles translations and Hölderlin habitually went back to earlier work and worked at it again. Rewriting was always intrinsic to Hölderlin's working method, but in this period it seems to have been adopted as a deliberate strategy for extending his writing into a new dimension. The activities of reworking and translation took place side by side, like Hölderlin and Hegel working at the same desk in the *Stift*, and as there, there was ample and productive interaction between the two. They almost came to be one activity, and the techniques of translation entered fully into the processes of writing.

Hölderlin's Present

Hölderlin's present is determined by the French Revolution and by Greek antiquity. The modern world is both condemned and affirmed by the force of the Greek achievement: it is hallowed by being the same soil on which the gods were once immanent in human affairs, but damned by the distance which separates it from that state now. The effect of landscape in *Hyperion*—radiant with loss, expressive in its beauty of both the existence and the disappearance of fulfilment— is a concentration of the effect of the present as a whole when coupled with memory.

In the illumination reaching from the Greek past, the present is a
'dürftige Zeit' (ii/94), sombre and lonely:

> es wandelt in Nacht, es wohnt, wie im Orkus,
> Ohne Göttliches unser Geschlecht. Ans eigene Treiben
> Sind sie geschmiedet allein, und sich in der tosenden Werkstatt
> Höret jeglicher nur
>
> ('Der Archipelagus', ll. 241–4)

> [we go round in night, we live as they do in
> Orcus, godlessly, all of us. To their own labours
> They are welded alone, and in the din of the workplace
> Each hears only himself]

This image of the present as night-time, worked into a full mythology
in 'Brod und Wein', allows a negative understanding to become
hopeful, because it fits the present into a cycle, or 'Zeitbild' [picture
of time] (iii/536), makes of it an age of transition. In this respect the
turmoil produced by the French Revolution and its consequences
make for an unusually promising world, in the throes of change. 'Man
kann wohl mit Gewißheit sagen', Hölderlin wrote to Ebel on 10 June
1797, 'daß die Welt noch nie so bunt aussah, wie jezt' [One can say
with some certainty that the world has never before looked as
colourful as now] (vi/229). Confusion and uncertainty are interpreted
as 'Gährung und Auflösung' [ferment and dissolution], preliminaries
to, and agents of, total change: 'Ich glaube an eine künftige
Revolution der Gesinnungen und Vorstellungsarten, die alles
bisherige schaamroth machen wird' [I believe in a future revolution of
ways of thinking and feeling that will make everything we have had
so far go red with shame] (vi/229).

Hölderlin never forgets that we are engaged in history, that we are
under way. But it is not simply that the present is an age of transition,
it is in and by virtue of transition that a new world can appear, as
elaborated in the essay 'Das Werden im Vergehen'. In the transitional
lies a great openness to possibility: 'im übergehenden ist die
Möglichkeit aller Beziehungen vorherrschend' (iv/282).[9] The present
holds the potential of all other worlds, and the task is to hold these
possibilities open, to prevent the 'ängstlich bornirte Zustand' [anxious
narrow-mindedness] (vi/304) which Hölderlin felt was prevalent and

---

[9] Cf. Novalis, ii 189: 'Alle *Wircklichkeit* hat ein Vor und ein Nach—beydes sind
Möglichkeiten—Nach *ist* Möglichk[eit]. Vor war Möglichkeit. In ihr ist aber alles
zugleich'.

the chief hindrance to realizing the opportunities of transition. If, as Hölderlin defines it in 'Das Werden im Vergehen', the present is characterized by fear and pain (iv/283), the lack which causes these feelings is also the means by which a better world, in the past or the future, is negatively present in the here and now. In the same way, the absence of god from the world imparts a negative knowledge of, or longing for, divine fulfilment. It is a radical view of the present which in the one movement faces up to the meaninglessness of existence as it is now and creates a space for understanding that meaninglessness as itself meaningful. This stems from seeing the present as a period of transition, and from seeing transition as a prerequisite for epiphany. The 'issue' out of the present is to be religious in nature—the new age Hölderlin believes to be imminent will be consecrated from outside[10]—but it can only come once the world is prepared and receptive to it. We must work to receive—the achievement of a fit world is congruent and synchronous with its being filled by divine presence again, but it is not *brought about* by this presence. The two things are one, inseparable and indistinguishable, because neither can be without the other, they are interdependent. Hölderlin's thought did not allow for what he called 'positive revelation', one which is all granting, wholly bestowed and not opened out to:

Alles greift in einander und leidet, so wie es thätig ist, so auch der reinste Gedanke des Menschen, und in aller Schärfe genommen, ist eine apriorische, von aller Erfahrung durchaus unabhängige Philosophie, wie Du selbst weist, so gut ein Unding, als eine positive Offenbarung, wo der Offenbarende nur alles dabei thut, und der, dem die Offenbarung gegeben wird, nicht einmal sich regen darf, um sie zu nehmen, denn sonst hätt' er schon von dem Seinen etwas dazu gebracht. (vi/300–1)

[Everything is interconnected, and is passive just as much as active, including the purest thought a human being can have; and strictly speaking an *a priori* philosophy, one entirely independent of all experience, is just as much a nonsense as a positive revelation, where the revealer does the whole thing and he to whom the revelation is made is not even allowed to move in order to receive it, because otherwise he would have contributed something of his own.]

A life 'voll göttlichen Sinns' (ii/111) is one of exact interrelation: 'meaning' ('Sinn') in that phrase is simultaneously conferred and

---

[10] Cf. Howard Gaskill, 'Hölderlin and Revolution', *Forum for Modern Language Studies* 12/2 (Apr. 1976), 118–36 (123).

construed. The unsettling and loosening of fixed structures and patterns of thinking in the wake of the French Revolution were thought by Hölderlin, and not only by him, to be propitious for the coming and creating of a new age.

It was the task of poetry to aid the traversing of the interim. In calling some of his poems 'Nachtgesänge' (vi/436) Hölderlin made this explicit: they were understood to be about the night-present, concerned with transition. 'Das Werden im Vergehen' investigates how art, specifically tragedy, may intervene in the course of the present and suggests that it benefits from the disjunction and incoherence by eliciting a configuration which points a way out, which hastens the transition into a 'new world'. The first objective of poetry is thus to interpret the 'reißende Zeit' [tearing times] (ii/112), the 'Wildniß' [wilderness] (ii/214) of the present, to try and catch a constellation of the released possibilities which might make sense of them and a space for hope. In the terms of 'An die Madonna', to see that the wilderness is 'göttlichgebaut/Im reinen Geseze' [built by the gods/In pure law] (ii/214). Part of this process is simply a critique of the prevalent state of affairs. But a poem may also gesture beyond the moment and forecast the future in images. To project into the future really is to forecast, because the projecting imagination carves out a shape which reality may thus be provoked into taking on. As expressed in 'Das Werden im Vergehen', the present is a gap, a 'Lüke' (iv/284), which the poem fills, enabling a transition across it: 'so gehet aus dieser Vereinigung und Vergleichung des Vergangenen Einzelnen, und des Unendlichen gegenwärtigen, der eigentlich neue Zustand, der nächste Schritt, der dem Vergangenen folgen soll, hervor' [and from this joining and comparing of the past-individual and the infinite-present proceeds the actual new state, the next step, which is to follow the past] (iv/284). The poem becomes itself an agent in history.[11] It becomes a focus of transition, a concentrated form of the present which also, and thereby, acts on the present.

Hölderlin's present is not our present, because ours lacks the luminous shadow of a pending time of fulfilment. We are thus likely to read his poems in a way slightly but importantly different from what we might envisage to be Hölderlin's understanding or expectation (but he knew his poems would have to wait, he was

---

[11] Cf. Mark Grunert, *Die Poesie des Übergangs: Hölderlins späte Dichtung im Horizont von Friedrich Schlegels Konzept der 'Transzendentalpoesie'* (Tübingen, 1995), 80–1.

handing them into the unknown). Though Hölderlin is a religious poet, the nature of his religion—with the premiss of absence and the drawing-into-one of divine epiphany and human fulfilment—makes for an easy translation into non-religious terms (or less obviously religious ones). We have in the main lost his belief in a near redemption, but his concentration on the present as a place of change and the sense of hope embodied in his poems are the more vital now that that belief has vanished. What gives pause is that the hope engendered in Hölderlin's poems is the closest we get to a modern ideal.

The Two Versions of the First Stasimon of *Antigone*

Beissner talks of four distinguishable layers in the Sophocles translations, the latest of which corresponds to the changes Hölderlin announced in the letter to Wilmans of 8 December 1803. With this last layer Beissner has in mind strongly interpretative translation such as Hölderlin himself draws attention to in the 'Anmerkungen', the translation of καὶ Ζηνὸς ταμιεύε-/σκε γονὰς χρυσορρύτους by 'Sie zählete dem Vater der Zeit/Die Stundenschläge, die goldnen' (*Antigonä*, ll. 987–8) for example.[12] Since we do not have Hölderlin's manuscripts of the tragedies but only the (badly) printed final versions, it is actually difficult to say which layer a given passage belongs to, and Beissner's distinction is more useful to describe different tendencies of style and method than as a real tool of chronological differentiation. This is especially true as many instances ascribable to the last stage (they diverge radically from the Greek) may well rest on error. The only possibility of really comparing Hölderlin's different approaches, and of getting an idea of what exactly he may have done to render the language of the tragedies 'lebendiger' (vi/434), is given by the existence of an earlier version of the first lines of the first stasimon of *Antigone*. It is the only passage of the Sophocles we have in two different versions, and a comparison permits some insight into the direction in which Hölderlin was translating.

> Vieles gewaltge giebts. Doch nichts
> Ist gewaltiger, als der Mensch.
> Denn der schweiffet im grauen
> Meer' in stürmischer Südluft

[12] Beissner points out that these divergences are 'den späten Varianten zu manchen Gedichten ähnlich' (105).

Umher in woogenumrauschten
Geflügelten Wohnungen.
Der Götter heilge Erde, sie, die
Reine die mühelose,
Arbeitet er um, das Pferdegeschlecht
Am leichtbewegten Pflug von
Jahr zu Jahr umtreibend.

Leichtgeschaffener Vogelart
Legt er Schlingen, verfolget sie,
Und der Thiere wildes Volk,
Und des salzigen Meers Geschlecht
Mit listiggeschlungenen Seilen,
Der wohlerfahrne Mann.
Beherrscht mit seiner Kunst des Landes
Bergebewandelndes Wild.
Dem Naken des Rosses wirft er das Joch
Um die Mähne und dem wilden
Ungezähmten Stiere.

(v/42)

[Much that is mighty there is. But nothing
Is mightier than man.
For he wanders around the grey
Sea in stormy air from the south
In winged dwellings surrounded
By the sound of waves.
The holy earth of the gods, her,
Pure and effortless earth,
He works over, driving the race of horses
Round from year to year
With the manoeuvrable plough.

Delicate birdkind,
He sets it traps, pursues it,
And the wild tribe of the beasts,
And the salty sea's race
With cunningly woven ropes,
The experienced man.
Masters through his art the country's
Mountain-roaming game.
On the neck of the horse he throws the yoke
Round the mane and on the wild
Untamed bull.]

Ungeheuer ist viel. Doch nichts
Ungeheuerer, als der Mensch.
Denn der, über die Nacht
Des Meers, wenn gegen den Winter wehet
Der Südwind, fähret er aus
In geflügelten sausenden Häußern.
Und der Himmlischen erhabene Erde
Die unverderbliche, unermüdete
Reibet er auf; mit dem strebenden Pfluge,
Von Jahr zu Jahr,
Treibt sein Verkehr er, mit dem Rossegeschlecht',
Und leichtträumender Vögel Welt
Bestrikt er, und jagt sie;
Und wilder Thiere Zug,
Und des Pontos salzbelebte Natur
Mit gesponnenen Nezen,
Der kundige Mann.
Und fängt mit Künsten das Wild,
Das auf Bergen übernachtet und schweift.
Und dem rauhmähnigen Rosse wirft er um
Den Naken das Joch, und dem Berge
Bewandelnden unbezähmten Stier.

(ll. 349–70)

[Monstrous is much. But nothing
More monstrous than man.
For he, over the night
Of the sea, when towards winter blows
The south wind, he puts out
In winged and roaring houses.
And the heavens' sublime earth
Unperishable untiring earth
He rubs sore; with the striving plough,
From year to year,
He does his business, with the race of horses,
And the world of the dreaming birds
He snares, and hunts them;
And the passage of wild beasts,
And the creatures happy in Pontus' salt
With spun nets,
The knowing man.
And catches with arts the game
That wanders and sleeps in the mountains.
And round the neck of the rough-maned horse

He throws the yoke, and round the mountain
Roaming untamed bull.]

According to Beissner, the earlier version belongs to the second
phase of translation, one in which an attempt is made at the Greek
metrics.[13] That attempt is given up in the published version of these
lines, but traces of it seem to remain, especially in the opening lines.
And in fact the first version is to be found throughout the second.
Böschenstein mentions the retention of 'bergebewandelndes' in
'Berge/Bewandelnden' as making it likely that Hölderlin referred to
his earlier version the second time round.[14] (Of course it is quite
possible there were intermediate versions and that the earlier
encounter with such a famous passage should have stayed present in
Hölderlin's mind without the help of a manuscript—there is an echo
of it at 'Am Quell der Donau', ll. 46–8.) That would mean that the
retranslation was also a rewriting, a revision of his earlier
understanding, not just searching for hidden aspects of the original
Greek but writing against a version which had been complicit in the
Greek's obfuscating of its origins.[15] At the same time, the second
version clearly takes off from the first and conserves as much as it veers
away from: the metrics and structure of the first two lines, which in
both versions pass over the sense of movement in πέλει (πολλὰ τὰ
δεινά. Κοὐδὲν ἀν-/θρώπου δεινότερον πέλει—'Many horrors. And
nothing more horrible *moves* than man'); the mistranslation of
οἴδμασιν ('swell', not 'Wohnungen' or 'Häußern', though Hölderlin
makes the same mistake at *Antigonä*, l. 611—'eine Hütte'); the phrase
'wirft [...] um' for Greek ἄξεται in the last few lines.

As with a palimpsest, the earlier text looks through the later one.
But the divergences, the way the second translation reaches into the
understanding testified by the first and disturbs it, bringing to light an
urgent and harsh stratum residing in the Greek, are even more telling.
The enigmatic, 'dark' nature of choral lyric, its gnomic expression and
stretched syntax, invites probing, and as with Pindar, different
translations can yield several, even contradictory, interpretations.
Hölderlin marks the tendency of his new version at the outset by his
translation of πολλὰ τὰ δεινά: 'Ungeheuer ist viel'. Monstrous itself,

---

[13]   Beissner, 96.
[14]   Bernhard Böschenstein, '"Die Nacht des Meers": Zu Hölderlins
Übersetzungen des ersten Stasimons der Antigonae', in: *'Frucht des Gewitters':
Hölderlins Dionysos als Gott der Revolution* (Frankfurt a. M., 1989), 37–53 (45).
[15]   See pp. 60–4 above.

the word 'ungeheuer' stands at the head of the strophe, far outbidding 'Vieles gewaltge giebts' (though virtually retaining that rhythm). It brands the stasimon, as 'Gemeinsamschwesterliches!', the tragedy's untranslatable first word, brands the play as a whole.[16] Apart from the lexical difference, 'gewaltge' is much diminished by standing in the middle of the sentence rather than first, or last as in the Greek; and accordingly, quite what is monstrous about man appears submerged in the lines that follow, when compared to the printed version. The work the second version does to make the Greek manifest is evident in the repeated, sometimes agrammatical pronouns referring to 'der Mensch', who is thus made to impinge on the text just as his activities forcefully impinge on 'der Himmlischen erhabene Erde'. In the nine lines following 'der Mensch' there are twice as many such pronouns as in the first version. This bias culminates in 'mit dem strebenden Pfluge,/Von Jahr zu Jahr,/Treibt sein Verkehr er', where 'er' is wrenched to our attention by its unusual position, which is further emphasized by 'sein' in 'sein Verkehr' (and also by the rhyme). 'Verkehr' also draws attention to itself: uncommonly, it is neuter, not masculine (at the end of the eighteenth century the gender was unfixed), which in itself could be seen to make man's 'trade' appear more instrumental. It is a rich word in this context: the root sense of turning is exactly what the plough does, and so it brings out what is also the root of the Greek πολεύων.[17] Hölderlin brings the original meaning of the Greek word to the surface by using a German word on which the context, and the reader, have to repeat the work of the translation by remembering its root elements. There is thus a double movement; the translation simultaneously goes to the source of the Greek and revives German by making its etymology resonate.[18] 'Verkehr', emphasized as it is, also contains a further connotation which suggests that man is raping the earth with his plough.

The focus on man's activity, his unending abrasive mastery of nature, coupled with assertive, interpretative translation which marks out its difference from the original and from its more conventional ancestor, invite a comparison between what the passage describes and the activity of translation it is engaged in, the way the German masters

[16] George Steiner calls 'Gemeinsamschwesterliches' a 'willed monster': *Antigones* (Oxford, 1984), 85.

[17] Cf. Böschenstein, '"Die Nacht des Meers"', 43.

[18] Cf. Berman, 'Hölderlin, ou la traduction comme manifestation', 141: 'la traduction [...] ressuscite l'archaïque de l'allemand pour accueillir l'archaïque du grec'.

its Greek material. The two seem to fuse when man's exploitation of nature is not simply described, but mimed by the verse: 'Und der Himmlischen erhabene Erde/Die unverderbliche, unermüdete/ Reibet er auf'. Translations such as 'über die Nacht/Des Meers' (first version: 'im grauen/Meer'), 'wenn gegen den Winter wehet/Der Südwind' ('in stürmischer Südluft'), 'Häußern' ('Wohnungen'), 'reibet er auf' ('arbeitet er um'), 'Rossegeschlecht' ('Pferdege- schlecht'), 'jagt sie' ('verfolgt sie'), 'Das Wild,/Das auf Bergen übernachtet und schweift' ('des Landes/Bergebewandelndes Wild'), as they intensify or expand, deflect overtly from the original and from an ordinary or dictionary understanding, and in so doing isolate the transformative process of translation under way. This is underlined by the traces of the earlier translation in the second: in revising not just the Greek original, but a previous version too, the text Hölderlin published holds within its dynamics a criticism and examination of its status as translation. We are only able to speak of traces of an earlier translation because that translation exists still and has not gone astray, as the rest of Hölderlin's working-papers have. For most of the translation they must have existed, but one cannot point with any certitude to places where they have left their mark, simply because there are no means of comparison.[19] Lines 349–70 can thus be read in a privileged way, a way that becomes implicit for the rest of the tragedies, but which can only be practised in this one case. This privileged reading is also a very different sort of reading in that it unsettles the text by adding an extra dimension, one which, once published, it has to be able to do without, but which it cannot escape entirely. The tricks of transmission have preserved the extra dimension, but its role is limited because the later text is complete and so constructs for itself a kind of autonomy. The problems are similar to those concerning a poem and its variants and earlier versions. They become very much more complicated when there is no final, authoritative text, which is the case with many of Hölderlin's later poems.

Böschenstein reads the second version of the stasimon in an extremely tendentious manner which my reading corroborates without going so far. He asks the good question why, in the second version, night should twice have been adduced over and above the original and the earlier version: 'über die Nacht/Des Meers' rather

---

[19]   Nor is it sure which edition of Sophocles Hölderlin translated from.

than 'im grauen Meer'' and 'das Wild,/Das auf Bergen übernachtet und schweift' rather than 'des Landes/Bergebewandelndes Wild'. He notes that both mentions of night are associated with crossings (over the sea and over the mountains), and continues:

Ich vermute nun, daß Hölderlin, wie vielleicht auch in einigen seiner wichtigsten Elegien und Hymnen, den Akt des Übersetzens aus dem Griechischen als ein eigentliches Über-Setzen mitreflektiert, als ein Über-Setzen, das durch die Nacht führt, in Verbindung mit einem Durchgang durch den Winter, durch das Meer, vielleicht auch durch das Gebirge. Das Übersetzen wäre dann eine Überfahrt.[20]

[My guess is that Hölderlin (perhaps also in some of his most important elegies and hymns) understands the act of translation from the Greek as an actual trans-lation, as a trans-ference which goes through the night, together with a passage through the winter, over the sea, perhaps also through the mountains. Translation would then be a crossing.]

To translate from Greek to German is obviously to forge a link between Greece and Hesperia and to assist in the transition from one to the other which the modern age is engaged in. Böschenstein sees the translation as betraying an awareness of its role in its *themes*, most evidently by adding the references to night. He talks of a 'Reflexion der Übersetzung über ihren eigenen Sinn innerhalb ihres eigenen Mediums' [reflection made by the translation on its own meaning within its own medium] (p. 53). Further, he sees translation as an instrument of analysis of the period of night: Hölderlin's translation of the stasimon makes man's exploitation of nature into an over-exploitation which disrupts the relationship between humans and gods. Thus, the translation comes to illustrate the nature of the situation it is trying to help to resolve, or to reflect the conditions of the transition it is part of. Böschenstein even tentatively suggests that the word 'Verkehr' could contain 'eine weitere semantische Schicht [...], nämlich die Arbeit der Übersetzung als einer Umwendung von einer Sprache und Vorstellungsart in die andere, welcher Vorgang den 'Verkehr' zwischen diesen Vorstellungen zustande bringt' [a further semantic layer: the work of the translation as a turning of one language and way of thinking into another, which process brings about the 'commerce' between them] (p. 43).

Böschenstein's essay is sensitively suggestive of how intimately the process of translation is connected with Hölderlin's cardinal themes,

---

[20] '"Die Nacht des Meers"', 40.

and of how a consciousness of this seems to be discernible in the texture of some of his writings, pre-eminently in the printed version of the first stasimon of *Antigone*. But it also seems to succumb to irresponsibility in imputing an inherent reflection on translation to any and every mention of a transition or crossing or journey in Hölderlin's poetry. There are undoubtedly poems, such as 'Patmos', whose logic and structure seem to be conceived according to the underlying analogy of translation, and which thus also offer some reflection on translation itself. But if the concept of translation is expanded so broadly that it becomes possible to perceive traces of and references to it at every turn in Hölderlin's work, its real significance as an agent in the development of the work is in danger of becoming diffuse or invisible. Particularly obscured is the fact that translation has an important place in Hölderlin's work not because it can be readily aligned to many aspects of it, but because it is so related in a specific way. Böschenstein sees translation as relating to the various aspects of Hölderlin's work not through analogy but intrinsically, as if translation were his theme. As the Pindar translation allowed a realization of Hölderlin's poetics precisely because it constituted an *analogue* of their workings, the relation between Hölderlin's translations and what can be seen as the central preoccupation of his poetry, the transition into a new world, is crucially one of analogy. Historical transition is bound up with the dissatisfactions of the present, never complete, not even certainly discernible as such at all. Poems can satisfy, and preempt actual movement out of one thing and into the next, but only in images, which, the more persuasive they are, betray their insufficiency with respect to the present. Translations from Greek to German on the other hand, though they also function like poems and in this regard share their limitations, do perform a certain transition, imbuing German with sense that was once housed in Greek. They thus offer a paradigm of transition as a completed act, of a crossing that has been made. It is a crossing which is at once sufficiently like and sufficiently unlike the grand historical shift into a new era. That is, although it can be seen as actually a minuscule part of the shift, it is essentially in analogy to it. It is as analogy that it has force, because it exceeds what it analogizes, forming the hope that a full transition may be made in the real world. The movement of translation embodies hope by extending into a domain which in the historical world is exclusively future, and showing the possibility of its habitation. At the same time it is a reflection on the mechanics of transition, and that is why it is so interesting that the retranslation of the *Antigone* stasimon should accentuate, as Böschenstein points out that it does, the ideas of crossing and pernoctation as indices of the present.

The changes which Hölderlin worked into his Sophocles translations in the last phase seem to involve a new consciousness of translation as a modern activity with a particular role in the interim. It is privileged as a mode of writing because it shadows forth into the future while being intrinsically homogeneous with the processes of the present, searching for links, forming dialogue, and provoking an interaction with the past. The *Antigonä* stasimon is at once a rewriting and a retranslation, the two activities meet here in obvious correspondence. It is emblematic of a relationship which defines Hölderlin's work at this stage. Returning to his own poems obsessively, he seeks to unsettle their structures and rewrite them into new ones, to write a poetry of the present which is in flux and open to change, a process into which the reader is drawn.

Hölderlin's Syntax of Transition

To read a poem by Hölderlin is to enter into a complex process which cannot necessarily be precisely defined afterwards. It is probably true that no poem should yield anything which may then be remembered instead of it, except things peripheral to what the poem is peculiarly the enactment or expression of. This means that a poem can render many valuable and interesting things which are extrinsic to its purpose, even as these things go towards the total constitution of the poem. All poems only exist fully when performed as wholes, when they are read (and possibly when they are being written). This is the case with all texts if they are not to remain closed books, but once the books have been opened there are degrees to which a text thrives or wilts after its reading. On such a scale, if didactic works are put at one end (in so far as their main intent is to deliver a message, retaining it answers the intent), many of Hölderlin's poems, and certainly his conception of poetry, stand at the other. Countless phrases and images and rhythms may be carried away from them, but what they are really about, their substance and breath, is only to be found in the act of reading.

The poems demand a lot of their reader. This is partly because he or she frequently has to abandon the logical sense, the proceeding according to preconceived ideas and expectations, which we rely on for everyday life. Most good writing will challenge or actually seek to disrupt such habits, since they are usually in the way of the sort of realization it is attempting to bring about; but some of Hölderlin's poems, as they are read, engineer a suspension in the mind which makes it particularly open and susceptible to change. That is to suggest that certain poems effect in the reading an unfixing, a suspension, similar to that pertaining in a period of transition, where 'das Mögliche' becomes 'real' [the possible becomes real] (iv/283).

As in the Pindar translation, there are moments in Hölderlin's poems which involve the reader in a contract that becomes peculiarly binding. Syntax and diction are employed in such a way that a reading must continually revise the positions it adopts as it progresses. The full meaning of a poem grows out of the checks and changes we experience as we make our way along its course. The making of sense does not proceed step by step, but by imagining forward and remembering back, by altering and substituting and extending the elements the poem forces it to go through. In that process of reading, the mind must be changeful, is *rendered* changeful, as it performs and is taken up by the rhythms of the poem. In order to read the poem, the reading mind must give itself almost entirely to the poem's movements in an act of faith that these movements will resolve themselves. Hölderlin was quite lucid about the anti-logical intention of an unconventional syntax:

Die logische Stellung der Perioden, wo dem Grunde (der Grundperiode) das Werden, dem Werden das Ziel, dem Ziele der Zwek folgt, und die Nebensäze immer nur hinten an gehängt sind an die Hauptsäze worauf sie sich zunächst beziehen,—ist dem Dichter gewiß nur höchst selten brauchbar. (iv/233)

[The logical ordering of periods—when the cause is followed by the development, the development by the goal, the goal by the end, and the subclauses are always simply put after the main clauses they immediately refer to—is certainly only very rarely of use to the poet.]

A small example of what I mean, the way a reading has to correct itself as it comes on new information, occurs in a distich from 'Heimkunft' (ll. 49–50):

Warm ist das Ufer hier und freundlich offene Thale,
    Schön von Pfaden erhellt grünen und schimmern mich an.

[Warm the shores are here and welcoming open valleys,
  Beautifully brightened by paths, glint and attract me with green.]

The hexameter presents two parts in parallel: the valleys appear to be 'freundlich' as the edge of the lake is 'warm'. But in the pentameter 'freundlich' becomes retrospectively an adverb and 'Thale' is attracted to the verbs 'grünen und schimmern' rather than the implied 'sind' of line 49. And were one required to parse the sentence, one would have to assign the words the functions they fulfil from the perspective of the pentameter. Poetically though, they have a double function, 'freundlich' is both an adjective and an adverb and the distich articulates itself over that shift: the pentameter plays on and modifies the words above it as its metre echoes and varies the hexameter's. Perhaps the couplet even gains some of its supple force from the way the attractive openness of the 'offene Thale' is enacted syntactically, the words drawing on both lines. The point, though, is that the reader must balance both grammatical functions, and that this involves an openness and a suppleness in him or her which, as well as being extended by the reader, is created by the syntax. As we revise our reading, or adjust it, there is a moment of uncertainty, almost even of helplessness, which is also the moment when we are drawn right into the poem.

Such an effect is obviously much further-reaching when a poem extends its syntax over several lines or strophes. The odes, with their strict forms, give the most striking examples, because the syntax is tensed and contradicted by the movement of the metre, which offers patterns the words can either comply with or override. There are several passages in the odes where a sentence spans four or five strophes, and it is in these long stretches that the energy syntax can generate is at its highest.[21] And also, that the greatest attention and suspension is exacted from the reader. There are poems which seem to exploit syntax in a particularly conscious manner, where its movements are congruous with the actual theme of the poem. 'Ermunterung' encourages the heart, which is 'wie ein kahl Gefild' [like a bare field], to become an 'Echo des Himmels' [echo of heaven], to make a gesture of hope which can then be answered, thus creating a correspondence between inner and outer which intimates the

---

[21] See 'An die Deutschen', ll. 24–40, 'Der Main', ll. 9–32 (6 strophes), 'Diotima', ll. 1–17.

greater correspondence of epiphany. The last four strophes of the poem project this hope along a single sentence; as it unfolds, its rhythms even more than its lexical sense anticipate the desired communion. It bodies forth a link which is actually missing:

> bald, bald singen die Haine nicht
> Des Lebens Lob allein, denn es ist die Zeit,
> Daß aus der Menschen Munde sie, die   15
> Schönere Seele sich neuverkündet,
>
> Dann liebender im Bunde mit Sterblichen
> Das Element sich bildet, und dann erst reich,
> Bei frommer Kinder Dank, der Erde
> Brust, die unendliche, sich entfaltet   20
>
> Und unsre Tage wieder, wie Blumen, sind,
> Wo sie, des Himmels Sonne sich ausgetheilt   22
> Im stillen Wechsel sieht und wieder
> Froh in den Frohen das Licht sich findet,
>
> Und er, der sprachlos waltet und unbekannt   25
> Zukünftiges bereitet, der Gott, der Geist
> Im Menschenwort, am schönen Tage
> Kommenden Jahren, wie einst, sich ausspricht.
>
> [and soon the copses will not sing
> To honour life alone, for now it is time
> That from the lips of human beings
> A more beautiful soul proclaim itself,
>
> And then in loving alliance with our kind
> The element will form, and rich again then
> With the gratefulness of children the
> Earth's breast, which has no limits, will unfold
>
> And our days they will be like flowers again
> Where the sun up in the heavens sees itself
> Distributed in quiet reflection
> And in joy once again the light resumes,
>
> And he, who moves without language and unknown
> To us prepares what comes, the God, the Spirit
> In the human word, to coming years
> In the days of beauty, as once, will speak.]

These lines describe an arc out of the present dilemma of listlessness through an evocation of a full, correspondent life 'im stillen Wechsel' to the moment of epiphany itself, but this moment is also a return to the present, and what in the reading had transiently seemed real is pronounced definitively absent, no longer and not yet: 'wo [...] der Gott [...] kommenden Jahren, wie einst, sich ausspricht'. 'Sich ausspricht' harks back to the verbs ending the three previous strophes, which are a sort of gradual arrival—'sich neuverkündet', 'sich entfaltet', 'sich findet'; but, almost in mockery, instead of confirming and crowning the sequence, 'sich ausspricht', deflecting past and future, makes plain that the only utterance is to be found in the poem.

So the movement of the last four verses is shown to be an illusory event, even within the larger artifice of the poem. This honesty, though, and fidelity to the unideal present, does not undo the effect of the syntactic passage of the last four strophes. There a passage is opened for the reader into a condition where a real transition beyond the present seems envisageable, if only momentarily. The syntax creates a flux which on one non-semantic level opens onto the future, though the opening is closed by the words' lexical meaning. No one syntactic 'trick' as striking as in the couplet from 'Heimkunft' , but an intricate, varying structure in which a constant wavering is produced. To attempt to describe the main features, the fluctuations which a reader goes through: there is a conflict between words which seem to mark the stages of a clear progressive statement—'dann [...] Dann [...] dann [...] wo', together with the chain of verbs already mentioned— and the counter-flow of anastrophic genitives ('des Lebens Lob', 'der Erde/Brust' etc.) and pronouns anticipating the nouns they properly belong to. The effect of these latter two devices is to retard the forward motion which the apparently key elements of the period prompt. A genitive of the form 'des Himmels Sonne', apart from fleetingly suggesting a construction which will determine the genitive ('des Himmels') otherwise than as a possessive, makes a miniature dynamic pause as understanding awaits completion, especially if it is preceded by a preposition as in 'aus der Menschen Munde' or 'bei frommer Kinder Dank', where the genitive is an interruption. These two phrases perform *in nuce* the delaying, suspending movement of the poem as a whole. This is increased by the pronouns 'sie' (l. 15), 'sie' (l. 22) and 'er' (l. 25), which, though they predict their nouns, put off their actual enunciation and cause a lift in the rhythm. A counterpart to these anticipatory words is the extension of nouns once they have fallen, as signally in 'der Erde/Brust, die unendliche, sich entfaltet' (ll. 19–20), where the syntax acts out the sense of unfolding. Again, the effect is of a slowing-down of the syntactical flow, so that a sense of progression is almost absent. A point reached is spun out, the sentence builds up and gathers before going on, like a stream flowing through a pool, 'im Stillstande der Bewegung' [in the stillness of movement] (iv/265). Lines 25–6 combine the two, anticipation and extension: 'der Gott' is announced by 'er', deferred further by a relative clause, and renews itself in 'der Geist', so that for two lines the poem is at rest, though it is the kind of rest Hölderlin called 'die lebendige Ruhe, wo alle Kräfte regsam sind' [living rest, when all faculties are alert] (vi/305).

To speak of syntax is inevitably to speak of its effect in the reading mind. There is a paradox whereby the slowing of syntactical progress *increases* a sense of movement by postponing the final cadence which will bring the period to a standstill. Though the sentence pauses, the mind is kept in 'a sort of vigilant torpor' (like Hölderlin's 'lebendige Ruhe') as it strives to hold on to the thin syntactic thread which runs through the last four verses *at the same time* as being lulled by the meditative, pondering movement of the words.[22] Great concentration is demanded of the reader, the mind's capacity for holding syntactical structures is stretched, probably beyond what is possible, so that in order to proceed, in order to read, certain words have to be taken on trust in the faith that in the course of the sentence, once articulated, they will collect the meaning they do not have on their own. By the time the end of the sentence (and of the poem) has been reached, its words have fallen into place—the trust extended in their meaningfulness has been rewarded. But they have not fallen into place definitively: each reading involves the same uncertainty, the same wavering between meanings and grammatical roles, and the poem can only be read through a submission to this uncertainty. There is a useful comparison to be made, I think, with music: the shift out of harmony into dissonance and into new harmony. The state of abeyance, of hanging on waiting for release, created by the phase of dissonance, is not just a preliminary to the second harmony, but intrinsic to experiencing it, the only course along which it is reached. It is a

---

[22]   The words 'a sort of vigilant torpor' are Thierry-Maulnier's, quoted in Donald Davie, *Articulate Energy: An Inquiry into the Syntax of English Poetry*, 2nd edn. (London, 1976), 31. Hölderlin's is the better phrase.

transition in which the need for harmony is generated.

In 'Ermunterung', the itinerary of the final long sentence, though moving out towards the future, remains true to the present. It is true also to a certain experience of the present, attracted and unsettled by an imagined future whose elements derive from a remembered (but also necessarily imagined) past. The future 'Ermunterung' conjures is a conjunction of god and man in language ('der Geist/Im Menschenwort'), but the present is defined by unconnectedness, by the very absence of that coming-together. The absence, though, gives the poem its impetus: the words 'wie einst' in the last line are cruelly abrupt in their reminding that divine immanence can only really be spoken of in the past, but at the same time they seem to intimate that for this very reason it may once again occur in the future. 'Einst', referring both back and forward, to past and future, but only uttered in the present, holds in its ambiguity the spirit of the present as it is embodied in the poem.

The way the present is articulated in 'Ermunterung' corresponds to Hölderlin's understanding of the present in general: as a period of transition, rich and confusing. Through its syntax, the poem creates a 'zaudernde Weile' [hesitant time] (ii/91). The feeling of living in the modern world is one of disarray and bewilderment, but, Hölderlin thought, the flux out of which this feeling stems is also the precondition for the forming of a new world. There is a fundamental instability, but the very lack of fixity opens up all kinds of possibilities. To read through the long sentence of 'Ermunterung' is to be cast into a similar condition, where there are no fixed points and, even worse, words present themselves as fixed points only to have this status revised as the sentence proceeds. Again, in order to read, the reader must become acquainted with uncertainty and be possessed of a 'reading faith'. The poem puts us into a flux. During that moment of hesitation, of abandonment to the intricacies of syntax, when we are obliged to ignore the demands of reason and let the rhythm carry us, the poem is an interim, a small gap in the logic we try to rule our lives by. It thus corresponds to the 'indessen' (ii/94) of the transitional age, and creates a state of mind in the reader peculiarly open and undefined. Hölderlin, as we have seen, associated such a state (a 'state' of flux in fact) with the possibility of manifestation, of the arrival of something new. This dynamic is also operative within the poem in that the poem works ('der Gesang [...] glükt', ii/119) at the moment or moments I spoke of when the reading mind, from progressing logically, step by step, word by word, relating the poem to experience outside it and verifying it according to this knowledge, is forced to give up such strategies and adopt the movements, the rhythm, of the poem itself. Then, the reader is drawn in and for an instant *becomes* the poem, the present state of uncertainty is indistinguishable from that which the poem engenders. The act of reading generates one indivisible present; momentarily the everyday world and the world of the poem cohere, but the coherence disappears as soon as it is felt, and can be recovered, if at all, only by entering again into the process of reading.

The syntax of 'Ermunterung', and of other poems in which syntax has a similar function, leads us into flux; but it also leads us out again. There is a moment of suspension, but this settles at the end of the poem, and the faith extended to its course is justified as the sentence comes to rest at a full stop (like a final chord). The syntax reaches a resolution, and from the vantage-point of the ending its fluctuations make sense. The uncertainty felt while reading has been traversed and some clarity gained, in the sense that the sentence has proved itself readable. What the poem does then, is recreate an interim, a state of confusion, and show a way out of it, show that what appears directionless is in fact a transition. The reader acquires experience, becomes knowledgeable, of the dynamics of transition, and the successful emergence from uncertainty in the poem reflects hopefully on the outcome of the processes of the world itself. The reader undergoes a transformative process, learns that complex and contradictory modes of feeling (brought about within the poem) can have an issue, and to some extent this may equip him or her for living in the present and seeing there the locus of a positive transition. Simply, through a similarity in dynamics, the poem makes change in history seem a real possibility. The poem anticipates in its movements, in the rhythm of its syntax, the hoped-for transition into a better world; and it helps create the conditions for that to be possible by supplying the reader with a hopeful sequence of feeling.

But it is only a poem. The resolution that comes at its end does not actually effect a transition in the real world, any more than the projection of fulfilment in the 'Brautfest' [bridal feast] of the poem 'Der Rhein' does. And on one level, the resolution the syntax reaches is just a return to normality, out of a sense of fidelity towards the unideal state of affairs. The syntax resolves itself, but that is not the point. Reaccepting grammatical convention is an admission that the 'ideal' syntax cannot under the present circumstances be sustained and that the vision it holds is illusory. The transformative process it initiates, and wants, can be hinted at, presented in poetic parallel, but cannot be assumed to exist outside the workings of the poem. 'Ermunterung' anticipates, and that is where its encouragement lies. But nothing it does can ensure the experience of reading the poem will be extended into everyday life. Thus, at the end, the return to present reality in both the syntax and the story of the poem, as it admits its anticipation and in honesty concedes. This may seem to contradict what was said before: from being understood as 'akin' to the present, the syntax of 'Ermunterung' becomes 'ideal', that is, it is aligned with a projected future. These two understandings derive from a difference between the *effect* of the syntax on the reading mind and the *status* of the same syntax in grammatical terms. Reading the poem leads to a transient identification of the life of the reader in and outside the poem. But as a whole the poem is still to be distinguished from the real world (among other things by its grammar); part of its power comes from its working on a different plane.

There is an obvious congruence between the hesitation, the deferral, of the syntax and the theme of the poem. 'Ermunterung' imagines a human speech in which the divine will be present, but the life of the poem takes place in the interim before that, during which the god 'sprachlos waltet und unbekannt/Zukünftiges bereitet' (ll. 25–6). Its own language takes its rise from the absence of that full one which would render it unnecessary, and, as it were, tries to fill the gap, so that the desire, the project, comes close to being the fulfilment. It is not the god who 'sich ausspricht' at the end, but only the poem. The final sentence works as a resistance to speaking directly of what would constitute fulfilment: 'der Gott, der Geist' (and even this formulation refuses to be definite). It is in the slow transition to this (muted) culmination that the essence of the poem occurs, for as the god is named the poem comes back to earth, as it must, and shifts what had come to appear present into the future of 'kommenden Jahren'. The poem closes, but remains open in that what would really seal it, 'der Geist/Im Menschenwort', is still distant.[23] As such, it constitutes the required response—the 'Echo' (l. 1)—to the good weather and invites a further response; but it can do no more than

[23] One could even argue further, as Hans-Jost Frey does, that the delaying allows what is 'sprachlos' (l. 25) to express itself in the poem. See his '*Ändern*: Textrevision bei Hölderlin', in: *Der unendliche Text* (Frankfurt a. M., 1990), 76–123 (86).

beckon. It is an openness that is both hopeful and painful since it exposes itself to the possibility that the only fulfilment pending is the limited one of the poem itself, that there may be no answer; but the movement of the syntax, if we understand it as creating an interim and guiding us out of it, expresses through its whole rhythm a hope which the lexical sense of the words does not dare pronounce as it finally reaches the resolution it had for so long been putting off. The syntax, carrying beyond the interim, overrides the sense it articulates.

Lines 13–28 of 'Ermunterung' only found their final form in the last of several fair copies. As clearly set out in the Frankfurt edition, previous versions presented the last four strophes in three sentences, with full stops at the end of lines 16 and 20. It is stunning, and very instructive, to observe how such small changes can utterly transform the dynamics of a poem. In three separate blocks, the final four verses are a slightly lame evocation of an envisaged future. Isolated, lines 17–20 are wooden and appear to be an unnecessary insertion. Only when the whole sequence is articulated do the lines come to life and take on the passing ability to convince us that they are enacting something in the present. The syntactic difficulties which are at the heart of the poem simply come from Hölderlin's having taken out the punctuation. The attention span demanded of the reader is then much greater, and the poem becomes much the richer for it. Instead of syntax and form coinciding, with stops coming at the end of the strophes, there is conflict between the two, with the sentence extending over natural pauses. The deletion of the full stop after 'sich entfaltet' (l. 20) is particularly telling, as the energy and growth evoked there is allowed to flow over into the next strophe. Perhaps we should say that the removal of the full stops brings out an existing tendency, since the formulation of the lines hardly changes from the second fair copy (*FA*, v/766–7) onwards, but in fact it does render them much more complex, subjecting the whole construction to 'denn es ist die Zeit,/Daß...' (itself a complex expression). The suspension of the long sentence is thus arrived at in the process of composition, and not something Hölderlin had in mind from the beginning.

Rewriting

From very early on, rewriting was an intrinsic part of Hölderlin's working method. Perhaps his whole work can be seen as an obsessive reworking of the one theme, a continuous search for more effective means of handling his material, circling round and round the ideal poem, which if attained, would fulfil the whole project. Hölderlin hardly wrote anything without going through several versions. The composition of *Hyperion* was a long, laborious process involving a metrical version.[24] *Empedokles* went from version to version, with shifts from blank to free verse and back again, and remained in transit, never finding a final form. As we have seen, Hölderlin set about altering his Sophocles translation at a late stage, and it is likely that it had already undergone some revision. The *Frankfurter Hölderlin-Ausgabe* makes it particularly clear that most of Hölderlin's poems involved many stages and only got written by continually retracing their steps and starting out again.

It is true that rewriting is important to many writers' manners of working, that the genesis of a poem, particularly, often comes gradually, and through a lot of hard work. Very many poets have altered their writings retrospectively, most notoriously perhaps, Wordsworth. And what we can say about the history of a poem is also dependent on what manuscript material has survived to us (partly, what individual writers have *allowed* to survive). But in Hölderlin rewriting seems to be vital to the poetic process—very often elements of a final version arise from suggestive juxtaposition or promptings in earlier drafts[25]—and the poem only constitutes itself gradually. The process of composition forms the poem, rather than its being given more or less from beginning to end, further drafts essentially consisting of improvements to an already defined whole.

Long before 1803/4, Hölderlin had also gone back to completed poems as the basis for new ones. Most of the short 'epigrammatic' odes he wrote while in Frankfurt received thorough expansion two years later, in 1800. 'Stimme des Volks', in its last version eighteen strophes long, starts off as two strophes, self-contained and published in Neuffer's *Taschenbuch*.[26] 'Rewriting' is not an apposite term here—really a wholly new poem is developed out of what proves to be only the beginnings of one. These very short poems are like first lines, from which the poem then later ensues. If Hölderlin wrote them originally

---

[24] See Beissner's account: iii/296–318.

[25] E.g. through rhyme: in 'An die Parzen' (l. 8) 'gelungen' replaces 'gesungen' (*FA*, v/540–1); and in 'Diotima' ('Du schweigst...'), strikingly, 'Doch eilt die Zeit' (l. 6 of first version) becomes 'Die Zeit doch heilt' (l. 18 of the second).

[26] Cf. i/563.

with Goethe's advice 'kleine Gedichte zu machen' [to write short poems] in mind (vii,2/109), which is possible, then their startling extension shows what restraint Hölderlin had been persuaded to exercise, and to what extent he was repressing his poems' potential. With most of these expansions the original short poem becomes, unchanged or only slightly, the first strophe or strophes of the later poem. (Once, expanding 'An unsre großen Dichter' into 'Dichterberuf', Hölderlin copied out the first poem—making very slight changes—as a base, and then wrote in between the lines the divergences which would allow the development of the new ode. This anticipates a later practice.) The original unit then provides the starting-point, but not the end-point, for the later addition, which nevertheless remains within the parameters of the root poem. The continuations are generally expanded treatments of the original theme, taking up the terms of the initial poem and enlarging their scope. Even 'Stimme des Volks', the development which seems most to exceed the bounds of its seed—it was reworked in two phases, brought first to thirteen, then to eighteen strophes—can be understood as a meditation on questions opened by the Frankfurt ode. The Xanthus story is an extreme version of the river's course into the sea and oblivion, which is 'meine Bahn nicht, aber richtig' [not my way, but right] (FA, v/580, first version). Often the new poem is a response to the old one, most clearly in 'Die Heimath', where the original constitutes an unanswered question: 'Ihr [...] Ufer [...]/Stillt ihr der Liebe Leiden?' [you banks,/Can you relieve love's sufferings?] (ll. 5–6), to which the further strophes reply that for all its comfortings, home, once the traveller has arrived there, will not be a remedy to sufferings which are existential: 'Ein Sohn der Erde/Schein' ich; zu lieben gemacht, zu leiden' [A son of the earth/I seem to be; made to suffer, to love] (ll. 23–4). 'Das Unverzeihliche' is an admonitory epigram, ending 'doch stört nur/Nie den Frieden der Liebenden' [but never/Break the peacefulness of lovers]. Its expansion, 'Die Liebe', tones this down to 'doch ehret/Nur die Seele der Liebenden' [but always/Respect the souls of lovers] and then continues with a kind of poetic explanation of the importance of this precept. In going back to the original poems, Hölderlin seems to have sought a stimulus, and each time he embodied the stimulus in the new poem, rather than starting afresh on the same theme. The new work is in dialogue with the old. It is odd, on the face of it, that he preserved the originals as openings (and even more surprising that they, finished poems, can serve as openings at all without there being a hiatus between them and the following text). That he did seems to betoken an extreme thrift, an unwillingness to reject any poetic material.

It is a thrift which amounts to a poetic technique. The poems derive from their beginnings, never forget their origins as they proceed. In this respect they are very like poems such as 'Brod und Wein' and 'Patmos', which contain in their first strophes, in concise, ungerminated form, the elements out of which the dynamics and tensions of the complete poems unfold. Perhaps this practice was even influenced by these reworkings, in that they encouraged a particular manner of composition and poetic thinking that worked from a source set at the beginning of the poem. The reworkings of the Frankfurt odes are also very close to what Hölderlin did later in his *Pindar-Fragmente*. In both cases a short text is conserved by being integrated into a new text, and the integration takes the form of an extended meditation on the terms given by the originating lines.[27] This anxiety to preserve and remain faithful to beginnings does appear to be a constant pattern in Hölderlin's work. Very often, the process of reworking ends up at a position very near to the original one, or, having passed through various possibilities, finds its way back to the first materials, though they may be considerably transformed.[28] A related case is the transcription of the hymn 'Wie wenn am Feiertage...' from prose to verse: the original prose is simply written into verse-lines and strophes with very minor changes, that is, it is already rhythmically structured, remarkable when one considers that Hölderlin was adopting a strictly Pindaric metrical scheme. (This resembles Goethe's putting of the prose *Iphigenie* into verse—again, few changes were necessary—or, inverted, Novalis's rewriting of his 'Hymnen an die Nacht' from verse to prose.) The composition of *Hyperion*, was, like the structure of the finished novel, circular, finally coming to rest in a form corresponding to the original idea.[29]

Only one of the reworked Frankfurt poems expands its original in a manner which is perhaps more what one would expect: 'Diotima'. Inflation might be the word to use here, rather than extension. The two strophes of the original become six, whereby the first is also, with

[27]   On the *Pindar-Fragmente* (Sattler: *Neun Pindar-Kommentare*), see Ch. 6 below, pp. 245–53.
[28]   Cf. Frey, 82.   [29]   Cf. Sattler's description, *FA*, xv ff.

some alterations, the first strophe of the new poem, and the last two and a half lines of the last strophe are transferred, verbatim, to the end of the new version. The remaining one and a half lines (5 and 6) of the first poem reappear in lines 13 and 18 of the reworked poem. The original poem is split up, but reappears almost in its entirety, with the important difference as against the other poems of this group that not only the beginning forms the beginning, but the end the end, of the new poem.[30] The status of the original ending as ending is corroborated by the manuscript evidence, which shows the first trace of 'Diotima' to be a preliminary version of the last two lines: 'Die Helden könt' ich nennen/Und schweigen von der schönsten der Heldinnen' [I could name all the heroes/And pass over the most beautiful heroine] (FA, v/420).

'Diotima' was worked over once more, in pencil, very probably in the winter of 1803/4.[31] Apart from a change in grammatical case, those elements carried over from the very first version remain untouched. But the new changes are of a quite different kind from the expansions of the Frankfurt odes—they are not additive, rather they replace words while retaining the form of the original, and they are written in between the lines of a fair copy. They are at odds with the version they insert themselves into, they even contradict it directly: the Greeks, if that is who they are, spoken of before in the past, are now emphatically claimed for the present—instead of 'sonst' [once] in line 6 'noch jezt' [even now], and in line 8 'freuten' [enjoyed] has become 'freuen' [enjoy]. There is also a startlingly unconventional syntax: 'Tönt denn zu freuen nicht schon/Leben?' [Rings then to gladden not now/Life?] (ll. 19–20).[32] It is difficult to make sense of the corrections if they are integrated into a new version, though they seem to be an attempt to reinstate the poem's meaningfulness after Susette Gontard's death. The poem is certainly rendered much more complex. It seems to introduce another group of people: 'die Dankbarn' [the thankful ones] (l. 10), in the first (six-strophe) version apparently referring to the Greeks, are now themselves 'ausgegangen

---

[30]   This is almost certainly due to the fact that Susette Gontard's initials are written into the beginning and end of the last line of the first verse (S) and the last line of the last verse (G), which gives 'dich nennt' in the final line a special resonance. See Michael Franz and Roman Jakobson, 'Die Anwesenheit Diotimas: Ein Briefwechsel', LpH 4/5 (1980), 15–18.   [31]   Cf. FA, v/419.

[32]   This follows the FA's reconstructed text (FA, v/426), one reading of the manuscript material, which is not clear. Cf. FA, iv/364 and StA, ii/439.

von jenen' [issued from them] (l. 10), and it is these 'jene' who must
be the Greeks. Perhaps the poem can be read if Diotima is thought of
as dead, victim to the uncomprehending age, and the 'Freigebornen'
[freeborn] (l. 5) are taken as those few people in the present, such as
the poet, who remembering her and the Greeks, still hope to bring
on the arrival of the 'Himmlischen' [gods] (l. 18). Whether this is
tenable or not, the poem has become troubled and lost its obvious
coherence. The corrections add a layer whose relationship to the
original whole is indeterminate. Hölderlin did not, so far as we know,
give them the authority of a fair copy.

Reworkings of this kind, but even more radical and disruptive,
become a main feature of Hölderlin's writing in the winter of 1803–4.
The rewriting that was always part and parcel of his work seems, as I
said, to be taken up quite consciously as a means of energizing his
poetic development, and for a while composition and revision are
virtually synonymous. The practice stands in the closest relation to
translation, not only within the general evolution of Hölderlin's work
(the Sophocles translations are reworked at the same time as the
'Durchsicht' [look-through (vi/436)] of the 'Nachtgesänge', and
further revision of poems in the *Homburger Folioheft* is probably
concurrent with translation of *Ajax* and the *Pindar-Fragmente*), not
only thus, but as regards technique. In order to rework 'Der gefesselte
Strom' into 'Ganymed', Hölderlin wrote out the first poem fair and
then put in his new version between the lines, like an interlinear
version.[33] This was also his method with the elegies and the other
revised poems in the *Homburger Folioheft*. In each case the basis for the
revision is a finished (sometimes published) poem, an original to be
worked upon. Hölderlin translates himself into a new idiom. As with
the Pindar translation, a new departure, forcing the language into new
territory, is instigated by the agency of translation. To recapitulate,
there comes a point in Hölderlin's work when rewriting is deliberately
brought into the process of composition, and that is also when writing
and translation are most tightly linked.

The analogy between revision and translation perhaps needs to be
scrutinized a little more closely. It exists through an equation of
original and translation with earlier version and revised poem. When,
over lines 65–6 of 'Stutgard'—'die See schikt/Ihre Wolken, sie schikt

---

[33]   See the facsimile, *FA*, iv/373–4.

prächtige Sonnen mit ihm' [the sea sends/Its clouds, it sends magnificent suns with him]—Hölderlin puts 'Ungeheures' and 'krankende' so that the lines then read 'die See schikt/Ungeheures, sie schikt krankende Sonnen mit ihm' [the sea sends/Monstrosities, it sends sickening suns with him],[34] both revisions appear to diverge in the same direction, to be twisting the original text with a similar intent, but while semantically they depart considerably from the text (contradict it, more or less), as parts of speech they remain consistent with what they replace—the grammatical structure of the original sentence is followed. The shift in meaning is comparable to the inevitable modification a text undergoes as it gets translated. But though this is the natural analogical relation, the revisions seem to invite, in their oddity, the further association with words which have been strongly affected by a foreign language, by something behind them pushing them out of conventional usage. However, the words they stem from ('ihre Wolken', 'prächtige') offer nothing of the sort. In revising them, 'translating' them into a new register, Hölderlin transposes into a *language of translation*, as if this external pressure were bearing upon them. The language is not furnished by the mechanics of the revision itself, but is in an idiom related to his translations from the Greek; at a similar tangent to accepted usage, but without the obvious cause. The warping of German observable in the Pindar translation now appears to occur spontaneously. Or almost, because it still happens within, and seems to need, a process of rewriting. The revision operates according to the analogy with translation, but the relationship is not reducible to it alone. Hölderlin is rewriting out of his *experience* as a translator, actually conjoining the two modes of writing, original composition and translation. He takes the technique (of reworking) from his normal practice, and the language derives from his translations. But the reworking technique is clearly akin to translation, and more so in 1803/4 than before, because Hölderlin is working from finished poems.

This fact is vital to the strength of the analogy. It is what separates the late rewritings from the process of rewriting in Hölderlin's work in general. Hölderlin actually returns to poems he had already brought to a state of completion, which have a status of wholeness. As in translation then, there is an original from which to work, and usually

---

[34] As in the *FA*'s final text (vi/200).

the form of the original is preserved.[35] Yet the inner dynamics of the relationship are not quite the same. A translation, while being unavoidably different, is nevertheless aiming at a similarity with its original. It is attempting to approach. A rewriting, on the other hand, is by definition working away from its original, the poem is altered precisely to differ. The intent is not the same.

Both impulses though, towards and away from the text, equal an effort of manifestation in the new language arrived at through the rewriting/translating process. In rewriting his old poems, Hölderlin is trying to drive them into new expressiveness. The heightening and intensification of the tone as the translation out of the old into the new is made is obvious. The language becomes precarious, exposed, in its desire to be expressive. It is also violent in its relationship to the poem it derives from. Indeed the whole undertaking of revision represents a violence. The original poems have already found a form, and in order to extend them their form must be broken into. There is something unsettlingly destructive about even those revisions, like that of 'Der gefesselte Strom' or 'Der blinde Sänger', which end in a new form and are unquestionably successful. When it comes to poems such as 'Brod und Wein' or 'Patmos', where no new version is reached, damage is done, though damage is not the only result. The violence inherent in the act of rewriting seems to be part of the rationale behind the whole practice of revision. There is disagreement with the earlier text; but perhaps there is also disagreement with the whole concept of a complete, rounded text. Whereas the 'Nachtgesänge' revisions find a new crystallization, later ones seem to solicit unfixity.

The revisions can be seen as a very consistent and extreme consequence of Hölderlin's poetic theory. As often, Hölderlin is taking something through to its logical conclusion. His interest in transition as a place of manifestation is extended into the process of composition; rewriting undoes the fixity the original text has reached and puts it into flux again, so that from out of the possibilities opened a new constellation can form. At their most ideal, Hölderlin's poetics

---

[35] The additions to 'Der Archipelagus' seem not to replace, but to extend the original (FA, iii/241). Where the FA decides they do replace, it seems not to be in the manner of a translation (FA, iii/243–4). In the course of being rewritten into 'Blödigkeit' the last two strophes of 'Dichtermuth' get compressed and transformed into one.

would have the poem adopt a constellation capable of rendering the Spirit, and according to this criterion his poems had failed. Rewriting them was a kind of angry attempt to make them work, and some of the revisions, especially in 'Brod und Wein', do seem to be like spurs, provoking the poem, and at the same time disrupting it. But even at a less absolute level, Hölderlin's poetics do not tolerate stasis, and though most of his poems do not close but, read properly, come to an end which points outwards, as finished poems they can nevertheless appear specious. Hölderlin's thinking about poetry, about the nature of manifestation, turns on the paradox of holding something that cannot be held, the vessel of an epiphany breaking as it contains. The breaking *is* the manifestation and allows the onward passage of the Spirit: 'das Leben [durchläuft] alle seine Puncte [...], und um die ganze Summe zu gewinnen, auf keinem verweilt, auf jedem sich auflöst, um in dem nächsten sich herzustellen' [life runs through all its points and, in order to gain the total sum, dwells on none of them but dissolves each time to reconstitute itself in the next] (iv/284). No one form can serve. The breaking open of the poems is a radicalization of this kind of thinking. Hölderlin's poems, in their whole nature and project, await completion from outside, they attempt to encourage, to engender a response which will then fulfil them and make them whole. In a sense then, finished form does not suit them and goes against their meaning. That is obviously an extreme argumentation, and I do not mean to set up unfinishedness, fragmentation, as an end in itself. But I do think that at one level it is what Hölderlin's late work implies. His most successful poems are still the finished, coherent ones, in which the need for completion is balanced by the complete form, in itself an anticipation of what is hoped for, and part of the gesture demanding response. And at first, in the revisions that made the 'Nachtgesänge', whole poems were translated into whole poems.

Of these, the most purely translational revisions are of 'Der gefesselte Strom' into 'Ganymed' and of 'Der Winter' into 'Vulkan'. Fair copies of already completed poems are prepared, and the revision takes place within the formal limits thus set. The revisions are then, as with all the 'Nachtgesänge', published with Hölderlin's authority. For other of these poems, the revisional process is more complex: an unfinished draft is reworked and brought to completion ('Thränen'),[36] a poem is reduced ('Blödigkeit'), or a revision returns not to the most recent version of a poem, but to an earlier point in its genesis ('Chiron').[37] Different altogether is the case of 'Hälfte des Lebens', which seems to owe its existence to a 'zufälliges Nebeneinander verschiedener Entwürfe' [chance juxtaposition of different drafts].[38] This is not a revision at all, but it is the eminent example of a poem evolving within a fluid textual situation, and Hölderlin seems to be searching for a similar openness in returning to his poems and dissolving the particular forms they had settled into. Out of the dissolution new forms could rise.

Der gefesselte Strom.

Was schläfst und träumst du, Jüngling, gehüllt in dich,
  Und säumst am kalten Ufer, Geduldiger,
    Und achtest nicht des Ursprungs, du, des
      Oceans Sohn, des Titanenfreundes!

Die Liebesboten, welche der Vater schikt,
  Kennst du die lebenathmenden Lüfte nicht?
    Und trift das Wort dich nicht, das hell von
      Oben der wachende Gott dir sendet?

Schon tönt, schon tönt es ihm in der Brust, es quillt,
  Wie, da er noch im Schoose der Felsen spielt',
    Ihm auf, und nun gedenkt er seiner
      Kraft, der Gewaltige, nun, nun eilt er,

Der Zauderer, er spottet der Fesseln nun,
  Und nimmt und bricht und wirft die Zerbrochenen
    Im Zorne, spielend, da und dort zum
      Schallenden Ufer und an der Stimme

Des Göttersohns erwachen die Berge rings,
  Es regen sich die Wälder, es hört die Kluft
    Den Herold fern und schaudernd regt im
      Busen der Erde sich Freude wieder.

[36] Cf. David Constantine, 'The Meaning of a Hölderlin Poem', *Oxford German Studies* (1978), 45–67 (50–2).
[37] On the rewriting of 'Der blinde Sänger' into 'Chiron', see Frey, 89–96.
[38] Beissner, ii/663.

Der Frühling komt; es dämmert das neue Grün;
    Er aber wandelt hin zu Unsterblichen;
        Denn nirgend darf er bleiben, als wo
            Ihn in die Arme der Vater aufnimmt.

                                    (*FA*, v/834)

        [The shackled river.

Why, youth, do you sleep and dream, wrapped in yourself,
    And linger at the cold edge too patiently,
        And neglect your origin, you, the
            Son of Ocean, the friend of the Titans!

The bearers of love, the ones your father sends,
    Don't you recognize the life the breezes breathe?
        And doesn't the word come, that bright from
            Above the wakeful god sends down to you?

And now a sound, a sound from within his breast,
    As when he used to play among the rocks, it
        Wells up in him and he thinks of his
            Strength now, the power he had, now he hurries,

The ditherer, he laughs at his shackles now,
    And takes and breaks and flings the broken pieces
        In anger, easy, here and there to
            Both of the roaring banks and at the voice

Of the gods' son the hills round about wake up,
    The woods begin to stir, the chasm hears the
        Herald distant and with a shudder
            Joy moves again in the bosom of the earth.

Spring is coming; the green begins to show through;
    But he is going to where they never die;
        There is nowhere he can stay, except
            Where into his arms his father takes him.]

            Der gefesselte Strom.

Was schläfst und träumst du, Jüngling, gehüllt in dich,
    Und säumst am kalten Ufer, Gedultiger!
        Und achtest nicht des Ursprungs, du des
            Ozeans Sohn, des Titanenfreundes?

Die Liebesboten, welche der Vater schikt
  Kenst du die lebenathmenden Lüfte nicht,
    Und trift das Wort dich nicht, das hell von
      Oben der wachende Gott dir sendet.

Schon tönt, schon tönt es ihm in der Brust. Es quillt
  Wie da er noch im Schoose der Felsen schlief
    Ihm auf, und nun gedenkt er seiner
      Kraft, der Gewaltige, nun, nun eilt er

Der Zauderer; er spottet der Fesseln nun
  Und nimmt und bricht, und wirft die Zerbrochenen,
    Im Zorne, spielend, da und dort zum
      Schallenden Ufer, und an des Herolds

Bekannter Stimme wachen die Hügel auf
  Es regen sich die Wälder, es hört die Kluft
    Den Stromgeist fern und schaudernd regt im
      Busen der Erde sich Freude wieder.

Der Frühling keimt.[39]

      [The shackled river.

Why, youth, do you sleep and dream, wrapped in yourself,
  And linger at the cold edge too patiently!
    And neglect your origin, you the
      Son of Ocean, the friend of the Titans?

The bearers of love, the ones your father sends
  Don't you recognize the life the breezes breathe,
    And doesn't the word come, that bright from
      Above the wakeful god sends down to you.

And now a sound, a sound from within his breast.
  As when he used to sleep among the rocks, it
    Wells up in him and he thinks of his
      Strength now, the power he had, now he hurries

---

[39] Reconstructed according to the transcription of the manuscript in *FA*, iv/372–5.

The ditherer; he laughs at his shackles now
　　And takes and breaks, and flings the broken pieces,
　　　　In anger, easy, here and there to
　　　　　　Both of the roaring banks, and at the herald's

Familiar voice the hillside wakens up
　　The woods begin to stir, the chasm hears the
　　　　River spirit and with a shudder
　　　　　　Joy moves again in the bosom of the earth.

Spring is budding.]

Ganymed.

Was schläfst du, Bergsohn, liegest in Unmuth, schief,
　　Und frierst am kahlen Ufer, Gedultiger!
　　　　Denkst nicht der Gnade, du, wenn's an den
　　　　　　Tischen die Himmlischen sonst gedürstet?

Kennst drunten du vom Vater die Boten nicht,
　　Nicht in der Kluft der Lüfte geschärfter Spiel?
　　　　Trift nicht das Wort dich, das voll alten
　　　　　　Geists ein gewanderter Mann dir sendet?

Schon tönet's aber ihm in der Brust. Tief quillt's,
　　Wie damals, als hoch oben im Fels er schlief,
　　　　Ihm auf. Im Zorne reinigt aber
　　　　　　Sich der Gefesselte nun, nun eilt er

Der Linkische; der spottet der Schlaken nun,
　　Und nimmt und bricht und wirft die Zerbrochenen
　　　　Zorntrunken, spielend, dort und da zum
　　　　　　Schauenden Ufer und bei des Fremdlings

Besondrer Stimme stehen die Heerden auf,
　　Es regen sich die Wälder, es hört tief Land
　　　　Den Stromgeist fern, und schaudernd regt im
　　　　　　Nabel der Erde der Geist sich wieder.

Der Frühling kömmt. Und jedes, in seiner Art,
　　Blüht. Der ist aber ferne; nicht mehr dabei.
　　　　Irr gieng er nun; denn allzugut sind
　　　　　　Genien; himmlisch Gespräch ist sein nun.

(FA, v/837–8)

[Ganymede.

Why sleep, son of the hills, awkward, in a mood,
    And freeze there at the bare edge, too patiently!
        Have you forgotten the grace you had
            At their tables, when the gods were thirsty?

Down where you are don't you know what your father
    Wants, in the chasm the quicker play of air?
        Doesn't the word come, that full of old
            Spirit a much-travelled man sends to you?

But now a sound from deep within his breast. Like
    When he used to sleep high up in the rock, it
        Wells up. In anger he clears himself,
            Shakes his shackles loose, and now he hurries

Who was so clumsy; he laughs at the slag now,
    And takes and breaks and flings the broken pieces
        Drunk with anger, easy, there and here
            To the watching banks and at the stranger's

Own special voice the flocks all jump to their feet,
    The woods begin to stir, the deep land hears the
        River spirit and with a shudder
            Life moves again in the navel of the earth.

Spring is coming. And everything, in its way,
    Flowers. But he is distant; no longer with us.
        Far gone now; for they are all too kind,
            The angels; now he's talking in heaven.]

As is also the case with 'Der Winter'/'Vulkan', the writing out of
the fair copy is already the beginning of the work of revision, as if the
copying process were a way of passing the poem under review. This is
depicted by the breaking off at the end; by then, in the course of
writing out, the poem had already taken a new direction and the
original ending had become unviable. This direction begins to make
itself felt in the 'anticipatory' revisions at lines 10 ('schlief' instead of
'spielt') and 19 ('Stromgeist' for 'Herold') of the *Reinschrift*. Its
transitional status is held in the small correction of the *d* to a *t* in
'Gedul(d)tiger' (l. 2). The previous fair copy had a *d*; 'Ganymed' has
a *t*, which, interestingly, reverts to the first drafts of the poem.

The violence of the act of rewriting is given a clear image in the curtailed form of the *Reinschrift*. But though it is the text from which Hölderlin immediately derived 'Ganymed' (as can be seen from the facsimile—*FA*, iv/373–4—he wrote the new poem in and around it), to print it here is really only a convenience: earlier stages of work are still present (as the *Reinschrift* itself in ll. 16–17 borrows from versions earlier than the one it mainly follows), and the final form of the last strophe, though it differs greatly from previous endings, obviously relates to elements of them which have not been copied down. Really the reader needs to have all the drafts and versions to hand (*FA*, v/827–38).

The revision 'Der gefesselte Strom'—'Ganymed' has received a lot of critical attention.[40] The very last touch to it, the new title, only appears from the publishing of the poem in Wilmans's *Taschenbuch*, and it is difficult to know how to integrate it into the poem as a whole. The revision had Ganymede in mind, as the question 'Denkst nicht der Gnade, du, wenn's an den/Tischen die Himmlischen sonst gedürstet?' (ll. 3–4) reveals. Ganymede was the gods' cupbearer. The new title acknowledges a turn the poem has taken, but it also has a deep effect on the way we are likely to read it. In all its versions, the poem enacts a return of energy, aligned with the coming of spring. From the beginning this was to work through the metaphor of a frozen river melting at the end of winter (the earliest title was 'Der Eisgang' [The Thaw]—*FA*, v/829), but the river is personified, addressed as 'Jüngling'. The title indicates this ('shackled' not 'frozen'), and we are reminded of it regularly, by the epithets and names associated with the river in the course of the poem; but the personification figures chiefly as a poetic device beneath which we always perceive the river itself, running down the poem and out towards the sea, 'wo/Ihn in die Arme der Vater aufnimmt' (l. 24). We have been clearly told at the beginning of the poem that the river is 'des/Ozeans Sohn' (l. 4), and have no trouble distinguishing between the main metaphor (the river) and a figurative or mythological layer which is laid loosely over the top. In 'Der gefesselte Strom' it is the

[40]   See Alfred Romain, 'Ganymed', *HJb* (1952), 51–84; Jochen Schmidt, *Hölderlins später Widerruf in den Oden 'Chiron', 'Blödigkeit' und 'Ganymed'* (Tübingen, 1978), 146–76; David Constantine, 'Translation and Exegesis in Hölderlin', *MLR* 81 (1986), 388–97 (396–7); Jean-Pierre Lefebvre, 'Der Fährmann und die Hebamme: Ein Vergleich der Oden "Der gefesselte Strom" und "Ganymed" auf Grund der komparativen Übersetzung', *HJb* 29 (1994–5), 134–49; Grunert, 149–62.

noun that is important, the adjective merely an adjunct. The poem 'Ganymed' is much more complex, and allows no simple separation of different strands or layers of meaning as we read. We come to the poem ignorant of the river, and it only makes itself felt gradually, indefinably perhaps. The poem still seems to speak of a river, but we cannot escape into the information of the title for confirmation; the poem has distanced itself from any clear referent outside its workings.

Hölderlin's returning to, or turning on, 'Der gefesselte Strom' indicates a dissatisfaction with the poem which can be measured by the degree to which the later realization corrects the first. 'Ganymed' animates the old structure and makes the release of energy more manifest. It is an intrinsic critique of the earlier version. The transition out of stasis into movement which 'Der gefesselte Strom' seeks to, and 'Ganymed' really does, enact is also the transition the work of revision brings about: the form of 'Der gefesselte Strom' is unfixed and enlivened into more dynamic form. The act of rewriting, therefore, has a particularly intimate relationship with the meaning of the poem: each revision at once alters 'Der gefesselte Strom' (animates it) and provides the means through which a process of animation is realized in 'Ganymed'.[41] The correcting words have (at least) a double function; as well as constructing the meaning of 'Ganymed' they *act* upon 'Der gefesselte Strom'; they actually effect, in textual terms, what they signify. The two procedures can in the end hardly be distinguished—writing is rewriting.

When 'Ganymed' is read this intimacy extends to the transformation the poem works on the reader. A further process of enlivenment is realized: the quickening, the liberation, and also the fascination in the poem are felt, rendered 'fühlbar und gefühlt' (iv/243), by the rhythms and syntactic jumps. In what must be a unique way, the reader is bodily involved in the process of the poem. It runs through us reading as the river/Ganymede seams along the poem, and the change from 'schallenden' to 'schauenden' (l. 16) describing the riverbanks, which Hellingrath pointed to as characteristic of the effect of the revision (ii/547), describes also the new alertness aroused in the reader by 'Ganymed' as against 'Der gefesselte Strom'.

Such effects are arrived at via the revision process, and the method

[41]   In that sense I suppose I agree with Grunert when he says the poem 'Ganymed' represents 'seine eigene Genese' (149).

of revision Hölderlin adopts is that of translation. At times the translation really is of an interlinear nature: a word is replaced by a word with a grammatically identical role, as in: 'Der Zauderer, er spottet der Fesseln nun'—'Der *Linkische; der* spottet der *Schlaken* nun'. Elsewhere the revision is more complicated, positions are changed and new elements are introduced, but it is still possible to follow the broad derivation of one line from an other, as in the two versions of the first line. Apart from the last strophe, which is completely restructured, the changes mostly take place on the lexical level. The syntax, and even the rhythm, are surprisingly little changed considering the different total impression 'Ganymed' leaves. In verses 3 and 4, in which the awakening happens, 'Ganymed', though much more expressive of energy, moves in almost exactly the same way as 'Der gefesselte Strom'. As with the punctuation of 'Ermunterung', the slight changes in the position and number of pauses are instructive.

An idea of the lexical innovations that occur during revision can be gained from the concordance to Hölderlin's poems. 'Der gefesselte Strom' contains five words never used before in the poems ('Titanenfreund', 'Liebesboten', 'aufquellen', 'Zauderer', 'Herold'), 'Ganymed' nine, including 'aufquellen', but not 'schief' and 'frierst', both of which are used only once elsewhere ('Bergsohn', 'geschärfter', 'der Linkische', 'gewanderter', 'besondrer', 'Stromgeist', 'Nabel', 'allzugut', 'aufquellen'). But far more striking than numbers are the register and texture of the words: 'Der gefesselte Strom' has traces of a conventionally lyrical vocabulary in 'Liebesboten' and 'Herold'; 'Ganymed' replies with 'gewandert', 'der Linkische', 'Schlaken', 'Nabel', words which force themselves upon us in their strangeness. Their very oddity gives them an eruptive energy which fits the impulse of the poem exactly. Hölderlin's intention to go against accepted forms, to contradict them outright, is clear in the inversion of 'da und dort' (l. 15). Grimm calls 'dort und da' rare and gives one example.[42] The willed strangeness of the new diction is absorbed by the process it describes and enacts, and whose total meaning it contributes to. There is thus no sense here of the language being extreme for its own sake. There are adequate poetic grounds for its radicality, namely the movement and theme of the poem itself. Nevertheless the language and the attention it draws to itself point

---

[42]   From Rückert. *Deutsches Wörterbuch*, ed. Jacob and Wilhelm Grimm, 16 vols (Leipzig, 1860–1914), ii (1860), 650.

forward to later revisions where the context it occurs in accepts less easily the pressure and intensity being inflicted upon it, and where such language becomes an incursion, hurting the text it breaks into. In 'Ganymed' the language is just under control, and as the exceeding of limits, the breaking out of fixed form belong to the gesture of the poem, any 'excess', like the disruption of the ode metre in the last strophe, is immediately encompassed, the parts integrate into the whole.

The rewriting works against the template provided by 'Der gefesselte Strom', but even in its method it is not a straightforward contradiction. The revision is itself a process, opening up the text, making it changeable. That the final revisions (title, full version of last strophe) should only be available to us in the printing is very apt: only publication can really put a stop to a process that is potentially endless. Hölderlin's changes come gradually: in the opening lines 'Jüngling' becomes 'Sohn' before becoming 'Bergsohn', and 'in Unmuth' revises a first try, 'verdrossen' [annoyed]. The Ganymede myth is only introduced after a failed attempt to rewrite line 4 by reinstituting the dreaming motif cancelled in the first line. In line 8 the daring of 'ein gewanderter Mann' (translating 'der wachende Gott') is arrived at through a 'sinniger' [thoughtful] and then a 'wandelnder Mann' [wandering man] (*FA*, v/835). 'Herolds' becomes 'Fremdlings' via 'Wächters' [watchman's] and 'Wilden' [wild man's] (*FA*, v/836). 'Gewanderter' is a provable instance of the practice that occurs throughout the revisions: the adoption, while rewriting, of a language deriving out of Hölderlin's experience as a translator. As Beissner points out (v/547), 'gewandert' turns up as a translation of ἐρχόμενον in P5 17 and of στείχων in *Oedipus der Tyrann*, l. 815.[43] The word can thus be said to be borrowed from there, but Hölderlin still has to work towards it, to come at it through the process of the poem: the idea contained in the word first appears in the form of 'wandelnd', and only then can 'gewandert' come across from the translations as another possible layer. The manuscript of the reworking does not give us a new version but a loosening of the old text, a sifting of it into a spectrum of possibilities. Each word of revision is not a correction, but an addition, a further expansion of potential: neither base text nor

[43] In *FA*, l. 820. The word is also Voss's word for Odysseus in his first version of the *Odyssey* (see p. 27 above). Cf. also *Antigonä*, ll. 375–6: 'Allbewandert,/ Unbewandert', a (mis)translation of Παντοπόρος/Ἄπορος.

intermediate alterations are crossed out but left in suspension. Publication (with Hölderlin's authority) gives sanction to the final version 'Ganymed', and it is comforting to find that the latest (uppermost) alterations in the manuscript (like 'gewanderter' and 'Fremdlings') are those opted for in the printed version. Comforting because, for many of Hölderlin's poems existing only in manuscript, editors have had to make what is otherwise an arbitrary selection of the last (or presumptively last) variant; they have had to make a final decision on the direction of composition which Hölderlin preferred not to make. Hölderlin seemed always to want to extend the openness, the undecidedness, of a poem to the last possible moment, often to the point of renouncing a final, closing touch. This process can be followed in the manuscripts. He hardly ever crossed out at all, but underlined or bracketed or made a mark in the margin. To keep the maximum number of options and possibilities open for as long as he could seems to have been a principle of composition; to prolong the phase in which the poem could still strike out in a new direction; to put off the finality of decision. There seems to be an intention discernible to reconstitute something like the 'middle text' of the Pindar translation, a suggestive text, rich in its unfixity. From the first draft of a poem to the final version (if one is reached) the intermediate stages form a transition, and the poetic process makes the passage as slow as possible, holding the poem open. Here too, the idea of a manifestation in transition underlies Hölderlin's practice. To return to a finished poem is to attempt to reactivate the potential of this understanding of composition, to resist the closure which had put an end to it. The poem is returned to the transitional, undetermined phase.[44]

This 'state of composition', holding the different possibilities in parallel, is sometimes carried over into the final text, when a translation is found which combines different layers of earlier versions. 'Schlief' (l. 10) stays close to the sound of the word it replaces—'spielt'—while going right back to the sense of 'ruht' [rest], an early variant (FA, v/830). In line 21 'kömmt' reconciles 'keimt', the original word, and 'komt', which is adopted in 'Der gefesselte Strom' as part of a new version of that line. The form 'kömmt' negotiates between the two vocables, combines their sounds and thus perhaps even their meanings. Some of the sense of 'keimt', the sense of a

---

[44] Cf. the passage from the 'Verfahrungsweise' (iv/263–4), quoted on pp. 122–3.

gradual process, may be audible in the softer vowel-sound of 'kömmt'. Hölderlin's unhappiness with 'komt' is clear from the *Reinschrift*, which reverts to 'keimt', but 'kömmt' is given only in the printed version, and may stem from the typesetter. Hölderlin used both forms though, and which he chose was never arbitrary: there is even an example of his correcting himself from 'kömt' to 'komt'.[45]

Sound is an important factor in the dynamics of transition from poem to poem. Often new words are suggested by the shape and aural qualities of the words they replace. So 'am kahlen Ufer' is prompted by 'am kalten Ufer' (l. 2), 'stehen[...]auf' by 'wachen[...]auf' (l. 17), 'zum/Schauenden Ufer' by 'zum/Schallenden Ufer' (l. 16), or less obviously, 'irr gieng' derives from 'nirgend' (l. 23).[46] These echoes should also be thought of as a preservation of the original material, which is redistributed or transmuted, but not discarded.

The previous layers live on in the final version 'Ganymed', in various ways. There is a sense in which 'Ganymed' is *about* the earlier versions it rewrites, in which it actually seems to refer to its template and in so doing betrays an awareness of what it is engaged in, just as the retranslation of the stasimon from *Antigone* seems to dwell on the activity of translation. In both cases, and quite naturally, the deliberate repetition of a procedure (retranslation, rewriting) encourages a degree of self-reflection, of self-consciousness within the work. With 'Der gefesselte Strom'/'Ganymed', as I said, the propensity towards reflexiveness given by the rewriting is increased by the overlap between the theme and meaning of the poem and the intention of the revision. The poem can easily be read as illustrating its own workings. But this is only possible because the previous versions are available to us. The first readers of 'Ganymed' had nothing of this, and to interpret the poem wholly as 'eine Reflexion auf seinen Entstehungsprozeß' [a reflection on its own genesis], as Grunert does, is a very one-sided approach, tendentious in so far as it depends entirely on text the finished poem has isolated itself from.[47] To read it thus is to injure the autonomy Hölderlin gave it by having it published, represented by the new title. But since we do have the

---

[45] *FA*, v/696, line 21. Beissner (ii/537) does not have this reading.

[46] Cf. Frey, 90.

[47] Grunert, 149. Grunert calls 'Der gefesselte Strom' the 'Hauptperson' in 'Ganymed' (159). His interpretation is based on Schmidt's unlikely suggestion that the 'Wort' (l. 7) the 'Bergsohn' receives is 'Ganymed' (Schmidt, *Hölderlins später Widerruf*, 154).

earlier stages, and they have for years been printed side by side, it is equally tendentious to try and retrieve the naivety of those first readers and ignore the very pressing claims 'Der gefesselte Strom' makes on 'Ganymed'. Clearly, by its very nature as revision, 'Ganymed' is a palimpsest, in which 'Der gefesselte Strom' can be discerned, in the same measure that any translation must retain some transparency if it to be recognizable as a translation at all. Since 'Ganymed' *is* a revision, to say that what it revises figures in it is close to banality, since those are the very elements which allow us to link the two poems. There is though one word in 'Ganymed' which does look like a very deliberate reference to 'Der gefesselte Strom': 'der Gefesselte' (l. 12). This alters what from the very first draft had remained constant, 'der Gewaltige'. As the river/Ganymede surges free 'Ganymed' stresses its fetteredness, whereas all previous versions tell of its power. The word 'Gefesselte', coming at the precise moment when the fetters begin to be shaken off, seems to refer back to the poem it parts from, which remains caught in its linear progress towards the sea, and the new poem leaves the old one behind, moving on itself unfettered, and changing the 'Fesseln' to 'Schlaken' (l. 13). The process of rewriting is taken up into the poem, in so far as we can read 'der Gefesselte' as a reference to the earlier version (the complete title 'Der gefesselte Strom' is concealed in 'Ganymed', 'Strom' appearing in l. 19). The original poem is not just present but actually mentioned; but only, of course, audibly to readers who know 'Der gefesselte Strom'.[48] 'Ganymed' does not depend on the reference's being heard, but the reference enriches it because of the congruity of the effect of the reworking and the poem's metaphor of enlivenment.

A retreat from a sense outside the workings of the poem is a general consequence of the rewriting technique. The self-referentiality of which 'der Gefesselte' is an identifiable instance results naturally from the poem's development through self-translation. The poem takes its co-ordinates from itself, and the language thus turns in on itself, becomes denser, because it arises not just out of the needs of expression, but out of an inward relation to other words. The new intensity of all the rewritings stems partly from this: the derivation out of an ulterior text. In 'Ganymed' the tendency is compounded, as we

---

[48]   There are other examples of Hölderlin privately inscribing details into poems which enrich without being essential to them. See the article by Franz and Jakobson. Also: Pierre Bertaux, '"Sterbliche Gedanken"—S. G.', in: *Hölderlin-Variationen* (Frankfurt a. M., 1984), 89–93.

have seen, by the extra layer of metaphor that comes with the introduction of Ganymede into the poem. In both language and metaphor, then, the rewritten poem acquires more texture, it directs the reader's attention onto itself rather than deflecting it out towards a particular 'meaning'. It has become harder to read because no ready explanation, no exit to what the poem is 'about', is supplied, we cannot simply follow the course of the river as in 'Der gefesselte Strom'.[49] Something of the simultaneity of different possibilities of meaning cultivated in the manuscript of the revision is retained in 'Ganymed' in its aligning several metaphorical levels in parallel and refusing to give precedence to any particular one. An effect similar to that worked by syntax in 'Ermunterung', but here by other means, is produced: a moment of suspension in the reading mind, which is entirely taken up by the poem. The gap between Ganymede and the river, or the manner of their joining, which is not explained, leads the reader into a quandary from where links can no longer be made to a definite sense. Likewise, the opaque quality of individual words means that we are less disposed to look through them at what they signify but remain under their actual spell. The poem creates a pause in the mind, an openness of mind, as it is read, and this seems to be something the reworking sought to bring about. The more open the reading mind is held the more it is drawn into the poem and will itself realize the process the poem enacts and conjures.

In its embodiment of energy, 'Ganymed' is an obvious and clear counter to 'die träge Zeit' [the dull times] (i/175). It is a further instance of the tendency of Hölderlin's work at this time to distance itself from conventional utterance *in order* to have a political impact, combining a demanding form and a will to connect. Although the poem in its rewriting keeps within the form of the alcaic ode, in its last strophe it so contradicts the rules of alcaics that it can only be said to stick to them outwardly, in syllable-count and typography. As 'Ganymed' breaks free from 'Der gefesselte Strom', it also breaks out of its ordained structure and through syntax and rhythm, creates its own.[50] The lines are broken up into small paratactic blocks which override the ode strophe, or at least move in palpable conflict with it, so that once again, at the end, the poem enacts the liberation from

[49] Cf. Constantine, 'Translation and Exegesis', 397: 'we are kept *within* a work whose power to move us has been enhanced'.

[50] Romain sees both rhythm and language in the last lines as moving into those of the hymns (80–1).

fixedness and thus follows its own logic. The breaking off of the *Reinschrift* after the first half of line 21 is borne out by this movement out of metre, in which the apotheosis of the 'Stromgeist' is conveyed. An appearance of metrical form is kept up, but really the rewriting far exceeds the premises of the original, and in exceeding effaces them. A new form is reached, perfectly commensurate with the transfiguration the poem has undergone.

Revisions in the *Homburger Folioheft*

The poems among the 'Nachtgesänge' Hölderlin reworked were translated into new wholes. The intention of the reworking was always towards a new poem, as the titles reflect, and the corrections, the new versions, tend to reveal an insufficiency in the originals. These revisions were the last work Hölderlin did in the so-called *Stuttgarter Foliobuch*,[51] and also the last work in the ode form (which the reworkings begin to exceed). There were several pages left in the *Foliobuch*, but Hölderlin chose not to use them. By then most of his writing, though by no means all of it, was going into the so-called *Homburger Folioheft*, which seems in some respects to have been conceived as a whole.[52] The end of work in the *Stuttgarter Foliobuch*, though it does not correspond with the beginning of the *Homburger Folioheft*, marks a break in Hölderlin's production which is reflected in the style and intention of the revisions in the *Homburger Folioheft* and elsewhere. These slightly later revisions are thoroughly analogous to both the 'Durchsicht' (vi/436) of the 'Nachtgesänge' and the alterations in the Sophocles translations. Their idiom, though in places even more radical, shows the same urge towards greater compactness of expression and away from accepted norms. But all reworkings of poems after the 'Nachtgesänge' (and of Hölderlin's major hymns and elegies composed between 1800 and 1802 hardly any remain intact) result, in spite or even because of their intrinsic richness, in the disruption and fragmentation of their coherent original forms. Something like the successful translations of 'Dichtermuth' or 'Der gefesselte Strom' must have been behind the adoption of the interlinear strategy, but the incursions are not encompassed into a new homogeneous form. Rather than

---

[51]   *FA*, Supplement II, 17.
[52]   See Sattler's 'Einleitung' to *FA*, Supplement III, 9–20.

completion, there is an undoing which is particularly noticeable because the originals from which Hölderlin departed were already all but perfectly composed and achieved.[53]

Dissolution may be the result, but there is recompense. The *Homburger Folioheft* opens with fair copies of the already completed elegies 'Heimkunft', 'Brod und Wein' and 'Stutgard'. In between the lines of the beautifully fluent fair copies there then come corrections, at first isolated and then more continuous, which vary from straightforward shifts in intensity to entirely independent jumps in a new direction. There is an awkward and perplexing discrepancy between the sustained, even progression of the original elegiac couplets and the more irregular rhythms and inflammable language that get written in between the lines.

One of the first alterations to 'Heimkunft', and thus in the *Homburger Folioheft*, gives the direction of the reworkings and characterizes one aspect of them:

Heimzugehn, wo bekannt blühende Wege mir sind

[To go home, where blossoming paths are familiar to me]

becomes:

Heimzugehn, wo bekannt Weege mit Beeren mir sind
(l. 68: *FA*, vi/314)

[To go home, where paths with berries are familiar to me].

An obvious accretion of intensity is helped to expression by the advance of the season: from the general, diffuse blossoming the mind's eye shifts to the specifities of berries, the focus sharpens, and the change from participle to noun, towards concreteness, is of a piece with the transition.[54] 'Weege mit Beeren' calls actual details to mind, seems to refer to known paths in remembered vividness, whereas 'blühende Wege' is a general phrase less indicative of particular places. The more attentive gaze and the language needed to accommodate it ('Weege mit Beeren' is an odd phrase, it draws to itself a similar attention to that it results from) come at the point in the poem where

[53] The reworkings of and additions to 'Der Einzige' present a different case because the original form had a gap.
[54] Cf. 'Stutgard', l. 22, where 'Blumen' is changed to 'Beeren' (*FA*, vi/194). In its context this is a much more arbitrary change, perhaps no more than a memory of the revision in 'Heimkunft'.

home is evoked. As Groddeck points out, the revisions in 'Heimkunft', a 'streng hälftig komponierte Elegie' [elegy strictly composed in two equal parts], only occur in the second half of the poem, which is devoted to 'der Boden der Heimath' [the ground of home] (l. 55).[55] More precisely, apart from the apparently slight correction of 'hell' [bright] to 'breit' [open] in line 65, they begin exactly as the *Ich*'s imagination jumps forward beyond Lindau to his home proper, to the Neckar and the paths and trees he knows there. They attempt to lend the centre of 'den hesperischen *orbis*' (ii/876) a concrete particularity which in Hölderlin's earlier writing had been avoided for the sake of a more general, balanced poetic world. Details are now important in themselves and not just as efficient ciphers of a larger scene. The changes in the next few lines continue the process:

> Dort zu besuchen das Land und die schönen Thale des Nekars,
>   Und die Wälder, das Grün heiliger Bäume, wo gern
> Sich die Eiche gesellt mit stillen Birken und Buchen

> [To visit the country there and the lovely vales of the Neckar,
>   And the woods, holy greenness of trees, where oaks
> Join together with silent birches and beeches]

> Dort zu besuchen das Land und die rothen Ufer des Nekars,
>   Und die Wälder, das Grün luftiger Bäume, wo dann
> Tannenfarb' ist gesellt zu Buchen ekig und Birken
>   (ll. 69–71: FA, vi/314)

> [To visit the country there and the ruddy banks of the Neckar,
>   And the woods, airy greenness of trees, where fir-
> Colour is joined by beeches jagged and birches]

The generalizing, abstracting traits of the fair copy are suppressed (Hölderlin crosses out 'schönen Thale' and underlines 'heiliger' and 'Eiche') in favour of specific colours and shapes, movements and juxtapositions, so that in the mind a real landscape can be built up rather than just an idealized scene. The awkward syntax in line 71 means the reader feels the words being assembled to make up a picture. The deliberate effort of expression can be heard. This contrasts absolutely with the easy flow of the original lines, but we cannot speak of an improvement, a better realization, as in 'Der

[55] Wolfram Groddeck, 'Die Revision der "Heimkunft": Hölderlins späte Eingriffe in den Text der ersten Elegie im Homburger Folioheft', *HJb* 28 (1992–3), 239–63 (241).

gefesselte Strom'—'Ganymed'. The idealization of the home country in the *Reinschrift* of 'Heimkunft' belongs in a context: the joy and hope of the poem are only attainable in these general, universalized terms, in which the abstract and the concrete are deliberately confused and made to betoken each other: 'noch blühet die Sonn' und die Freud' euch' [the sunlight and joy flower for you still] (l. 75), 'das lebende Feld' [the living fields] (l. 82). These striking examples of hopeful synthesis are altered: 'die Freud' euch' to 'das Festlicht' [the feast-light] and 'das lebende Feld' to 'den Hof und das Feld' [the farm and the fields] (*FA*, vi/314–15); but the elegy cannot be transposed by correcting a few salient points, and the revisions mostly go too far in the opposite direction to sit happily alongside the lines that remain unchanged.[56]

The changes to 'Heimkunft' mentioned so far take place according to a process of substitution in which the connexion between original and variant is clear. In the details of the revisions (the intermediate stages, which are not always crossed out) the translational nature of this process emerges: the first shift from 'die schönen Thale' to 'die rothen Ufer' is 'die falbe Erde' [the dun earth]. The introduction of the colour of 'Tannenfarb' is first suggested by the correction of 'stillen' to 'blauen' [blue] (*FA*, vi/314). It is easy to see how a gradual manifestation of detail is drawn out of the general view of the fair copy. The landscape is made to impinge, as the translation of a foreign text brings home, in a like process of manifestation, the at first only vaguely apprehended contours of meaning. I suggested that the translation of Pindar was for Hölderlin the realization in his own language of the vessels of a former fulfilment; by the time he was reworking his elegies, the realization of his homeland, as a place of *imminent* fulfilment, was not less important, and the technique is in both cases essentially the same. The arrival of Pindar and Sophocles into German is itself hopeful, and the gathering of vividly exact details, fragments, of Hesperian landscape into language, making it seem to press for expression, contains a similar, though less confident hope. The language used, in its patent strangeness, seems to want to signify more than it really can, to make a gesture of meaning beyond what it holds, as if the redness of the Neckar's banks were 'unendlicher Deutung voll' [full of endless meaning] (ii/226). The revisions move

---

[56] Cf. in this context Hellingrath's remarks on '*harte* und *glatte fügung*': *Pindarübertragungen von Hölderlin*, 1–7.

from a style which suppresses detail, a style which really means less than it says and because of its role in the poem is only concerned to convey a general impression, to one in which the real constituents of the general impression are brought into the foreground and the detail cries out. The composure of the original lines is upset and there results a much less balanced text.

This practice is remarkably close to the intentions behind Hölderlin's Sophocles translations: 'Ich hoffe, die griechische Kunst [...] dadurch lebendiger [...] darzustellen, daß ich das Orientalische, das sie verläugnet hat, mehr heraushebe, und ihren Kunstfehler, wo er vorkommt, verbessere' (vi/434). Hölderlin thought Sophocles flawed by over-adherence to artistic convention and sought to correct the flaw by bringing out what this convention had suppressed: 'das Orientalische'. In the terms of Hölderlin's own poetics of manifestation, from which the remarks obviously derive, the total metaphor which Sophocles' tragedies represented had neglected the 'Grundton' [ground-tone] and placed too much emphasis on the 'Kunstkarakter' [art-character] (iv/266). The 'Kunstkarakter' had ended up concealing the 'Grundton' rather than expressing it.[57] The translation seeks to undo Sophocles's metaphor by changing the relation between 'Grundton' and 'Kunstkarakter', by underlining 'das Orientalische' and correcting the 'Kunstfehler', that is those points where the 'Kunstkarakter' is empty form. Hölderlin renders Sophocles's metaphor more dialectical (bringing out the 'Grundton', 'das Orientalische' so that there is more conflict), makes it newly expressive and unmuffled by 'Nationalkonvenienz' (vi/434). The revisions of 'Heimkunft' (and the late revisions as a whole) are in the same spirit. The changes amount to an undermining of the original poem's metaphor, the 'fremden analogischen Stoff' [foreign analogous material] (iv/150) into which the beloved world of Hölderlin's homeland had been transmuted. Hölderlin wrote of the lyric poem: 'Das lyrische, dem Schein nach idealische Gedicht ist in seiner Bedeutung naiv' [The lyrical poem, ideal in aspect, is in its meaning naive] (iv/266). The rewriting of lines 68–71 of 'Heimkunft' can be seen as a reversal of these poetics, which the original poem, here at least, had followed. The ideal 'Schein' is broken through ('die schönen Thale') and the 'Bedeutung', the bare, 'naiv' components

---

[57] At least to modern eyes. See above, p. 64.

('die rothen Ufer') emerge.[58] The revision of the poem goes further than the translation of the tragedies, or rather, it disrupts the original metaphor without reconstituting it, but the *intention*, of 'resetting' the metaphor in line with new insights, is identical.

The inversion of Hölderlin's Homburg poetics discernible in these particular corrections is part of a larger unsettling of the original poem 'Heimkunft'. The revisions looked at so far, through their intensity out of place, contradict the mode of the original, but in their divergence they remain within the same semantic field and essentially testify a new way of seeing.

Changes further down the elegy are of a different sort. There are two points where the work of revision is especially concentrated: lines 77–9 and 101–2. In the original elegy they are related: lines 79–80 ('Aber das Beste, der Fund, der unter des heiligen Friedens/Bogen lieget, er ist Jungen und Alten gespart' [*translation below*]) refer allusively to something which cannot, and should not, be named directly. Lines 101–2 then come to speak of and question this necessary tact: 'Schweigen müssen wir oft; es fehlen heilige Nahmen,/Herzen schlagen und doch bleibet die Rede zurük?' [Often we have to be silent; the sacred names are lacking,/Hopes are high in our hearts but speech stays behind?]. The revisions seem to be attracted by this reticence. Those in the first passage try to define what had been left undefined:

> Ja! das Alte noch ists! Es gedeihet und reifet, doch keines
> Was da lebt und liebt, lässet die Treue zurük.
> Aber das Beste, der Fund, der unter des heiligen Friedens
> Bogen lieget, er ist Jungen und Alten gespart.
>
> [Yes, all is still as it was! It prospers and ripens, but nothing
> That lives here and loves lets up in loyalty.
> But the best of all, the find, that lies under the bow
> Of holy peace, that is saved up for young and old.]

> Ständige.
> Ja! das Alte noch ists! das Männliche. Viel ist, doch nichts, was
> Liebt und berühmt ist, läßt beinerne Treue zurük.
> Blutlos. Aber der Schaz, das Deutsche, der unter des heiligen Friedens
> Bogen lieget, er ist Jungen und Alten gespart.
>
> (ll. 77–80: *FA*, vi/314)

[58] 'Schein' and 'Bedeutung' are equivalent terms to 'Kunstkarakter' and 'Grundton'. Cf. p. 88 above.

stalwart.
[Yes, all is still as it was! manly. There is much, but nothing that
  Loves and is famed lets up in bone loyalty.
Bloodless. But the treasure, Germanness, that lies under the bow
  Of holy peace, that is saved up for young and old.]

The changes show a great impatience ('Treue', before a good quality,
promising much, is now dismissed with the odd word 'beinern') and
are frankly antagonistic towards the original. They read like a
commentary on the earlier lines, explicating them violently. Line 79,
if that is how Hölderlin intended it, is now hypermetric.[59] Breaking
open the restraint of the *Reinschrift*, Hölderlin contravenes its metrical
form. The changes can be understood as consistent with the earlier
ones in that they seem to want to speak directly, and unlyrically, of
something 'underlying' the original words. Something concealed is
brought to light, but only at the cost of destroying the form. The
revisions of lines 101–2, a couplet which they seem to make to replace
entirely, are even odder and more complex. They retain the link noted
in the *Reinschrift*, referring again to Germanness ('Arm ist der Geist
Deutscher' [Poor is the Germans' spirit], *FA*, vi/316), but it is
doubtful whether a new distich can be constructed out of them, as has
been attempted (see the transcript: *FA*, vi/309).[60] They seem to be a
deliberate conundrum, as a response to the 'Zurückbleiben' of speech
the fair copy speaks of ('doch bleibet die Rede zurük?'). The new
words both promise something ('Geheimerer Sinn' [more secret
sense], *FA*, vi/316) and hold it back. The inwardness of the language
that arises from the reworkings is here taken to an extreme, and even
itself reflected on. The revisions are a kind of intense worrying at the
original, at once partaking in it (the words at least close to hexameters
and pentameters) and setting themselves apart from it (through their
diction and content). Unlike the first stages of the reworking, which
always keep in a clear relation to the fair copy, these last revisions are
esoteric; and though they mimic the translational process, they exceed
it, though no more, it must be said, than some of the interpretative
translations in *Antigonä*, which they strongly resemble. Common to all

[59]   There are many ways in which the line could be edited from the manuscript.
Cf. Groddeck, 'Revision', 248–9, and Friedrich Hölderlin, *'Bevestigter Gesang': Die
neu zu entdeckende hymnische Spätdichtung bis 1806*, ed. Dietrich Uffhausen (Stuttgart,
1989), 223–4.
[60]   Groddeck suggests a new reading of the lines and attempts an interpretation
('Revision', 259–62).

the alterations is an interest in a level of meaning the original, 'classical' poem has withheld, whether they attempt to reveal that level or ponder on the problem.

How should these late additions be read? Linked to this question is that of how they should be edited. The *Frankfurter Ausgabe* reconstitutes final versions of the three elegies in the *Homburger Folioheft* by amalgamating the revisions—that is, replacing the *Reinschrift* text where there is extra text written over it, but letting it stand if not. It thus presents these reworkings as a (completed) attempt to rewrite the poems. The *Stuttgarter Ausgabe*, on the other hand, publishes them in the appendix volume as variants. The course taken by the Frankfurt editors, fully explained in the two articles mentioned by Groddeck, has been attacked, especially in an article by Böschenstein, who argues that the manuscript of 'Brod und Wein', at least, represents a process of revision that was broken off.[61] No fair copies including the revisions survive of any of the elegies, but at least one may have existed: in 1807 Seckendorf published a version of 'Stutgard' that contains most of the revisions. At the same time he published 'Die Wanderung', which was also worked over, in a form which includes lines obviously Hölderlin's, although they do not appear in any of his manuscripts.[62] It is very likely Hölderlin did prepare fair copies with his late revisions, unless we are to assume that Seckendorf saw Hölderlin's working-papers and copied them down. If Hölderlin did write such versions out fair, he was attempting something very radical indeed, but he was also losing his judgement. Seeing that he was going mad, and that very little he had published had met with any understanding, this is not particularly surprising. However the Seckendorf printings may have come about, of all the elegies reworked, 'Stutgard' is the least affected, though the integrated version still makes very odd reading, especially in lines 65–6.[63] The reconstructed text of 'Brod und Wein' is not truly readable at all. I believe that Hölderlin set about rewriting his elegies in a way that has

---

[61] Bernhard Böschenstein, '"Brod und Wein": Von der 'klassischen' Reinschrift zur späten Überarbeitung', in: Valérie Lawitschka (ed.), *Turm-Vorträge 1989/90/91: Hölderlin: Christentum und Antike* (Tübingen, 1991), 173–200 (173).

[62] For example 'An strengstem Tage, staunendes Geistes' (l. 35: ii/714). Seckendorf also published the first strophe of 'Brod und Wein' (under the title 'Die Nacht') including the only change made to that strophe in the *Homburger Folioheft*.

[63] Quoted above, pp. 181–2.

its logic, but that if indeed he was working towards a whole revision, new completed poems at all, he never got there, certainly not in 'Brod und Wein'. Perhaps the process got interrupted, or perhaps by its very nature it proved impossible to terminate: the poems were opened too wide, or the additions were too foreign. In spite of this, fair copies may well have been made, as happened with 'Patmos'.

As we do not have these fair copies, we are obliged to read the manuscript material we do have. And the only way of really doing this justice is neither to conjecture a 'final' text, nor to study the revisions in isolation, but to read them and the verses they 'correct' together, as in dialogue.[64] The almost flawless transcription of the three elegies at the head of the *Folioheft* underlines the status they have in Hölderlin's work: of peculiarly finished, reposed works of art. As such they are at odds with most of the *Folioheft*'s contents, which are written in a later style, in free verse (with, for whatever reason, very few finished poems). Hölderlin seems to have written them out for the express purpose of revising them,[65] so that the aesthetic poise they represent could be questioned. The revision of the elegies at the beginning of the *Homburger Folioheft* thus marks the transition from the classical style to the new. The dissatisfaction with the old mode and its incompatibility with the direction Hölderlin's writing had taken comes to expression on the page: the even, flowing hand in which the elegies are copied out fair is disrupted by the thicker nib and darker ink in which the later corrections are written in.

These corrections work against the original poems even as they stem from them. They are like marginalia, except that they adopt the form of the text they comment on, at once criticizing, contradicting and participating. The alterations to 'Brod und Wein' reveal an anxiety about and dissatisfaction with not just the form of the original but the whole project it represents. One aspect of the process of rewriting, the unsettling of an established form, comes to a climax in 'Brod und Wein' in the absolute contrast between the homogeneous form of the original and the fragmentary, singular language of the revisions. The result is an unsettling of the poem, a reattainment of the transitional phase of composition, in which the possibilities of the poem are reopened. But the process remains in abeyance, and signs of

[64] For the elegies this is made possible by the transcripts in *FA*, vol. vi, and esp. by *FA*, Supplement III (facsimile and transcription of the *Homburger Folioheft*).
[65] Cf. *FA*, vi/203.

what prevented Hölderlin completing it are to be found among the revisions themselves. Written over the top of line 112 of 'Brod und Wein' are the words

> Sich
>   In sein
> Eine Kunst, Grab sinnt, doch, klug mit den Geistern, der Geist
> (FA, vi/230)

> [For himself
>   In his
> An art, grave plans, but, wisely with the ghosts, the Spirit]

which both Beissner and Sattler edit as 'Sich ein Grab sinnt, doch klug mit den Geistern, der Geist' [A grave the Spirit plans, wisely though with the ghosts, for himself] (FA, vi/255). The alignment of 'Kunst' and 'Grab' expresses drastically Hölderlin's doubts about the poem's ability to provide a vessel for the Spirit or the ability of humans to bear divine presence at all. Lines 111–14 of the original consider the dynamics of encounter between humans and gods in words which also refer to the role of the poem in bringing it on:

> Endlos wirken sie da und scheinens wenig zu achten,
>   Ob wir leben, so sehr schonen die Himmlischen uns.
> Denn nicht immer vermag ein schwaches Gefäß sie zu fassen,
>   Nur zu Zeiten erträgt göttliche Fülle der Mensch.[66]

> [Endlessly working there they seem to care very little
>   If we live, spared as we are by the gods in the sky.
> For a fragile vessel cannot always contain them,
>   Only at times can man bear the fullness of gods.]

A consoling explanation of absence which the later annotations cut right through with the question of whether 'die Himmlischen' can come into a human domain at all. The fear is that the fixed form of a poem ('Kunst') will no sooner embody the Spirit than it will stifle it ('Grab'). The only good form is a transient one, which avoids fixity, which undermines itself; and that is what the corrections do to 'Brod und Wein', undo it. The process is an extreme continuation of the search for 'das Lebendige in der Poësie' (vi/289), a consequential pursuit of the insight that 'das Reine kan sich nur darstellen im Unreinen' (vi/289), the attempt to make the poetry true. The search

---

[66]   Cf. 'Gefäße machet ein Künstler' (ii/221).

for an adequate form very radically deconstructs[67] the form that had been found, as too perfect and perhaps too sovereign, too monolithic. Some of the late variants introduce elements which might counter the definitiveness of classical form: over 'Göttern zu Lust der Gesang' [song for the pleasure of gods], 'schreitend in Winkeln Gesang' [song that steps in angles] (l. 60: *FA*, vi/226), which seems to refer to the verse-form the words appear in, and so lends the poem an awareness of its own workings that helps make it an overt fiction, and thus more truthful.[68] Similarly the ironic ambiguity of 'Schaal(e) ist Delphi' [Delphi a shell] (over l. 62: *FA*, vi/226).[69]

From these examples it can be seen that the language of the 'Brod und Wein' revisions is more and more peculiar and daring, loosening itself from the context it occurs in and taking on a self-sufficiency which does damage to its surroundings, a seemingly quite deliberate violence. Many words from this layer of work are nonce words in Hölderlin's vocabulary. It is as if the proximity to translation, which quite naturally furnishes new words and ways of saying, allows Hölderlin to extend his lexis extravagantly; and outside the translations themselves, no point in his writing, not even the late fragments, is in this respect so rich. But the abundance is a superabundance, the new elements do not just remain alien but shatter the coherence achieved, partly by vocabulary, in the original versions. The effect is not only similar, but related to the expansion Hölderlin's poetic world was undergoing at this time. To a fairly limited and well-defined arrangement of Greek and Hesperian (mostly German) places were added Lisbon and London, Tinian and the Tyrol. The old coherent world disintegrated under this sudden accretion, the desire to encompass everything made it fall apart.[70] 'Bäurisch' [boorish] (*FA*,

---

[67]   In the end it seemed impossible to avoid this word. There are correspondences between Hölderlin's practice here and the ideas of deconstruction. This is what interests Alice A. Kuzniar, *Delayed Endings: Nonclosure in Novalis and Hölderlin* (Athens, Georgia, 1987).

[68]   Schmidt explains 'in Winkeln' as a literal translation of *versus* (Jochen Schmidt, *Hölderlins Elegie 'Brod und Wein': Die Entwicklung des hymnischen Stils in der elegischen Dichtung* (Berlin, 1968), 181. And cf. Friedrich Schlegel: 'Was sich nicht selbst annihilirt ist nichts wert' (quoted by Grunert, 117).

[69]   Werner Almhofer detects 'eine Spur von Ironie' in the readings of ll. 87–92: '"Wildniß" und Vergnügen: Hölderlins mythologische Bildersprache in den späten Korrekturen von "Brod und Wein"', *HJb* 26 (1988–9), 162–74 (165).

[70]   See David Constantine, *The Significance of Locality in the Poetry of Friedrich*

vi/226), 'das Verzehrende' [what consumes] (*FA*, vi/226), 'zeitig'
[early] (*FA*, vi/229), 'beinern' [bony] (*FA*, vi/306), 'Handlungen'
[doings] (*FA*, vi/229), 'blutlos' [bloodless] (*FA*, vi/306) and many
others do the same.

The violence these words inflict on the *Reinschrift* seems to derive
from a new violence in the themes of the revisions. Coupled with an
anxiety about the status of art is an even greater fear that epiphany
would be unbearable, destructive, or simply annihilating.[71] This new
pessimism, which brands the reworkings, is an intrinsic criticism of
Hölderlin's poetics and of the hopes voiced in 'Brod und Wein'. The
corrections read like an angry, demonstrative reflection on the dangers
of what the project of the poem implies. Over

> Tausendfach, es ertrug keiner das Leben allein;
> Ausgetheilet erfreut solch Gut und getauschet, mit Fremden,
> Wirds ein Jubel, es wächst schlafend des Wortes Gewalt

> [Thousandfold, no one had to bear life alone;
> Distributed such things delight and exchanged, with strangers,
> Become pure jubilation, the word's power grows in its sleep]

is written

> Tausendfach kommet der Gott. Unt liegt wie Rosen, der Grund
> Himmlischen ungeschikt, vergänglich, aber wie Flammen
> Wirket von oben, und prüft Leben, verzehrend, uns aus.
>
> (ll. 66–8: *FA*, vi/226)

> [Thousandfold comes the god. Under lies like roses, the ground
> Awkward for gods, not lasting long, but like flames
> Works down from above consuming life, and tests us out.]

And over

> Zwar leben die Götter
> Aber über dem Haupt droben in anderer Welt.

> [The gods do live
> But over our heads, above in another world.]

Hölderlin (London, 1979), esp. ch. 3 ('The Coherent World, 1800–02') and ch. 6 ('The
Disintegrating World, 1802–06').

[71] Cf. a note of Coleridge's, as an instance of the proverb 'Extremes Meet':
'Nothing and intensest absolute being'—*Select Poetry and Prose*, ed. Stephen Potter
(London, 1971), 165.

Auch Geistiges leidet,
Himmlischer Gegenwart, zündet wie Feuer, zulezt.

(ll. 109–10: *FA*, vi/229)

[There is spiritual suffering,
The presence of gods, ignites like fire, in the end.]

The revision is a private act of self-criticism in which the poem turns in on itself and dissolves. A phrase written over lines 135–6 catches the destructive process which the manuscript contains: 'daß sich krümmt der Verstand/Vor Erkenntniß' [so that reason crumples/With insight] (*FA*, vi/230).

Most of the additions to 'Brod und Wein', while clearly relating to the base text, depart from the translational process of revision whereby individual words are forced into a new idiom. They have a more dynamic, conflictual relationship with the words they appear over, and sometimes they set off on a new track altogether, only to revert to the original, so that one is led to wonder whether for Hölderlin there were not a continuous connexion after all. The process is potentially endless, translations can be made of translations, so that the language gets pushed further and further out. It goes against any concept of completion, makes finishing, form, impossible. 'Das Ungebundne reizet' [Dissolution attracts] (ii/51), but in these late revisions it is all but given way to, in spite of attempts (in 'Brod und Wein') to appeal to the stay of 'Gränze' [limits] and 'Geseze der Erde' [laws of the earth] (*FA*, vi/226). There are no corresponding poetic limits, other than a residual hexameter and pentameter. It is certain that underlying the revisions is a desire to do away with such limits in the hope of opening the poem up to possibility, to put it in flux, to cultivate a 'Zustand zwischen Seyn und Nichtseyn' [condition between being and not-being] (iv/283) in which the unexpected might happen. Perhaps at this point Hölderlin even put a similar hope into a moving, indefinite state as he could into the turmoil of history (in the letter to Ebel of 10 January 1797 (vi/228–30), for example, or in 'Das Werden im Vergehen'), and saw his manuscript as imitating the process of history in an attempt to get near to it and be part of it, adopting its structures. The undoing of the perfected structures of the elegies was certainly due to their perceived inadequacy *vis-à-vis* the complex contradictoriness of the present, the expression of a desire to make them bear on the times like the shifting of *Antigone*, through translation, into a modern, Hesperian drama. But there the restructuring was completed, *Antigonä* was not only finished, but seen through the press and thus, potentially at least, delivered into society. Alignment with the transitional phase of history in the *form* inevitably means that the poem is virtually formless itself: the corrections to 'Brod und Wein' are only readable as a series of (interconnected) fragments, of metrical glosses. In that form the poem's ability, as a composed whole, to counter the prevailing confusion of things and transcend and point a way through it is neglected. Hölderlin's best poems, to which the three elegies in the *Homburger Folioheft* all belong, both partake in their time (ours) and work outside it, by allowing glimpses beyond to 'das Offene' [the open] (ii/91). That is how they function in the reading, filling our present but opening a hope towards the future. Perhaps Hölderlin's fragments can do something similar, but only because we can read them against the completeness represented by his finished poems and so as negatively summoning the whole they have failed to attain.

Hölderlin's rewritings of completed poems should be seen as formal experiments, inquiring after new possibilities by unsettling the ones realized, but not eradicating the old forms. The elegies still stand, the revisions have in the end taken nothing away from but only increased them, partly through the new material found, but also by the very fact of having challenged their workings. The process was a sort of wager in search of a point 'wo die ganze Gestalt der Dinge sich ändert, und die Natur und Nothwendigkeit, die immer bleibt, zu einer andern Gestalt sich neiget, sie gehe in Wildniß über oder in neue Gestalt' [when the whole shape of things changes, and nature and necessity, which are constant, incline towards another shape, whether they go over into wilderness or into new form] ('Anmerkungen zur Antigonä', v/271).

CHAPTER 6

The Meanings of Translation

Nicht ohne Schwingen mag
Zum Nächsten einer greifen
Geradezu
Und kommen auf die andere Seite.

('Der Ister', ll. 11–14)

Translation for Hölderlin meant translation from the Greek. This is obvious—after the summer of 1799 he did nothing further from the only other language he translated, Latin. But this focus on Greek is where the deepest meaning of the translations and the closest links between them and the poetry reside. More immediately than the poems, the translations bring together, into one form, the two poles of Hölderlin's poetic world. In a sense they short-circuit the preoccupations of his whole work, effecting the advent of the Greek into the German sphere.

This is the subject of a short poem from the *Homburger Folioheft*:

Wie Meeresküsten, wenn zu baun
Anfangen die Himmlischen und herein
Schifft unaufhaltsam, eine Pracht, das Werk
Der Woogen, eins ums andere, und die Erde
Sich rüstet aus, darauf vom Freudigsten eines
Mit guter Stimmung, zu recht es legend also schlägt es
Dem Gesang, mit dem Weingott, vielverheißend dem bedeutenden
Und der Lieblingin
Des Griechenlandes
Der meergeborenen, schiklich blikenden
Das gewaltige Gut ans Ufer.   (ii/205)

[As on seacoasts, when the gods
Of heaven begin to build and in

Ships unstoppably a splendour, worked
By the waves, one upon the other, and the earth
Increases, and one of the joyful ones,
With perfect pitch, putting it in order, so
On the poem, with the wine-god promising much and gesturing
And the darling
Of Greece, the one
Sea-born with her coy looks
An abundance crashes ashore.]

The bones of the poem are the complex simile (for want of a better word): 'Wie Meeresküsten [...] also schlägt es/Dem Gesang [...] Das gewaltige Gut ans Ufer'. The poem is remarkable for the unity of its gesture and its subject-matter: the simile and the difficult syntax only resolve themselves in the last line, at exactly the same moment as 'das gewaltige Gut' is washed ashore. As the simile comes together, the poem works, and the poem it describes, the 'Gesang', also accomplishes itself. They thus become inseparable, the 'Gesang' spoken of is the poem we read—a threshold onto the present over which the Greek world is conveyed. The epiphany of the poem is portrayed as an epiphany of the gods Dionysus and Aphrodite, as the arrival of Greek spirit and Greek form. This 'gewaltige Gut' comes into Hölderlin's German, is Hölderlin's German—the poem represents the ideal of the translations. But it speaks of a happening which occurs only in 'erfüllten Zeiten' [fulfilled times],[1] or which initiates them ('wenn zu baun/Anfangen die Himmlischen'), when the (poetic) epiphany is a true epiphany of the divine; however convincing the gesture and rhythm of the poem, such an event is not of the present. That is the achievement of the poem, to make apparently present what is absent, so that its success can seem to exceed the failure it really is if measured by the criteria it contains. In the unfulfilment of the present the nearest equivalent to a poem that would be accompanied by the gods is translation from the Greek. Against the Greek background there are two possible modes: translation of the forms in which previously the gods were manifest, and poetry such as 'Wie Meereküsten...' which attempts to bridge the gap by making fulfilment felt through its absence. 'Wie Meeresküsten...' is so powerful because of the rhythm of the sea that moves through it; the difficult syntax so stretches the simile that the

[1] Beissner (ii/838).

rhythm takes over and holds the poem together until the last line combines them all, syntax, simile, rhythm and sense in its final surge. To have written it, Hölderlin must have seen and heard the sea. He wrote many poems in which the sea is important, above all 'Der Archipelagus', but he only saw it late on, when he went to Bordeaux in 1801/2. The poem records his experience of the Atlantic there, but transposed into a Greek setting.

The journey to Bordeaux and the time Hölderlin spent there represent his only real encounter with the foreign. It was the nearest he got to a Grand Tour to Italy or Greece itself. The new landscapes and even the French language go into his poems, as foreign, and he thought the southern climate and people a clue to what he otherwise encountered only through his reading and the few statues he saw in Kassel—Greece and the nature of the Greeks.[2] In experiencing southern France and the French, Hölderlin felt closer to the Greeks; the foreign was identified with the Greek and translated into Greek terms. The letter Hölderlin wrote to Böhlendorff on returning from Bordeaux is quite open about this. Certain of the French he saw, especially the shepherds, had preserved a trace of what the Greeks were like:

Das Athletische der südlichen Menschen, in den Ruinen des antiquen Geistes, machte mich mit dem eigentlichen Wesen der Griechen bekannter; ich lernte ihre Natur und ihre Weisheit kennen, ihren Körper, die Art, wie sie in ihrem Klima wuchsen, und die Regel, womit sie den übermüthigen Genius vor des Elements Gewalt behüteten. (vi/432)

[The athleticism of people in the south, in the ruins of the ancient spirit, made me better acquainted with the true character of the Greeks; I got to know their nature and their wisdom, their bodies, the way they grew up in their climate, and the rules they followed to protect their exuberance from the violence of the element.]

This impression of encountering Greekness in France was compounded by the fact that on his way home to Nürtingen Hölderlin probably saw the classical statues Napoleon had stolen out of Italy and brought back to Paris:

---

[2] For French in Hölderlin's poems, see ii/878, 879 ('Kolomb'), 336, 340. Hölderlin briefly mentions what he saw in Kassel to his brother (letter of 6 Aug. 1796): 'einige Statuen im Museum machten mir wahrhaft glükliche Tage' (vi/216); see Beck's note as to what these might have been (vi/807).

Der Anblik der Antiquen hat mir einen Eindruk gegeben, der mir nicht
allein die Griechen verständlicher macht, sondern überhaupt das Höchste
der Kunst. (vi/432)

[Seeing the antiquities left me with an impression that has helped me
understand not only the Greeks themselves but all that is highest in art.]

Hölderlin's natural tendency to associate his experience of foreignness
with Greece was thus encouraged by actual geographical coincidence:
all we hear of Paris is that he saw 'Antiquen' there. Hölderlin went to
France for practical purposes, because the next tutoring job presented
itself in Bordeaux, but his return via Paris coincided with its
becoming a Mecca for artists, scholars and scientists from all over
Europe, particularly Germany. For a while, Paris displaced Rome as a
cultural focus as more and more of Western art ended up there and
attracted enthusiasts accordingly.[3] Hölderlin was witness to a crucial
shift, which Goethe identified at the time: the dislocation of works of
art from their (classical) ground, their 'Ort und Stelle', with which
they had always been perceived as continuous.[4] This shift was
inseparable from the political developments of the time, and part of
the rapid acceleration into modernity that was taking place.
Hölderlin's encounter with the 'Antiquen in Paris' (vi/437) was
essentially modern, and brushed a central experience of the Romantic
generation.

So the longest journey he ever undertook, though it led away from
Greece itself, brought him face to face with real Greek artefacts, actual
objects transported out of the past. It was a very figurative journey, in
which Hölderlin's life and work seem to mirror one another. 'Wie
man Helden nachspricht', he wrote to Böhlendorff on his return,
'kann ich wohl sagen, daß mich Apollo geschlagen' [As one says of
heroes I can probably say too: that Apollo has struck me] (vi/432). He
described the course of one of his poems: out from a starting-point,
home, the present, to a different time and place, where an encounter
is made which alters the perspective on the premises of the poem as
they are returned to. In miniature, 'Wie Meeresküsten...' performs a
similar outgoing and return. Its last word, 'Ufer', looks back
disconcertingly to the poem's beginning ('Wie Meeresküsten...') and

---

[3] See Ingrid Oesterle, 'Paris—das moderne Rom?', in: Conrad Wiedemann (ed.),
*Rom—Paris—London: Erfahrung und Selbsterfahrung deutscher Schriftsteller und Künstler in
den fremden Metropolen* (Stuttgart, 1988), 375–419.
[4] Goethe, 'Einleitung in die Propyläen', in: *Werke*, xii 38–55 (55).

so refuses to let the simile fall into two halves: the fulcrum, the 'Gesang', *is* the 'Ufer', is the poem itself.

Journeys

The pattern of 'Ausflug' and 'Rükkehr' (iii/38), of 'Progreß u Regreß' (ii/722) was one that shaped Hölderlin's life. The journey to Bordeaux was his fourth major 'Wanderschaft' (vi/406) away from home and back again. Home was Württemberg, his mother's house in Nürtingen and the Swabian dialect, and anything beyond its 'verehrte sichre Grenzen' [safe, revered frontiers] (ii/19) was technically foreign, abroad. It was the very strong sense of home that lent other places their foreignness. To be outside Swabia was to be 'unter Fremden' [among foreigners] (vi/312), and the periods he spent away, in Waltershausen, Jena, Frankfurt, Homburg, Hauptwil and Bordeaux, were experienced as self-imposed exile, to escape the claims of the *Konsistorium*. But though there was this practical reason for keeping outside, Hölderlin invested the pattern of his life with a larger significance so that the time away from home became a 'necessary period of trial and journeying abroad'.[5] From Frankfurt he wrote to his mother not to worry about her son 'der eben in der Fremde lebt, und leben muß, bis seine eigne Natur und äußere Umstände ihm erlauben, [...] irgendwo mit Herz und Sinnen einheimisch zu werden' [who is living abroad, and must do until his own nature and contingent circumstances allow him to settle down somewhere in body and soul] (vi/260). He tended to conceive of his whole life as a journey, especially as a sea-voyage: 'Auf dem Bache zu schiffen, ist keine Kunst. Aber wenn unser Herz und unser Schiksaal in den Meersgrund hinab und an den Himmel hinauf uns wirft, das bildet den Steuermann' [To navigate a stream needs no skill. But when our hearts and fates cast us down to the bottom of the sea and fling us up into the sky, that forms the helmsman] (vi/237).[6] The aim was always a final return, enriched and strengthened by the experience abroad. In the poems and later letters the scope of this pattern is widened still further, and it becomes one of Hölderlin's central metaphors, perhaps the central one. The wandering abroad is a spell of necessary estrangement, like the period of night that must be traversed. 'Es kehret umsonst nicht/Unser Bogen, woher er kommt' [Not for

---

[5]   Constantine, *Locality*, 79. On the journey see his ch. 4 (69–86).
[6]   See also the beginning of this letter (vi/235) and vi/232, 263.

nothing does our arc/Return to where it came from] ('Lebenslauf', ll.
3–4) and the path the arc traces is not in vain either. Having made it
to Bordeaux Hölderlin wrote home that he was 'nun durch und durch
gehärtet und geweiht' [now initiated and hardened through and
through] (vi/430). The traveller in the poem 'Rükkehr in die
Heimath' returns as 'der Geläuterte' [purified] (l. 20).[7] The idea of an
inevitable time away from home, while founded, as Hölderlin said it
should be (iv/150), on his personal experience, extends to offer a
framework in which the absence of the gods can be understood and
even affirmed: they too are away, absent, but only through necessity,
and they will return once the ordeal has been gone through, indeed
they *must* return, because a life in foreign parts cannot be endured for
ever:

> nemlich zu Hauß ist der Geist
> Nicht im Anfang, nicht an der Quell. Ihn zehret die Heimath.
> Kolonien liebt, und tapfer Vergessen der Geist.
> Unsre Blumen erfreun und die Schätten unserer Wälder
> Den Verschmachteten. Fast wär der Beseeler verbrandt.
>
> (*FA*, vi/257)[8]

> [and not in the beginning
> Is the Spirit at home, not at the source. His homeland eats him.
> Colonies he loves, and courageous oblivion, the Spirit.
> Our flowers delight and the shadows in our woods
> His parchedness. Almost the animator was burnt.]

The specific meaning of these lines from the revision of 'Brod und
Wein' is disputed, but whether they refer to a loop-like movement
out from Hesperia and back (Beissner) or to a single approaching
movement from east to west (Schmidt), the fundamental conception
of a transitional phase, a dearth, between a beginning and end of
fulfilment is common to both.[9] For Hölderlin, that transitional phase,
the present, demanded the kind of life he himself led, the restless
journeying, the resistance to home. Of marriage, which he equated
with a move back to Württemberg and taking a living there,
Hölderlin wrote to his mother: 'So wie ich jezt mich und *unsere Zeit*

---

[7] Cf. also 'Der Main', ll. 26–9.
[8] Cf. 'Friedensfeier', ll. 16–19.
[9] Cf. Beissner, 147–84 and Schmidt, *Hölderlins Elegie 'Brod und Wein'*, 200–8.
Beissner's interpretation rests entirely on the letter to Böhlendorff (vi/425–8) and is
less likely. Cf. also: Szondi, *Hölderlin-Studien*, 104–7.

kenne, halte ich es für Nothwendigkeit, auf solches Glük, wer weiß, wie lange Verzicht zu thun' [From what I know of myself and *our times* I hold it necessary to do without such happiness for who knows how long] (the underlining is Hölderlin's own, vi/362). In the poetry this unsettledness is characteristic of the age: the modern landscapes are crossed by the figure of the interval, the 'Wanderer' [traveller], and the heroes are navigators and explorers.[10] By contrast Greece enjoys a connectedness in which differences are already integrated. The sailors there are merchants, with established routes: 'Der Archipelagus' praises the 'fernhinsinnende Kaufmann' [merchant thinking into the distance]:

> die Götter
> Liebten so, wie den Dichter, auch ihn, dieweil er die guten
> Gaaben der Erd' ausglich und Fernes Nahem vereinte.
> (ll. 73–5)[11]
>
> [the gods also
> Loved, as much as the poet, him, because he was the one
> Equalized the earth's good gifts and joined up near and far.]

The narratives of Hölderlin's poems embark on journeys outwards to Greece to try and make connexions and bring it into relation with the present. In many poems, especially the hymns, this movement is announced:

> So gieb unschuldig Wasser,
> O Fittige gieb uns, treuesten Sinns
> Hinüberzugehn und wiederzukehren.
> ('Patmos', ll. 13–15)
>
> [Give us innocent water,
> Oh give us wings, to go across
> In all fidelity, and to return.]

The movement derives from Pindar. Hölderlin was knowledgeable of the structure of Pindar's poems and used individual odes as models for poems of his own.[12] He will have understood their rhythm much as Schelling did:

---

[10] Constantine, *Locality*, 79–80. Cf. ii/876.
[11] Cf. 'Andenken', ll. 41–3. There, the connecting is still to be done.
[12] In addition to his book, see Seifert's 'Die Rheinhymne und ihr pindarisches Modell', *HJb* 23 (1982–3), 79–133. This is yet another form of translation.

jede pindarische Ode [geht] von einem besonderen Gegenstand und einer besonderen Begebenheit aus, schweift aber von dieser ins Allgemeine ab, z.B. in den späteren mythologischen Kreis, und indem sie aus diesem wieder zum Besondern zurückkehrt, bringt sie eine Art der Identität beider, eine wirkliche Darstellung des Allgemeinen im Besondern hervor.[13]

[every Pindaric ode starts from a particular subject and a particular event, then deviates away from this into the general, into the later mythological sphere for example, and as it comes back from this to the particular again it produces a kind of identity of both, an actual representation of the general in the particular.]

It is the arc of a journey out and back, in which the initial point is given new meaning by being associated with another sphere.[14]

This is also the recurrent pattern of Hölderlin's Homburg poetics. In all genres, the progression of tones set out in the poetological tables reverts at the end to the original tone, so that the 'Kunstkarakter' (iv/266) is preserved.[15] The 'tragische Ode' (probably the Pindaric ode) in Hölderlin's description moves 'aus der Erfahrung und Erkentniß des Heterogenen' [from the experience and recognition of the heterogeneous] back into its 'Anfangston' [beginning tone] (iv/149). The passage outwards is the essential movement of a poem, it is what enables the development of the 'poëtisches Ich' [poetic I] (iv/253):

Alles kommt [...] darauf an, daß das Ich nicht blos mit seiner subjectiven Natur, von der es nicht abstrahiren kan ohne sich aufzuheben, in Wechselwirkung bleibe, sondern daß es sich *mit Freiheit* ein *Object wähle, von dem es, wenn es will, abstrahiren* kann, um von diesem durchaus *angemessen bestimmt zu werden* und es *zu bestimmen*. (iv/254)[16]

[Everything depends on the I not merely remaining in interaction with its subjective nature (which it cannot abstract from without losing itself), but

[13] Quoted in Peter Szondi, *Poetik und Geschichtsphilosophie II*, ed. Wolfgang Fietkau (Frankfurt a. M., 1974), 266.

[14] For obvious reasons this pattern is basic, and it has an intellectual history reaching back to the Neo-Platonists at least. See Werner Beierwaltes, *Proklos: Grundzüge seiner Metaphysik*, 2nd edn. (Frankfurt a. M., 1979), 158–64 ('Zur problemgeschichtlichen Herkunft der Trias μονή—πρόοδος—ἐπιστροφή'). Cf. also p. 96–8 above.

[15] The tables: iv/239–40. Cf. iv/243, ll. 30–3; iv/248, ll. 28–31.

[16] 'Das Ich' seems to include the writer of the poem and the subject in the poem. Cf. iv/263, ll. 3–5.

making the *free choice* of an *object* from which it can *abstract if it wishes to*, in order to be *determined* by this object in an absolutely *appropriate* way, and to *determine it.*]

The well-known thoughts in the first letter to Böhlendorff stem from such reflections (in this respect at least there is obvious continuation between Hölderlin's Homburg writings and his later poetic thinking).[17] There the paradoxical-sounding, but in fact fundamental notion of exposure to an other as a means to self-knowledge is developed for the relation between Germany and Greece: the movement of outgoing and return is distilled into a single movement in which encounter with 'das Fremde' [the foreign] is also encounter with 'das eigene' [what is one's own] (vi/426). We go to the Greeks to learn 'der *freie* Gebrauch des *Eigenen*' [the *free* use of what is *one's own*] (vi/426) and thus come to ourselves in the foreign. Hölderlin followed this itinerary in his Sophocles translations, where, translating Greek tragedy, he was able to write a modern form.

Translation was often seen as a journey, either abroad and home again, or as a visit from abroad, where the traveller, to a greater or lesser extent, adopts the customs and costumes of the host country. In the German tradition, an excursion followed by a return was the usual mode, the other being typically French. Herder conceived of translation thus,[18] and so did A. W. Schlegel:

So tun wir denn jetzt friedliche Streifzüge ins Ausland, besonders den Süden von Europa, und bringen von da poetische Beute mit zurück.[19]

[And so now we make peaceful expeditions abroad, especially to the south of Europe, and come back with poetic spoils.]

In both Herder and Schlegel there is a barely suppressed military metaphor; translators are not tourists but soldiers, as also in Hölderlin's comparison of translation with foreign service in his letter to Neuffer (vi/125). There the idea recurs of a period spent abroad from which return is always intended and finally imperative. The Pindar translation functioned in exactly that way, as a 'beugende Schule' [coercive schooling] (vi/425) in which Hölderlin's language underwent a transformation enabling the writing of poems peculiarly his own. The Sophocles versions are, as I said, more complex, and also

---

[17] On the letter see pp. 61–3 above.   [18] See p. 24 above.
[19] *Kritische Schriften*, iv 35.

more complete: they represent not so much a transition, as the Pindar does, but a combination of outward gesture towards the Greek and inward tapping of the resources Hölderlin had found in German, so that the act of translating is in no way to be separated from the act of writing.[20] But all the translations work to connect and relate the '*orbis der Alten*' and the 'hesperischer *orbis*' (ii/876), and are to be understood as intrinsic to the needs of their age, like the travellers and navigators that people Hölderlin's poems. They engage in a dialogue across time and space, make the journey out to the 'äußere Sphäre' (iv/256) of Greek, and this action draws the Greek into a new sphere of reference, just as the German is extended to encompass new ground. It is a potentially dangerous process, in which the language is exposed; contact with the vernacular can be lost, as Hölderlin warned Neuffer. The opening lines of 'Mnemosyne' seem to draw on the threat posed by translation and on the extreme experiences of the journey to France: 'Ein Zeichen sind wir, deutungslos/Schmerzlos sind wir und haben fast/Die Sprache in der Fremde verloren' [A sign is what we are, without meaning/Without pain and almost we have/Lost our language abroad] (ii/195). The 'fast' [almost] is crucial, and in keeping with the idea of a necessary return. Although the Sophocles translations can be understood as an end in themselves, Hölderlin still seems to have considered translation a phase, a schooling: 'Sonst will ich', he wrote dedicating the Sophocles to Princess Auguste of Homburg, 'wenn es die Zeit giebt, die Eltern unsrer Fürsten und ihre Size und die Engel des heiligen Vaterlands singen' [My further wish, if there is time, is to sing of the ancestors of our princes and their seats and the angels of our sacred country] (v/119–20).[21] The letters to Wilmans show that Hölderlin thought his translations of Sophocles returned the tragedies to their (neglected) roots.[22] On both sides then, encounter with the foreign was also a passage to the native.

---

[20] Rolf Zuberbühler, in *Hölderlins Erneuerung der Sprache aus ihren etymologischen Ursprüngen* (Berlin, 1969), shows how Hölderlin makes certain words in the Sophocles translations resonate with their Middle High German usage (20–1).

[21] Cf. the earlier pronouncements to Schiller, 2 June 1801 (vi/422, ll. 40–3) and in the second letter to Böhlendorff (vi/433, ll. 48–52).

[22] Cf. Wolfgang Binder, 'Hölderlin und Sophokles', in: *Friedrich Hölderlin*, 178–200 (184).

Gespräch

Relating, suggesting and thus facilitating points of contact, of exchange, are at the centre of Hölderlin's undertaking. Translation is one of the agents, among the most important because it deals directly with one of the phenomena which exact attention most urgently. It listens to the remaining traces of Greece and the ideal it had represented, which need to be kept in mind as much as the texture of the present, in which indications of the return of the ideal are to be discerned. 'Dichterberuf', a programmatic poem, lists in one breath three spurs which the poet must be equal to: 'des Orients/Propheten und den Griechensang und/Neulich die Donner' [the Orient's/Prophets and the songs of the Greeks and/The recent thunder] (ll. 34–6). The prophets (of the Bible), Greek literature, and the political events following the French Revolution ('neulich die Donner') are then the cardinal points which poetry must respond to and which must be brought into relation with each other. The business of the present is to overcome isolation and through connexion make things meaningful, putting them in their proper place, where their significance is apparent.[23] That is what Hölderlin's poems set out to do, 'organizing' by their rhythm and form and imagery into coherent wholes. Dialogue, interaction, constitutes the task, the mode, of the interim, as emerges in the beautiful lines from 'Friedensfeier':

> Viel hat von Morgen an,
> Seit ein Gespräch wir sind und hören voneinander,
> Erfahren der Mensch; bald sind wir aber Gesang.
>
> (ll. 91–3)
>
> [Many things from morning on,
> Since we have been a conversation and heard from one another,
> Humankind has learnt; soon though we'll become song.]

The present is a process of learning, of attentiveness, in preparation for the fuller state of 'Gesang'. But 'Gespräch' in Hölderlin's usage carries a peculiar weight: it is out of 'Gespräch' that 'Gesang' might come, or out of a situation won through the exact relation of living dialogue. 'Gespräch' is the preparation, but also the elements of the thing itself, which seek their proper constellation, in which: 'alles mehr Gesang und reine Stimme ist, als Accent des Bedürfnisses oder auf der anderen

---

[23] Cf. iv/235, ll. 4–6.

Seite Sprache' [everything is more song and pure voice than accent of need or on the other hand language] (from the *Pindar-Fragment* 'Vom Delphin', v/284). It allows a passage from 'Sprache' to 'Gesang'. In 'Menons Klagen um Diotima' the lovers feel 'den eigenen Gott/Unter trautem Gespräch' [their own god/In their intimate talk] (ll. 50–1). Like translation it is an exchange in which communion with an other enables return to oneself:

Schreibe doch nur mir bald. Ich brauche Deine reinen Töne. Die Psyche unter Freunden, das Entstehen des Gedankens im Gespräch und Brief ist Künstlern nöthig. Sonst haben wir keinen für uns selbst. (vi/433)

[Make sure you write to me soon. I need your pure tones. Psyche among friends, the formation of thoughts in conversations and letters, is vital for artists. Otherwise we have none for ourselves.]

'Gespräch' is a process then, in which the journey can be made out of the self and thus back, the communication which the passage into a new time of fulfilment depends on. Hölderlin wrote to his brother:

Die Augenblike dann, wo es uns endlich einmal gelingt, einander etwas Rechtes herausgesagt zu haben, die Augenblike, wo der Bruder dem Bruder, der Mann dem Mann, die menschliche Seele der menschlichen Seele als Zeuge eines Heiligen und Freudigen so gegenwärtig ist, die sind dann auch aller Hoffnung und alles Erfolges werth. (vi/420)[24]

[The moments when in our talks together we finally succeed in coming out with something proper and right, when as brother to brother, as man to man, as human soul to human soul we are present in living witness to all that is joyful and holy in the world, those moments are worth all our hopes and any measure of success.]

'Gespräch' equals a tiny, anticipatory realization in the present of what the future would be like, a glimpse. In this it corresponds to Hölderlin's poems, which are also to be understood as 'Gespräch' rather than 'Gesang' (there can be no simple division of translation and poetry into 'Gespräch' and 'Gesang'). The poems prepare for the new era and do not constitute it in the present; they endeavour to bring about a state of mind and body which holds a seed of what might come. In a letter to Seckendorf Hölderlin uses the word 'Gespräch' in a way instinct with superadded meaning, without an article (like 'Gesang' in 'Friedensfeier'): 'Ich wünschte Dich wirklich

---

[24] Cf. as well the 'Augenblike' Hölderlin described to Susette Gontard (vi/337, ll. 20–4 and 27–32).

einmal in Stutgard zu sehen und Gespräch mit Dir zu haben' [I should like to see you in person sometime in Stuttgart and have conversation with you] (vi/438).

Once (in a poem), the word appears in a sense more akin to what 'Gespräch' is usually seen as leading up to, at the end of 'Ganymed': 'himmlisch Gespräch ist sein nun' (ii/68). Violently issuing out of himself ('Irr gieng er nun', l. 23), Ganymede returns to the gods. 'Himmlisch Gespräch' is an encounter between the two spheres of human and divine.

Translation and tragedy

Tragedy, in Hölderlin's understanding, is the privileged place of such encounter. Within its dynamics the coming together of the two dissociated spheres, the human and the divine, should be re-effected. The 'immer widerstreitende Dialog' [ever-conflicting dialogue] (v/201), and the dialectical relations between this and the chorus, create the to-and-fro, the shifting possibilities, which permit this encounter. Tragedy is structured out of different levels of conflict—between the characters, and in the substance, the language, of the drama; but the central conflict, the *raison d'être* of tragedy, is the momentary one between the hero or heroine and the outer sphere of the gods. In that clash of opposites there is a momentary fusion, a joining which immediately becomes a dividing, like the intersection of two lines, or perhaps more accurately, the touching of two parabolic curves at their apices. There is an epiphany so violent and unmediated that it must at once be shunned, and the shunning is death, or, in Oedipus's case, blinding as anticipation and image of death. The god is present, Hölderlin says in the 'Anmerkungen zur Antigonä', 'in der Gestalt des Todes' [in the shape of death] (v/269). The experience of the absolute, the divine, is itself 'gränzenlos' [boundless] (v/201) and so unavoidably leads to destruction; the one sphere shows itself by breaking into the other and explodes its own means of manifestation. There has to be division for consciousness of fusion to be possible, but the consciousness that comes with division, with distance, is then necessarily of a unison which is over:

Die Darstellung des Tragischen beruht vorzüglich darauf, daß das Ungeheure, wie der Gott und Mensch sich paart, und gränzenlos die Naturmacht und des Menschen Innerstes im Zorn Eins wird, dadurch sich begreift, daß das gränzenlose Eineswerden durch gränzenloses Scheiden sich reiniget. ('Anmerkungen zum Oedipus', v/201)

[*The representation of the tragic relies above all on the enormity of god and man coupling and the force of nature and the innermost of man becoming One in boundless anger being grasped by the boundless process-of-becoming-One purging itself through boundless rifting.*]

The climax of tragedy is in the paradox of 'das gränzenlose Eineswerden', the paradox of trying to combine the radically different. From the time of *Empedokles*, Hölderlin understood tragedy thus, as a collision, a 'Kampf' [struggle] (iv/153), which is a means of revelation. The notes to the Sophocles translations continue that line of thought, and obviously it is in keeping with Hölderlin's thinking about poetry in general, much of which is developed in relation to tragedy.[25] But though the analysis of tragedy in the 'Anmerkungen' carries on from work such as 'Grund zum Empedokles' and 'Das Werden im Vergehen',[26] it also derives from having translated the tragedies *Oedipus the King* and *Antigone*. The description of the tragic process in the notes is one that seems knowledgeable of the actual practice of translation, and suggestive of the transactions between Greek and German.[27] The great intimacy with the plays, with their 'Rhythmus' [rhythm] (v/196) and their 'dialogische Form' [dialogic form] (v/269), which the 'Anmerkungen' betray and which sometimes make them esoteric, is due to the experience of having translated them, and the nature of the insights stems partly from the nature of the study, 'das innigere Studium der Griechen' [the most intense study of the Greeks] (vi/381), that translation is. Even the pronouncements in the letters to Wilmans regarding the translations, and the extremely theoretical remarks on the relations between Greek and Hesperian art in the first letter to Böhlendorff (4 December 1801), which belong with them, are to be seen as having grown out of the experience of translation.[28] These ideas were then applied retrospectively in the last stage of work on the tragedies. Translating Sophocles was a religious undertaking, a work of exegesis and prayer, aiming, like tragedy itself, at a manifestation, the reception into German of Greek sense and structure. The exact delicacy of the

[25] Cf. pp. 76–8 above.
[26] Cf. Meta Corssen, 'Die Tragödie als Begegnung zwischen Gott und Mensch: Hölderlins Sophokles Deutung', *HJb* (1948–9), 139–87 (142–3).
[27] Cf. Martin von Koppenfels, 'Der Moment der Übersetzung: Hölderlins *Antigonä* und die Tragik zwischen den Sprachen', *Zeitschrift für Germanistik*, Neue Folge 6/2 (1996), 349–67.
[28] Cf. Berman, *L'Epreuve de l'étranger*, 271–2.

encounter determined the form the work took at every point and overrode external considerations. Hölderlin's translational technique, especially the violence with which the two languages are made to meet, resembles the dynamics of the encounter between god and human which in Hölderlin's understanding is the core of tragedy.

The relationship is more than one purely of resemblance, but it is not easy to define. Berman suggests a correspondence when he quotes Hölderlin on tragedy to indicate the 'violence de la traduction [...], la délimitation mutuelle des langues et [...] leur métissage' [violence of translation, the mutual delimitation of the languages and their crossing].[29] The connexion has been heavily underlined by George Steiner:

> It emerges that Hölderlin's theory of translation is a 'tragic theory' exactly mirroring Hölderlin's model of tragedy and that the latter, in turn, is founded on the same dialectic of encounter, of self-destructively creative collision, which is central to Hölderlin's precepts and techniques of translation.[30]

The interwovenness, the mutual reflection, of the act of translation (and thus the dynamics of the finished version) and Hölderlin's understanding of the tragic action of the plays is grasped as it were instinctively by Steiner. His argument mimes the relationship rhetorically rather than examining it for its precise truthfulness. The imaginative pull of the idea, offering as it does an ideal of total coincidence such as Hölderlin's thinking on tragedy strives for but has to qualify, is so great that in Steiner's account it tends to draw attention away from the limits of the correspondence.

The limits are what give it its proper definition. Sophocles, like Pindar, represents for Hölderlin an embodiment of the Spirit which needs recovery into a modern tongue. The principal preoccupation of the translation is thus to make manifest, to find an expressive form. That is also the task and point of tragedy, to reveal for a moment the Spirit, to overcome 'die furchtbare Muße einer tragischen Zeit' [the terrible leisure of a tragic age] (v/270). The act of translation thus

---

[29] L'Epreuve de l'étranger, 272–3.
[30] Antigones, 75–6. See too 69, 105. Probably following Steiner, Böschenstein mentions a 'Verbindung von [...] Tragödienauffassung und übersetzerischem Verfahren' but simply means that Hölderlin translates according to his interpretation of the tragedy (Antigone): Bernhard Böschenstein, 'Göttliche Instanz und irdische Antwort in Hölderlins drei Übersetzungsmodellen: Pindar: Hymnen—Sophokles—Pindar: Fragmente', HJb 29 (1994–5), 47–63 (57).

shares in and repeats the tragic action, it acts out the drama of revelation. What is really compelling here is that it is tragedy that is being translated. An analogy between an understanding of the tragic and a practice of translation could be drawn wherever the necessary resemblance of structures between the two exists; it is the combination of the processes in one work which is telling, the significance of the business of translation is heightened simply by the nature of what is translated. Every successful moment in the translation stands in relation to the epiphanic intent of the plays as wholes. Just as the plays attempt to re-establish contact with the Spirit, to join what has come out of relation, the translation of them is an effort at retrieving the originality, the first effect of the Greek, to make them emerge in the newness of German. The dynamics of both operations resemble one another, but the different encounters (between divine and human, and between Greek and German) cannot simply be aligned. The hero makes the presence of the divine felt in death, or in the knowledge of it; the result of the tragic encounter is dissolution. As Hölderlin puts it in his note 'Die Bedeutung der Tragödien', heroes signify when they '= 0' (iv/274). But the same cannot be said of language, the medium of translation. If Hölderlin's translations work, it is precisely because they inhabit an area between disintegration and coherence in which the host language, German, however inflected, can survive.[31] A new language ensues, not 'Sprachverwirrung' [confusion of language] (ii/253) but an intelligible form able to convey the tragic action to us. It cannot quite be right to say that like the tragic character 'the translator's native tongue will perish in its wild motion towards a complete appropriation and 'ingestion' of the numinous source'.[32] In parts of the Sophocles translations the language comes perilously close to inarticulacy—for Hölderlin's contemporaries it was far gone—but it is almost always restrained by the precise gesture of the syntax and the frequent settling of the diction and rhythm into a tone very close to speech. Though the language is always exposed, it holds back sufficiently to relate the tragic encounter it takes part in, and so something is saved; revelation prevails over apocalypse even if the two are run very close together.[33]

---

[31] Perhaps the language of the translations could be compared to the blinded Oedipus.   [32] Steiner, *Antigones*, 83.

[33] Cf. Steiner, *Antigones*, 73; Constantine, *Hölderlin*, 295. And see Koppenfels (356): 'Das tragische Geschehen ist ein Bewußtseinsphänomen, und zwar ein

The movement of the translation is one outward *and* back, and the return is crucial if the true faculty of language is to be observed, which is to secure a 'Halt' [hold] (v/271) or as Hölderlin says in 'Im Walde', a prose poem in the *Stuttgarter Foliobuch*, to witness: 'Und darum ist [...] der Güter Gefährlichstes, die Sprache dem Menschen gegeben, [...] damit er zeuge, was er sei geerbet zu haben' [And for this reason is that most dangerous of goods, language, given to man, that he may witness what he is and what he has inherited] (ii/325).[34]

In the finished translations the drama of the encounter between German and Greek is discernible in a form which has preserved itself from dissolution. Here is a strophe from Sophocles' *Ajax*, of which Hölderlin translated three passages. The chorus imagines Ajax's mother hearing of his madness:

> Wohl wird gepfleget vom alternden Tage
> Schneeweiß aber an Jahren
> Die Mutter, wenn von seiner Krankheit sie
> Dem Wahnsinn etwas höret,
> Das klagende, klagende, nicht
> Trauergesang der armen Nachtigall
> Aussprechen wird die nun, sondern
> Scharftönendes Lied wird
> Die klagen, und von Händen
> Geschlagen werden auf die Brüste fallen
> Die Schläge und die Loken aus grauem Haare.
>   (v/279; *FA*, xvi/453)

> [Looked after by the ageing day
> Snow-white though in years
> She may well, his mother, when of his illness
> The madness she something hears,
> The wailing, the wailing, not the poor nightingale's
> Mourning cry
> She will pronounce then, but
> Shrill-sounding song she
> Will wail, and struck by
> Her hands on her breasts will come down
> The blows and curls from her grey hair.]

gefährliches, transgressives. Die Darstellung aber ist die Verleugnung dieses gefährlichen Gehaltes.'
[34] Thus the manuscript.

She is 'gepfleget vom alternden Tage', a delicate expression which goes to the root of ἔντροφος, a word more commonly understood and translated as 'acquainted with'. In Hölderlin's German it suggests a state of refined fragility, to be devastated by the news of Ajax's condition. This sense is underlined by 'schneeweiß', where the original λευκῷ simply means 'white': snow too is fragile and liable to disintegrate. The manuscript shows that Hölderlin worked at these two lines.[35] 'Gepfleget' begins a series of rhyming or half-rhyming words which is the burden of the strophe (a strophe isolated as such by Hölderlin against his own original, but in line with modern editions[36]): 'gepfleget [...] Tage [...] klagende, klagende [...] klagen [...] Geschlagen [...] Schläge'. These words bind the diffuse sentence that makes up the strophe into a unit whose agrammaticality becomes expressive of the dissolving effect of grief. The German follows the Greek very closely, whence the alogical syntax, but imposes its own structures. 'Das klagende, klagende' as a translation of αἴλινον αἴλινον mimics exactly the irruption of lament into the body of the sentence, but as Beissner indicates (v/515) it also reaches forward to 'Lied' three lines further down, a connexion not possible in the Greek. The German asserts itself over the Greek at other points, most notably at the end, where Hölderlin extends the reference of 'fallen' to include 'die Loken', something only intimated in the original: the word translated as 'Loken' is ἀμύγματα (literally, 'tearings') and it has a verbal force of its own. The actual tearing of the hair is passed over with an almost Kleistian detachment, which makes it more terrible. But despite these twists of Hölderlin's, the strophe seems transparently Greek, to derive from and open onto Greek, especially in its syntax.

There is a personal dimension to this understanding of translation, in which the encounter between languages is involved in the tragic conflict. It is in the Sophocles translations, particularly in *Antigonä* and the passages from *Ajax*, that Hölderlin lets drop, or confronts, the realities of his own mental state and connects it with a tragic fate. The Greek ἄτη meaning disaster or calamity is translated by Hölderlin into words meaning madness: 'Irrsaal' (e.g. *Antigonä*, l. 5), 'Wahnsinn' (e.g. *Antigonä*, l. 606), 'Irr" (*Oedipus*, l. 1305[37]) or 'Wahn' (e.g. *Antigonä*, l.

---

[35] See the variants (v/512). Both 'gepfleget' and 'schneeweiß' are alterations. Cf. 'schneehell' at *Antigonä*, l. 860: no Greek equivalent, but two lines before χιών (snow) is rendered as 'Winter'.

[36] The page-numbers Hölderlin affixed to his translations from *Ajax* prove which edition he used: the Juntina of 1555 (v/510).   [37] In *FA*, l. 1314.

1143). The *Ajax* translations seem specially selected for their focus on the hero's madness. Translation became a means of self-reflection, but also a means of battening onto a specific fixity, the comfort of a base text.[38] That Hölderlin was quite capable of seeing his life in tragic terms is evident from the two letters to Böhlendorff.[39] From a distance, the translation of Sophocles allows an investigation of this fantasy of identification, but also a resistance to its dangers, precisely because the Spirit is present only 'mittelbar/In heiligen Schriften' [indirectly/In holy scriptures] (ii/163) and not in threatening immediacy. A form is produced from the encounter which stands in relation to the source, but also in the present: a fresh manifestation is achieved, precariously resistant to collapse. Translation offered a shift into form, whereas the translation of original work (revision) led in the end towards dissolution. That last possibility is always present in the Sophocles versions too and seems intrinsic to the kind of translation Hölderlin practised. He was writing 'gegen die exzentrische Begeisterung' [towards eccentric enthusiasm] (vi/439), in a radically disruptive fashion and that outward impulse is sometimes only barely mastered. Some readers would probably hold that Hölderlin's control, or tact, was occasionally too slight,[40] that he failed to assert the claims of the vernacular sufficiently at all points. But for most of the translation, Benjamin's implicit argument in his translation essay that Hölderlin had so joined the languages that a hint of a 'pure language' could be heard, while not ratifiable, does seem to correspond to a sense we have, when reading the translations, of contact with something which moves in ways very close to the deepest movements of our psyches.[41] They keep seeming to come home to us new and fresh, but recognized at some level, like memories.

Relation

The Sophocles translations are a marvel of relation. The problem of how to relate, of what constitutes a relation between things,

---

[38]   Cf. Harrison, 280.

[39]   See vi/427 (Tantalus) and vi/432 (struck by Apollo). Long before, Hölderlin had translated with his own predicament in mind, doing part of a letter of Leander to Hero (from Ovid's *Heroides*) after the separation from Susette Gontard (see v/327–30).

[40]   Cf. Steiner, *Antigones*, 81.   [41]   Benjamin, iv 18.

particularly Germany and Greece as emblems of dearth and plenitude, is partly met in them. They make a connexion while showing the incompatibility of what is connected, the ineluctable differences which define the relation. The paradox of estranged proximity, which is how Hölderlin experienced the present, as a time in which fulfilment was imminent but unremittingly absent, is the situation 'Patmos' makes an image for in its opening strophe:

> Nah ist
> Und schwer zu fassen der Gott.
> Wo aber Gefahr ist, wächst
> Das Rettende auch.
> Im Finstern wohnen
> Die Adler und furchtlos gehn
> Die Söhne der Alpen über den Abgrund weg
> Auf leichtgebaueten Brüken.
> Drum, da gehäuft sind rings
> Die Gipfel der Zeit, und die Liebsten
> Nah wohnen, ermattend auf
> Getrenntesten Bergen,
> So gieb unschuldig Wasser,
> O Fittige gieb uns, treuesten Sinns
> Hinüberzugehn und wiederzukehren.
>
> (ll. 1–15)

> [Near is
> And hard to grasp the god.
> But where there is danger,
> A remedy also grows.
> In darkness live
> The eagles and not afraid
> The sons of the Alps go over the abyss
> On lightly-built bridges.
> Thus, since heaped round lie
> The peaks of time, and our dear ones
> Live near, becoming faint
> On separate mountains,
> Give us innocent water,
> Oh give us wings, to go across
> In all fidelity, and to return.]

The poem as a whole tries to counter this predicament by using the island of Patmos, on the edge of antiquity, as a node connecting to the Christian era, which, focusing on Christ himself, is recounted through to the present. Having mentioned the 'stillleuchtende Kraft' [gently shining power] that falls 'aus heiliger Schrift' [from holy scripture] (l. 194), the source of most of the poem's details, it closes quietly, offering a definition of its course:

> der Vater aber liebt,
> Der über allen waltet,
> Am meisten, daß gepfleget werde
> Der veste Buchstab, und bestehendes gut
> Gedeutet. Dem folgt deutscher Gesang.
>
> (ll. 222–6)

> [but the father
> Who governs over all
> More than anything loves the solid letter
> To be tended, and what is left
> Interpreted well. This German poetry does.]

Like 'Patmos', the translations respond to the dilemma of estrangement: in this light, poetry and translation are part of the same undertaking, which attends to 'der veste Buchstab', to 'bestehendes'. It is even possible that there is a specific reference to translation. *Deuten* in the Grimms' dictionary includes among its definitions: 'dem volk, den Deutschen verständlich machen, verdeutschen' [to render comprehensible to the people, the Germans, to do into German].[42] This sense is encouraged by being immediately followed by 'deutscher Gesang'. In that word then, the parity of poetry and translation for Hölderlin is held.

This parity also allows the process of translation to illuminate that of poetry, or one aspect of it. The Sophocles translations demonstrate how an exact attention to the letter of the original—'der veste Buchstab'—can result in a radical unsettling and transformation of the fixity it represents. The 'tending' of the letter is not necessarily gentle, and its 'solidity', though it is what has allowed it to endure, is also what threatens to leave it in petrifaction. Translation and interpretation (*deuten*), though they depend on something which appears fixed, are engaged in unfixing, even undermining, the apparent fixity, and precisely so as to permit tradition. Hölderlin's sometimes wilful readings of myths in his poems, his turning them to his own purposes, should be seen in this light: as an enlivenment. Later I shall look at this more closely, with regard to the *Pindar-Fragmente*.

---

[42] Quoted by Constantine, 'Translation and Exegesis', 395.

In its relation of Hölderlin's two centres of preoccupation, Germany and Greece, translation must have been particularly attractive. For how, in fact, are two spheres quite different in space and time to be brought together, even in the imagination? Translation seems to offer the possibility of relating them, by (in simplistic terms) mingling Greek sense and German language. The finished translation is a product of that relationship, a new form in which it is brought to bear, an actual nexus. Hölderlin's method of translation, its mixture of close cleaving and violent parting, aims at a point at which what I have called a just relation can be found. In the Sophocles it does this far more dynamically than in the Pindar, and in a much more sustained manner. The Pindar translation can be seen as a kind of graph responding to and charting the interaction between German and Greek: it is essentially passive, but this passivity itself does a violence to the original.[43] Having such experience behind it, the Sophocles is freer to adopt different modes at different points—a word-for-word approach where it works, but embracing other possibilities when they present themselves. It makes greater use of the differences between the languages as a means of expression, and through this dialectic constitutes a form. With amazing consistency, the Sophocles translations manage to navigate a course on which the two languages inform each other and the gap between them becomes expressive. Even at moments when the German really does assert itself—as, most famously, at *Antigonä*, ll. 987–8: 'Sie zählete dem Vater der Zeit/Die Stundenschläge, die goldnen'—it is still coloured Greek (the position of the adjective 'die goldnen'). In miniature, a productive relationship between antiquity and modernity has been found, 'reelle Wechselvereinigung' (iv/222) and not 'tyranny of Greece over Germany'[44] nor insouciant assimilation of convenient classical material.

It is a process in which a realization is brought about. Perhaps recourse to a phrase from the 'Verfahrungsweise' essay would help elucidate what is going on: 'das Reine, das dem Organ an sich widerstritt, [ist] in eben diesem Organ sich *selber gegenwärtig* und so erst *ein Lebendiges*' [the pure, which was in conflict with the organ in itself, is in precisely this organ *conscious of itself* and so only then *a living thing*] (iv/250). The Greek plays come alive in Hölderlin's translation,

[43] Cf. Ch. 4 above, esp. pp. 127–30.
[44] E. M. Butler, *The Tyranny of Greece over Germany* (Cambridge, 1935).

and as Greek has lost its spoken context the process of renewal is a necessary one: the Greek attains a new manifestation. 'Das Reine', a word Hölderlin sometimes uses for the Spirit, which he thought embodied in Sophocles' plays, reappears in the 'Organ' of the German language. The German is an entirely effective metaphor of the Greek. The success achieved in the translations of bringing German and Greek into just relation, where each assists the other into expression, provides an instance of what could be a larger reciprocity between the German and Greek spheres, which poetically is how Hölderlin imagined the recovery of a full life. The contact the translations make is an anticipation of the fulfilling of the whole poetic project, the 'Gespräch' that intimates 'Gesang' (iii/536).

A relation of the kind effected in the Sophocles translations was the ideal Hölderlin pursued in all his dealings. It is at the heart of his poetics, of his historical thinking, and of his understanding of the nature of revelation and thus of the moment in which a better life might begin. It is out of such a relation of words in a poem that what Hölderlin calls 'das Lebendige' arises. That is, the poem intermeshes with life, it works, and the words affect us with apparent presence, creating a sensation which for a moment we give credence to. It is then that an image of the fulfilled life, a feeling of it and its possibility, occurs, a foreshadowing of what Hölderlin also thinks of as being the function of a just relation: the coming into human affairs of the Spirit, something that can only happen safely when the social world is ready and actively involved. Revelation (those are the terms in which Hölderlin understands it—not 'positiv' but reciprocal[45]), divine immanence, is the form under which a new period of fulfilment, a life 'voll göttlichen Sinns' (ii/111), would commence, when the transition into a new age would have been made: 'Einheimisch aber ist der Gott dann/Angesichts da, und die Erd' ist anders' [But native the god is then, local,/There in our faces, and the earth is changed] (ii/57). Translation is so important because these two related concerns coincide there: the precise constellation of words which brings the Greek across, which manifests it, is also the realization of an obvious equivalent of the Spirit.

Words like manifestation and epiphany, used of poetry, are particularly apt in Hölderlin's case because moments when 'der Gesang [...] glükt' (ii/119) are almost always depictions of divine

---

[45] Cf. the letter to Sinclair of 24 Dec. 1798, quoted in Ch. 5, p. 157 above.

presence in the world, of a world beautiful because of its religious significance. There is thus a curious complementarity between the poetic means and what they evoke: the poem's 'epiphany' describes an epiphany and each lends force to the other. According to Hölderlin's theoretical poetics taken seriously, there would be no distinction; the moment of a poem's success would reveal the Spirit. It would incarnate it as Christ did God and so usher it into the world; the whole work of Hölderlin's poetry would have been accomplished. So, questions of poetic technique become all-important: putting the right word in the right place could change the world.

But these extreme hopes are not allowed purchase in the poems themselves. Such an all-or-nothing poetics, if it was ever seriously entertained (more likely, the essays in which it was investigated were a form of wishful thinking, an experiment in speculative thought), would be easily disproved simply by the failure, on those criteria, of the poems. A sort of nostalgia for the grand view can nevertheless be felt to survive into the poetry. Especially as the counterpart to such a poetic belief, if it is pursued with the same completeness, must be radical doubt. What link is there between the processes of the poem and those of the Spirit? Or: How can poetry relate to reality at all?

Partly, these questions were answered in the last chapter, in my attempts to describe the effects of reading the poems 'Ermunterung' and 'Ganymed': in the act of reading the life of the reader and the rhythm of the poem can coalesce. Something more general, more objective too perhaps, can be said about how Hölderlin's poems relate. Or, as words cannot but relate on some level, about how the poems contrive a relation which can make them effective, or truthful.

If translation can satisfyingly relate, and thus create an analogue of the relation an ideal poem would achieve between its own processes and those outside it, the poem itself cannot live up to this analogue. Hölderlin seems to have allowed himself, on occasion, to think of the poem as a sort of incarnation, incarnation being perfect relation. Christ, Dionysus, and depictions of other gods showing on earth in human form, generate in the poems in which they appear a longing that the poem might be like them and embody the Spirit.[46] Similarly,

[46]   See 'Wie wenn am Feiertage...', ll. 34–5, or the first strophe of 'Der Einzige'. The *locus classicus* for poetry as incarnation in Hölderlin is probably his version of the opening of the *Bacchae* (and the derivation of 'Wie wenn am Feiertage...' out of it).

the poems, 'imperfect' as they are, desperately want the shape of reality to correspond to their fictions. But both these desired coincidences are only ever wishful thinking. They are analogies, and, by definition, analogy is a linking of things in some respects quite different from each other. The gap between reality and poem cannot be bridged directly, and it is possible that it can never really be bridged at all. The successful depiction or realization of a state of fulfilment in a poem is in itself no guarantee of its pertaining in the political world. It is against the horror of non-relation that Hölderlin's poems compose themselves. The fundamental discrepancy between the images the poems can body forth and the actual conditions in the world outside is the source of Hölderlin's poetry, it is what gives impetus to its continual generation of analogies. Analogy, or a form of saying which both relates and emphatically does not relate to the way things are, is one of the few modes open to him as a poet who is aiming at change. A kind of counter-reality, a 'dargestellte höhere Welt' [higher world of representation] (vi/329), is created within the economy of the poem; but just as in a translation the counter-world of the receiving language, if it is to be truthful, has to avoid total appropriation and allow something of the conflict of the two languages to be felt, the gap between them, so the images of the poem, since they correspond only to the utopian imagination, that is, to themselves, must put right this one-sidedness by admitting their fictiveness. It is then, by breaking through the fabric the poem has woven, that the real world can appear. The evocation of fulfilled life and then the retreat from it in the poem, exposing it as imaginary only, effects a true relation between the poem and the political reality it hopes to influence: the failings on both sides are made to play on each other and so allow passage between the two spheres. It is because of the imperfect nature of things as they are that the poem is forced to renounce its achievements, to show that it has exceeded itself; and the renunciation, by pointing out that the poem's images can be equated with nothing in the present, makes plain the inadequacy that pertains.[47] While admitting its inability to quite reach fulfilment the poem creates an experience of what fulfilment might be like if it were attained in history, the only place it ever could be attained but which

---

Again, it is important that this is a *translation*. In general see: Bernhard Böschenstein, 'Die *Bakchen* des Euripides in der Umgestaltung Hölderlins und Kleists', in: '*Frucht des Gewitters*', 72–90 (esp. 72–7).   [47] Cf. Adorno, 463.

is now unfit. The admission that poetry is not capable of bodying forth in the present enables a turning to history, it is a way of making space for reality to impinge in the poem, even if the present is not the overt subject, or even mentioned as such.

'Die Wanderung'

'Die Wanderung' works in this way. The journey it is structured by forms, as often, the narrative which allows the characteristic poetic dynamic to unfold. It begins boldly analogizing Swabia and Lombardy:

> Glükseelig Suevien, meine Mutter,
> Auch du, der glänzenderen, der Schwester
> Lombarda drüben gleich,
> Von hundert Bächen durchflossen!
>
> (ll. 1–4)

> [Blessed Suevia, my mother,
> Like your sister over there, Lombardy,
> Who shines more strongly, you too
> Flowed through with a hundred streams!]

Its attempts to relate the classical landscape with the modern one are reinforced by the texture of the language: the Latin form for Swabia, the anticipatory epithet 'der glänzenderen', 'Von hundert Bächen durchflossen'—a Homeric-sounding phrase—all seek to make connexions, to emphasize the similarities found in the landscapes lying on each side of the Alps. To uncover, or construct, such relations between Hesperia and Hellas (in this case Italy, further south and east, points to Greece) is an undertaking which fuels the poem's longing that the correspondences should be meaningful. It is part of the old desire that the poem might effect incarnation, since the Greek past is consistently seen as a time of fulfilment and the present as terribly wanting. Sometimes, particularly in later poems, this process can appear rather desperate and unconvincing, as in the blatant pseudo-etymologizing of Mount Ossa and the Knochenberg in 'An die Madonna' (ii/214): the desire that the two might relate so overrides the strength of the link that all that remains is a sense of wilfulness, and of the fact that there is *no* link.[48] But in 'Die Wanderung' the practice comes off, the desire and the connexion seem to complement

---

[48] That could conceivably be the point.

each other, and the poetic synthesis can work forward into the rest of the poem as its founding, hopeful, image.

From that small correspondence the poem then moves out 'dem Kaukasos zu' [for the Caucasus] (l. 25) in search of a larger one, encouraged by another analogy, between poets and swallows, and by a myth relating the emigration of 'die Eltern [...], das deutsche Geschlecht' [our ancestors, the German people] (l. 32) down the Danube to the Black Sea. The journey of the poem thus repeats an earlier one, in fact the two seem to merge as the recounting of the myth becomes the poem's own progress into the Greek world. But whereas the mythical ancestors made a one-way journey, a passage outwards which met with fulfilment and needed no return, the present journey keeps true to the comparison with the swallows, which come back in lines 83–5, as they punctually do in spring. The deepest sense of the identification lies in the almost mechanical return of swallows to the exact point they leave in autumn. Likewise the poet's visit is not to be an emigration but is paid only under the understanding that there will be a return. 'Doch nicht zu bleiben gedenk ich' [But I do not think to stay], the poet says (l. 91), and the swallows, and Swabia's towns, which 'alle meinen, es wäre/Sonst nirgend besser zu wohnen' [all say nowhere else/Would be better to live] (ll. 23–4), have already made that clear.

The middle of the poem (it is carefully divided into three distinct triads) is given over to the climax of the myth, a myth of encounter between the Germans and the 'Kinder der Sonn'' [children of the sun] (l. 36). The meeting leads to the exchange of weapons, commerce, and the mingling of language and blood from which the Greeks arise, 'schöner, denn Alles,/Was vor und nach/Von Menschen sich nannt'' [more beautiful/Than anything stemming/From humans before or since] (ll. 58–60). The poem tells it as something the poet heard in his youth, but in fact its only vehicle is the poem itself. The merging of the two stories I referred to is thus perhaps better called a way the poem finds of distancing itself from its culmination:

> Doch als sich ihre Gewande berührt,
> Und keiner vernehmen konnte
> Die eigene Rede des andern, wäre wohl
> Entstanden ein Zwist, wenn nicht aus Zweigen herunter
> Gekommen wäre die Kühlung,
> Die Lächeln über das Angesicht
> Der Streitenden öfters breitet, und eine Weile

Sahn still sie auf, dann reichten sie sich
Die Hände liebend einander.

(ll. 43–51)

[But when their clothing had touched,
And no one could begin to make out
The other's peculiar speech, there might well
Have arisen a fight, if down from the branches
There had not settled the coolness
Which often alters the faces
Of quarrellers into a smile, and a moment
They looked up in silence, then reached
Each other their hands in love.]

It is not an accident that this sequence—the confrontation of opposites ('die eigene Rede des andern'), near conflict ('wäre wohl/Entstanden ein Zwist'), and then the reconciliation and blending of the opposites—recalls the terms of Hölderlin's poetics. The encounter is after all a poetic one, and the joining of northern and southern realms out of which a new form of life proceeds is the hope of Hölderlin's poems. The myth thus relates the project of the poem, shows its possible realization, but leaves it suspended in the aura of the mythical past. This suspension is also brought about by the poem's main rhythm, the journey. Having been conveyed to the Black Sea by the myth, the poem admits the illusoriness of what it has evoked:

Wo aber wohnt ihr, liebe Verwandten,
Daß wir das Bündniß wiederbegehn
Und der theuern Ahnen gedenken?

(ll. 61–3)

[But where do you live, dear ones of mine,
That we might enter into the union
Again and cherish our ancestors' memory?]

A final attempt is then made to override this faltering in a hymnic summoning-up of Greece and its development from east to west. But in the first line of the last triad, 'O Land des Homer!' [O land of Homer!], the poem pivots from praise to implicit lament as it is made clear (by the tense) that the subject is back in the present, surrounded by hopeful linking signs (the cherry-tree, the peaches, the swallows) but essentially separate. The purpose of the excursion was to invite the 'Gratien Griechenlands' [Graces of Greece] (l. 99) westwards to

Hesperia, to prompt a journey in the other direction, but even the artifice of the poem cannot depict this. It seems an outlandish hope: 'wie kommt/Ihr, Charitinnen, zu Wilden?' [why do the Charities/Come to barbarians?] (ll. 108–9). That ultimate, intensely wished-for relation, must be deferred. The poem ends in waiting. 'Gegenwärtiges' [present things] (l. 87) forces it into a sort of retreat.

Poetic doubt

It is an awareness of poetry's insufficiency that, in large part, makes Hölderlin seem so modern. But the shortcoming is also a strength. In answer to his own question 'Ne faut-il pas condamner [...] la prétention de la poésie?' [Shouldn't we condemn the pretension of poetry?], the French poet Yves Bonnefoy said (in 1959):

Je crois qu'il faut plutôt reconnaître ses limites et, oubliant qu'elle a pu être une fin, la prendre seulement pour le moyen d'une approche, ce qui, dans nos perspectives tronquées, n'est vraiment pas loin d'être l'essentiel. Il y a une vertu possible du manque, c'est de connaître qu'il est un manque et d'accéder ainsi à un savoir passionnel.[49]

[I think we should rather recognize its limits and forgetting it was once an end in itself take it simply as the means of an approach, which in our present reduced perspective is not so very far from being the thing itself. There is a possible virtue in lack which is to accept that there is a lack and to accede thus to a passionate knowledge.]

This statement is very general, and perhaps tiresomely familiar now, but it is particularly relevant to the sense and project of Hölderlin's poetry. In Hölderlin too, it is when poetry is exposed, when it challenges itself, that it becomes most capable. Thus, it does manage to get some purchase on the world both as it is *and* as it might one day become. The 'savoir passionnel' in Hölderlin's poems is mostly longing, but even longing is a form of knowledge, it has an object, and by providing images to feed it the poems help make its satisfaction in the present more necessary. The 'manque' inherent in poetry, freely recognized by the workings of a Hölderlin poem, is intrinsic to its role in an age of transition, or a 'dürftige Zeit' (ii/94). The poem 'Menons Klagen um Diotima' imagines at its end a future age 'Wo die Gesänge wahr, und länger die Frühlinge schön sind,/Und von neuem ein Jahr

[49]   Yves Bonnefoy, 'L'Acte et le lieu de la poésie', in: *L'Improbable et autres essais* (Paris, 1983), 107–33 (126)

unserer Seele beginnt' [Where the poems are true, and the springs are nice for longer,/And once again a year of our souls will begin] (ll. 129–30). The implication that until then poems are essentially 'untrue' gets very close to identifying the mode of Hölderlin's poems. Deriving entirely from their place in the interim, they forge analogies to the way things are not. This 'untruth', by being shown to be such in the course of each poem, is a form of truthfulness towards the present (and a criticism of it). The 'untruth' is a vital imagining forward which allows a space of hope to be kept clear. The poems look forward to a time when the self-undermining would no longer be necessary for them to be true, when they could quite simply proclaim what was there (poems like Hölderlin's would in fact be obsolete).[50]

More and more, after the return from Bordeaux and increasing markedly after about 1803, a scepticism about the viability of this mode creeps in. Since the poems construct analogies to utopias, they cannot in any way be proven; there is only their own persuasiveness to argue for them. Even though they may still be 'le moyen d'une approche', allowing the building of utopias to act on developments in the present, there is the possibility that the analogies are false not just in the sense that they do not hold at the present moment, but absolutely. They relate quite simply to nothing, perhaps. This is to entertain the thought that the transitional nature of the present is not just a phase but a permanent state of affairs with no resolution, near or far. Next to the hubristic hope that the poem might embody the Spirit, and so in a sense complete history, that concession is devastating. Its effect can be discerned in the later poems.

They are less confident, more anxious and complex. Many of the poems from Hölderlin's period of greatest clarity and coherence contain moments of doubting and hesitation which contradict their main gestures. The last lines of 'Die Wanderung', in a programmatic sort of way, affirm an attitude towards epiphany which avoids any form of certainty or intention in favour of an unknowingness:

> Zum Traume wirds ihm, will es Einer
> Beschleichen und straft den, der
> Ihm gleichen will mit Gewalt;

[50] On the tension between proclaiming and undermining see David Constantine, 'Saying and Not-Saying in Hölderlin's Work', in: David Jackson (ed.), *Taboos in German Literature* (Oxford, 1996), 43–58 (esp. 47–51).

Oft überraschet es einen,
Der eben kaum es gedacht hat.

[It turns to a dream, if someone tries
To steal up on it and punishes
Whoever tries to reach it by force;
Often it surprises someone
When their mind is hardly on it.]

This attitude of undetermined readiness shrinks from the boldness of the journey and the imaginative constructions of the body of the poem. Instead of making analogies, attempting to preempt the moment, 'Die Wanderung' relaxes into poetic modesty and patience, contenting itself with little. It shifts into a mode which from being a counterweight, one element in a total economy ('Die Wanderung') to balance it towards the demands of the prosaic world, will become a disposition which marks whole poems in their language, syntax and rhythms.

This change can be characterized on the one hand as a turning away from the main project of the poetry thitherto, and on the other as a turning towards concrete details. The large scope of the elegies and completed hymns is renounced, along with the utopian analogizing which defines it. Poetry *as* project is no longer trusted, it seems; instead, synthesis appears to be resisted as too beguiling. The poems (or fragments, as they mostly are), such as 'Das Nächste Beste', 'Vom Abgrund nemlich...', or 'Wenn über dem Weinberg...', focus more on what is knowable, on what the senses can have, on what can be described without the help of analogy. The end of 'Die Wanderung' abandons the art of active relation, evades it even, and surrenders itself to a more casual or aleatory course, which is essentially one of receptiveness, of openness to eventuality. Instead of constructing a set pattern to which history might correspond, the later poems expose themselves, perhaps rather helplessly, to possibility and variety.[51] Like the reworkings of the elegies and of other poems, it implies a humbler (less demanding) idea of the nature of history. Doubt about the likelihood, or even about the possibility, of imminent change on the grand scale, the disappointment and uncertainty that encroached as time went on and hopes released by

---

[51]   Paul Celan's statement 'La poésie ne s'impose plus, elle s'expose' refers perhaps to a similar shift of mode: Paul Celan, *Gesammelte Werke*, ed. Beda Allemann, Stefan Reichert and Rolf Bücher, 5 vols. (Frankfurt a. M., 1983), iii 181.

the French Revolution began to sour, lead to a concentration on
things and the attempt to render them intensely in poetry:

> Reegen, wie Pfeilenregen
> Und Bäume stehen, schlummernd, doch
> Eintreffen Schritte der Sonne,
> Denn eben so, wie sie heißer
> Brennt über der Städte Dampf
> So gehet über des Reegens
> Behangene Mauren die Sonne
>
> Wie Epheu nemlich hänget
> Astlos der Reegen herunter.
>
> (ii/254)

> [rain, like a shower of arrows
> And trees stand slumbering, but
> The sun comes striding in,
> For exactly as it burns with
> Greater heat above the haze of the towns
> The sun goes up above the walls
> Of the hanging rain
>
> Like ivy you see the rain
> Hangs down without branches.]

Something similar to the fixing on a given text that translation
provided occurs here in the poetry; realizing phenomena in language,
making them manifest, becomes a kind of comfort, an alternative. It
is itself, on a much diminished scale, a hopeful activity, but it is one
which refuses to accept larger, extraneous significance, though it
seems to be crying out for it. All the hopes and projections of the
hymns and elegies contract into those highly charged details. Much of
what is familiar in Hölderlin disappears, or is displaced: the Greek-
German world begins to give way to one defined by Germany and
France, which has thus lost its cultural-historical aspect and import.
The writing, by its very nature, settling on particulars, tends towards
the fragmentary. Though the manuscripts indicate in some cases the
intention to compose large poems not unlike the finished hymns, it is
hard to see how the different bits could be related into coherence as
before. That capacity, or even propensity, seems to have gone.

The language of the late writings seems often to have a peculiar
quality, a kind of detached or disembodied feeling. In the rewritings,

Hölderlin looked to be using an idiom which derived from his practice as a translator, where the German words were often inflected by the Greek they rendered. This idiom seemed to be provoked by the translational technique used for the rewritings. Here, it occurs even without that framework: many of the fragments, in whole or in part, seem to read like translations, or as if they were subject to some foreign influence which cannot be identified.[52] This is true not only of their diction but of their syntax:

> Blumen fangen
> Vor Thoren der Stadt an, auf geebneten Wegen unbegünstiget
> Gleich Krystallen in der Wüste wachsend des Meers.
>
> (ii/254)

> [flowers start
> Before the gates of the town, not much favoured by levelled roads
> Like crystals in the desert growing of the sea.]

When it works, which is often, the oddness coincides with an intense poetic language, and perhaps the comparison with a language of translation is a way of describing it rather than a proper definition.

Still, it is possible to trace a sort of history of the place of translation in Hölderlin's work. At first, before the Pindar translation, it is a secondary and separate activity, little more than an exercise. Then with the Pindar Hölderlin seems to turn to translation more deliberately, as a main means of getting his writing to a new stage, and the undertaking has a larger significance deriving from the poetic theory. The Sophocles is no longer a means, it is primary, and writing and translation converge. This parity continues in a different form in the rewriting of the group of poems in the 'Nachtgesänge', where the techniques of translation are adopted. Later revisions (such as of 'Brod und Wein') then depart from this interlinear, the alterations sometimes bear no discernible relation to the words they make to replace, but they retain the language of translation none the less, apparently helped by the context of translational revision. Finally (at about the same time), this language becomes available without the context, without the explicit analogy of translation.

Not included in this history are Hölderlin's *Pindar-Fragmente*. They are such a curious work that it is difficult to fit them in anywhere, they are in the real sense of the term *sui generis*. But the language of

---

[52] Cf. Constantine, 'Translation and Exegesis', 395.

translation pertains especially to them, and many of the preoccupations and patterns of thought I have been concerned with, what could be called the dynamics of translation, are involved in their workings.

The *Pindar-Fragmente*

The second period of concentrated dealing with Pindar which the *Pindar-Fragmente* represent betrays a very different relationship to the source texts from that of the Pindar translation of 1800. This emerges first of all from the manner of translation.[53] Like the pieces from P1 (v/291–2: perhaps done as late as 1805), which can be compared with the earlier version of the whole poem, most of the translations of Pindar's fragments are composed and self-sufficient. There are different modes of translation in operation, with varying dependence on the Greek: the translation in 'Das Alter', for example, keeps to the Greek word-order after the fashion of the Pindar translation, and all the fragments orient themselves towards it. But more concession is made to German demands than before, above all in the longest, 'Die Asyle', in which twice the elements of a verb are separated by several lines ('haben [...] geführt' and 'Hat [...] geboren'). In spite of this the syntax is rarely quite German, and the translations preserve a foreign feel which also extends to the prose, even though this is not translation but of Hölderlin's own composition. All but two of the original fragments appear in prose in the edition Hölderlin used, the Stephaniana of 1560, but he puts them all into verse.[54] The two already in verse-lines, under the titles 'Von der Wahrheit' and 'Von der Ruhe', are rearranged by the translation. This in itself serves to demonstrate the greater freedom Hölderlin allows himself towards his originals compared with his practice in 1800. He is out to create entities, to render the Greek less 'fragmentary' than it was before, without appropriating it entirely. Each translated fragment is a single sentence (as also in the Greek, apart from in 'Das Höchste', whose

---

[53] Cf. Benn, 45–6. The *Pindar-Fragmente* are to be found at v/281–90; line-numbers given are those here.

[54] Hölderlin owned this edition (vii,3/388). It is a tiny pocket-book, and the pages are so narrow that the prose can look like verse. The lineation of the fragment in 'Vom Delphin' may have been influenced by Hölderlin's edition of Plutarch, who preserves this fragment: see Michael Franz and Michael Knaupp, 'Zum Delphin: Eine hermenautische Expedition', *LpH* 8 (1988), 27–38 (28).

original Greek is divided by a full stop), and the rhythm and composure of each sentence is such that even when the syntax gives difficulties, as in the fragments in 'Von der Ruhe' or 'Die Asyle', the reader is carried through to a satisfying, conclusive end. The translations thus assert their own form, and the verse moves with a steady, measured step, fitting the tone of the Pindar, which has been preserved, mostly, for its sententious quality.

The *Pindar-Fragmente* consist of nine scraps of Pindar handed down by other classical authors, and translated into German verses by Hölderlin. To each is added a continuation in prose which takes up the words of the translated fragment and meditates on them, spinning them out into a new context which often seems very distant from the original one. The prose adopts the postures and gestures of an academic commentary, which it nearly always belies by refusing to allow a distinction between the two parts: instead of moving out into discursive explanation, it weaves a greater whole in which all parts demand equal attention. This unity is clearest in 'Vom Delphin' but proper to all the texts. The prose is lyrical and rhythmical, and its syntax and diction have the same strangeness about them, the same 'foreign' or extra-German taste, as the verse. For example, in 'Das Alter':

Eines der schönsten Bilder des Lebens, wie schuldlose Sitte das lebendige Herz erhält, woraus die Hoffnung kommet; die der Einfalt dann auch eine Blüthe giebt, mit ihren mannigfaltigen Versuchen und den Sinn gewandt und so lang Leben machet, mit ihrer eilenden Weile.

[One of the most beautiful pictures of life, how innocent custom maintains the living heart, from which hope comes; which then gives simplicity a flowering too, with its manifold experiments and makes the mind agile and so long life, with its hastening slowness.]

The whole each text represents is recognized as such by a title, also of Hölderlin's invention, though sometimes inspired by the context given in his edition. Title, verse translation and original prose come together in each case to make up what amounts to a new genre.[55]

Of Hölderlin's writings they are among the most resistantly strange, but also—two or three of them especially—the most fascinatingly beautiful. They are very hard to define: verse and prose come

---

[55] Cf. Jeremy Adler, 'Philosophical Archaeology: Hölderlin's "Pindar Fragments"': A Translation with an Interpretation', *Comparative Criticism* 6 (1984), 23–46 (24): 'a new form of text, a hybrid work, part poetry and part exegesis'.

together, but the usual distinctions between them are reduced to a minimum (essentially, to the way they are set out on the page); translation and original composition combine, but both are of the same complexion. They escape the usual categories, and it is hard even to find a satisfactory name for them. Beissner calls them the *Pindar-Fragmente*, Sattler, in his edition, *Neun Pindar-Kommentare*. Neither name quite works, as they both draw attention to only one aspect of what have to be taken as wholes. Perhaps they should simply be called *Pindar Texts* in recognition of the difficulty of pinning them down, but also to indicate the weaving together of different modes and genres. In a very Hölderlinian manner, opposites meet and manifest themselves in a new form.[56]

As if in reference to this mixed genre, the centaurs are important. Half-human and half-horse they are like an emblem of the heterogeneous texts which, in the order established by Beissner and accepted by Sattler, they open and close: 'Untreue der Weisheit' and 'Das Belebende' have to do with centaurs, in particular Chiron.[57] In the poem 'Chiron', the centaur's hybrid form ('zweigestalt', l. 35) mirrors his position in the interim, awaiting and almost experiencing the transition from 'night' (l. 4) to 'light' (l. 2). Chiron's role of educator and poet, preparing for a better world, also belongs to the transitional age. Living, as 'Das Belebende' tells us, by streams and rivers, the centaurs are useful for transporting people from bank to bank, their horse-half allowing them to ford the waters. So their form, as well as symbolizing transition, lets them carry it out, and in this they are like translation and its place in Hölderlin's work. The texts they frame, the *Pindar-Fragmente*, incorporate the dynamics of translation and are in a form which comprises transitions and invites reflection on transition; some of their themes revolve round the problems that go with a transitional age, particularly the problem of how to anchor oneself, preserve one's identity, within it.[58] Like the 'Nachtgesänge', also nine in number and with which they are often paired,[59] they relate to the interval and are perhaps a genre devised specially for it.

[56]   Cf. Walther Killy, 'Welt in der Welt: Friedrich Hölderlin', in: *Wandlungen des lyrischen Bildes* (Göttingen, 1956), 30–51 (47).
[57]   Cf. Adler, 'Philosophical Archaeology', 32, 34; also Bernhard Böschenstein, 'Le Renversement du texte: Hölderlin interprète de Pindare', *Littérature* 99 (Oct. 1995), 53–61 (58).   [58]   Cf. Harrison, 286–7.
[59]   Sattler, *FA*, xv/331; Michael Franz, 'Die Schule und die Welt: Studien zu

All of the *Pindar-Fragmente* in their form, and certain of them in their subject-matter also, are involved with a problem raised by the translations: that of the paradox of preservation and change. It is a paradox inherent in the nature of translation, which both preserves its original, by helping it to a new manifestation, and, doing so, radically changes it. It goes to and leads away from its source in the same movement. This is emphasized in the *Pindar-Fragmente* because the fragments themselves are a wonder of survival, handed down by other authors in contexts which may be foreign to them and then collected later in editions such as the one Hölderlin used. Hölderlin's *Pindar-Fragmente* continue this process of transmission by selecting nine of Pindar's fragments and putting them into a new constellation, giving them another lease of life (we are reading them now) but sometimes making of them something rather different from what we are told the originals 'really' mean. Hölderlin enters into a tradition: the fragments have only come down to us because they were excerpted and given a new setting, made relevant to a need, and Hölderlin channels them again. In his Pindar edition, which prints the source of each fragment and also provides a facing Latin translation, the process is manifest. Hölderlin then extracts the fragments from the Renaissance, scholarly milieu and redirects them into a post-revolutionary, poetic one. Amalgamating them into his own contexts he continues a tradition, but its character, despite, perhaps, appearances, has been much changed: rather than submitting to the fragments in respectful exegesis, Hölderlin's texts create for them a living tradition which restores them as poetry rather than as mere vehicles of wisdom.

'Untreue der Weisheit' [Unfaithfulness of Wisdom], the first of the *Pindar-Fragmente*, explores in its form and in its themes this tension in tradition. The title excises the fragment from its original context, and the translation leads it out further, into a modern language:

> O Kind, dem an des pontischen Wilds Haut
> Des felsenliebenden am meisten das Gemüth
> Hängt, allen Städten geselle dich,
> Das gegenwärtige lobend
> Gutwillig,
> Und anderes denk in anderer Zeit.

Hölderlins Pindarfragment "Untreue der Weisheit"', in: Christoph Jamme and Otto Pöggeler (eds.), *Jenseits des Idealismus: Hölderlins letzte Homburger Jahre (1804–1806)* (Bonn, 1988), 139–55 (140).

[O child, whose mind is on the skin
Of the pontic beast who loves the rocks
More than anyone's, to all towns ally yourself,
Praising the present
Freely, and think
Other things in other times.]

The encounter between languages intrinsic to translation is then made visible by the juxtaposition of the translation (which, though in German, represents the Greek and retains a Greek action), with the prose section, which is the modern (German) interpretation.

Fähigkeit der einsamen Schule für die Welt. Das Unschuldige des reinen Wissens als die Seele der Klugheit. Denn Klugheit ist die Kunst, unter verschiedenen Umständen getreu zu bleiben, das Wissen die Kunst, bei positiven Irrtümern im Verstande sicher zu seyn. Ist intensiv der Verstand geübt, so erhält er seine Kraft auch im Zersteuten; so fern er an der eigenen geschliffenen Schärfe das Fremde leicht erkennt, deßwegen nicht leicht irre wird in ungewissen Situationen.

[Capacity of the solitary school for the world. The innocentness of pure knowledge as the soul of intelligence. For intelligence is the art of remaining true under different circumstances, knowledge the art of being certain of one's reason amid positive errors. If reason is exercised intensively it will maintain its strength even in diffuseness; inasmuch as it easily recognizes the foreign against its own well-honed sharpness and for this reason is not easily confused in uncertain situations.]

The prose conducts the fragment yet further from its origin by continuing the work of the translation and converting it into quite new terms. It also introduces, or makes explicit what we can see as implicit in the translation, themes which relate to the movement I have been describing. Pindar's fragment is generally taken to be the advice of a father to his son to the effect that he should be adaptable, as sensitive as the octopus's colour is to its surroundings.[60] It is slightly ambiguous, and Hölderlin's translation makes it more so; the interpretation then turns it into something like its opposite, making its theme the 'Fähigkeit der einsamen Schule für die Welt' (l. 7). The prose and the quotation from P4 which follows furnish a context in which the fragment is associated with a specific story, that of Jason leaving the protection of the centaur Chiron and going out to reclaim

---

[60] Clemens Menze, 'Weisheit und Bildung: Eine Interpretation von Hölderlins Pindarfragment "Untreue der Weisheit"', in: Jamme and Pöggeler, 157–71 (159).

the usurped throne of his father:

> So tritt Jason, ein Zögling des Centauren, vor den Pelias:
>   ich glaube die Lehre
>   Chirons zu haben. Aus der Grotte nemlich komm' ich
>   Bei Charikli und Philyra, wo des
>   Centauren Mädchen mich ernähret,
>   Die heilgen; zwanzig Jahre aber hab'
>   Ich zugebracht und nicht ein Werk
>   Noch Wort, ein schmuziges jenen
>   Gesagt, und bin gekommen nach Haus,
>   Die Herrschaft wiederzubringen meines Vaters.

[This is how Jason, a pupil of the centaur, appears before Pelias:
>   I think I have
>   Chiron's learning. For I come from the cave
>   By Charikli and Philyra, where the
>   Centaur's girls nourished me, and
>   They are holy; twenty years I spent
>   There and not one work
>   Or word or anything dirty to them
>   Did I say, and have come home
>   To restore my father's rule.]

The lines of Hölderlin's translation now shift in this new light: 'das pontische Wild' is no longer an octopus, but Chiron the educator;[61] 'das gegenwärtige' is not so much 'whatever you happen to come across, the present moment' but the present as opposed to the past; and 'anderes denk in anderer Zeit' not just an instruction to be opportunistic but a call to develop into a new stage of being, to step out into the world. All relates to the transition out of the 'einsame Schule' into 'die Welt' and the necessary change to be undergone. This is also the dynamic of the text itself and the modulation the original goes through, the combination of preservation and change. One must appear different in order to remain the same, that is, to remain true to oneself. The interpretation is a manifesting of the base text, and obeys the same dynamic, that of Hölderlin's poetics, according to which something can appear not as itself, but only as something else.[62] This is the sense of the title 'Untreue der Weisheit'.

---

[61] Cf. Markus Fink, *Pindarfragmente: Neun Hölderlin-Deutungen* (Tübingen, 1982), 17–18.   [62] Cf. pp. 90–2 above.

The movement outwards seems to be a form of 'Untreue' towards the source, but it is the only way in which the 'Weisheit', meaning both the gist of the fragment and the teachings of Chiron, can be tested and realize itself in the world of experience. In fact the 'Untreue' is 'eine scheinbare' [only apparent];[63] it keeps to the law of manifestation. The end of the prose opens onto the quotation from P4: the derivation out of Pindar returns to him.[64]

The last *Fragment*, 'Das Belebende', reflects similarly on the necessary passage away from a source, the passing from a primitive to a cultivated condition. The prose takes up the elements of the verse and re-routes them, enacting a process of 'enlivenment'. Again, the process is a violent one: the centaurs (with some classical encouragement) are immediately converted into rivers, and really the sense of the whole fragment is inverted: 'die Gewalt/Des honigsüßen Weins' [the power/Of honey-sweet wine] (ll. 3–4) leads not to intoxication and the rejection of civilization (thrusting the table away, and then the subsequent attack on the Lapiths) but to the finding of 'Bewegung und Richtung' [movement and direction] (ll. 30–1), 'Bestimmung' [purpose] (l. 38) and the quitting of the primitive, pastoral state.[65] The apparent fixity of the fragment is aligned with stagnant waters: 'die Gewässer suchten sehnend ihre Richtung' [the waters, full of longing, sought their course] (l. 22). The prose is a quickening of it, the lending of form, as the gradual formation of banks gives shape and movement to the work of the water: each imparts definition to the other and the result is an even flow, or rhythm: 'die gestaltete Welle verdrängte die Ruhe des Teichs' [the calm of the pool gave way to the shapely wave] (ll. 32–3). Seen in these river-terms, the manipulation of the fragment seems anything but wilful and to make perfect sense: however far the prose runs from it, there is always a direct link back to the source, and the movement away is necessary for the source to be knowable at all and for its whereabouts and nature to become an object of enquiry. Hölderlin seems to have retraced the etymology of the word centaur to find

---

[63] Fink, 28.

[64] Interestingly, this corresponds to Steiner's 'final stage' in what he calls 'the hermeneutic motion' of translation: 'compensation, the offertory turn of the translator towards the original which he had penetrated, appropriated and left behind'—*After Babel*, 395.

[65] Cf. Böschenstein, 'Le Renversement du texte', 56–7.

suggestions for his prose continuation.[66] And like 'Untreue der
Weisheit' it issues into poetry at the end: 'Die Gesänge des Ossian
besonders sind wahrhafftige Centaurengesänge, mit dem Stromgeist
gesungen, und wie vom griechischen Chiron, der den Achill auch das
Saitenspiel gelehrt' [The songs of Ossian especially are true centaur-
songs, sung with the river's spirit, and as if by the Greek Chiron, who
also taught Achilles to play the lyre] (ll. 39–41).

The originating fragments, the bits of Pindar, *are* the main concern
of the *Pindar-Fragmente*.[67] They are 'bestehendes' (ii/172) and need to
be kept in mind. Though fragmentary themselves, they bear traces of
a past unity and for that reason they provide a hold and a focus in an
age beset by dissociation. Hölderlin goes to them for the same reasons
as he went to Pindar's odes and Sophocles' tragedies, to test the
relation between the old and the new worlds and actually to connect
them. 'Die Asyle' deals with such traces, 'Ruhestätten' [places of rest]
(ll. 12 and 20) which give some sense of a continuity between past and
present. They can be fixed upon. But again, Hölderlin arrives at his
interpretation through radically changing the Greek as he translates.[68]
There are in Hölderlin two opposed tendencies: one towards a
shoring up, a need for fixity, and one towards openness, a mode
entirely receptive and associated with chance, but risking dissolution.
The former is perhaps simply a reaction to the latter, as in these lines
from 'Der Einzige': 'immer jauchzet die Welt/Hinweg von dieser
Erde, daß sie die/Entblößet; wo das Menschliche sie nicht hält' [the
world always shouts/Away from this earth, so that it/Strips it bare;
where humankindness does not hold it] (ii/163). Whereas at one stage
Hölderlin's writing mediated between these poles to create the
tension which made his most coherent poems, later they tend to
appear each in isolation, or as separate aspects of the same piece of
writing: on the one hand, the emphasis on 'Maas' [measure] (ii/158)
and 'Gränze' [limits] (ii/603) and 'Halt' [a hold] (ii/163) and the
turning towards visible things and the specific ground of classical texts;
on the other, the undoing of finished poems in rewriting, and the
fragmentary impulse of the poems after that. The *Pindar-Fragmente*,
with their attachment to the law (see 'Von der Ruhe', 'Das Höchste'

---

[66] See Killy, 43. Cf. also 'Der Ister', l. 68, and Beissner's note (ii/816). Etymology
plays a major part in 'Die Asyle'.

[67] Beissner (38) seems to think of them as only pretexts.

[68] See Harrison, 287.

and 'Die Asyle') and to tradition may seem to form part of the 'conservative' pole, and it is true that in many ways they feel like an entrenchment.[69] But the dissolving action of their prose-parts works against this so that the two tendencies hold each other in dialectic relation and a (new) form is found. In many ways the *Pindar-Fragmente* are also the culmination of the relationship between poetry and translation in Hölderlin's work. The two coexist, both clearly separate and inextricable.

---

[69] Cf. Albrecht Seifert, '"Die Asyle": Überlegungen zu einer Interpretation des Hölderlinschen Pindarfragments', in Jamme and Pöggeler, 173–8 (177). Seifert suggests that this facet of the *Pindar-Fragmente* could be considered as lying 'jenseits der Tragödie'.

BIBLIOGRAPHY

Editions of Hölderlin

Sämtliche Werke, ed. Friedrich Beissner and Adolf Beck, 8 vols. (Stuttgart: Kohlhammer, 1943–85) [='Große Stuttgarter Ausgabe'].
Sämtliche Werke, ed. D. E. Sattler et al., planned in 20 vols. with 3 supplements (Frankfurt am Main: Roter Stern, 1975–) [='Frankfurter Ausgabe'].
'Bevestigter Gesang': Die neu zu entdeckende hymnische Spätdichtung bis 1806, ed. Dietrich Uffhausen (Stuttgart: Metzler, 1989).

English translations of Hölderlin

Poems and Fragments, tr. Michael Hamburger, 3rd edn. (London: Anvil, 1994).
Selected Poems, tr. David Constantine, 2nd edn. (Newcastle upon Tyne: Bloodaxe, 1996).
An edition of Hölderlin's essays and letters, translated by Jeremy Adler, is forthcoming from Penguin.

Translations, and works bearing on translation, before or contemporary with Hölderlin

BODMER, JOHANN JAKOB, *Der Mahler der Sitten* (Zürich, 1746; repr. Hildesheim: Olms, 1972).
BREITINGER, JOHANN JAKOB, *Critische Dichtkunst*, 2 vols. (Zürich, 1740; repr. Stuttgart: Metzler, 1966).
Encyclopédie, ou Dictionnaire raisonné des sciences, des arts et des métiers, par une société de gens de lettres, 17 vols. (Paris: Briasson, David, Le Breton, Durand, 1751–65).
GOETHE, JOHANN WOLFGANG, *Werke*, ed. Erich Trunz, 14 vols. (Munich: Beck, 1988).
GOTTSCHED, JOHANN CHRISTOPH, *Ausführliche Redekunst*, 4th edn. (Leipzig: Breitkopf, 1750).
HAMANN, JOHANN GEORG, *Entkleidung und Verklärung: Eine Auswahl aus*

Schriften und Briefen des 'Magus im Norden', ed. Martin Seils (Berlin: Eckart, 1963).

HERDER, JOHANN GOTTFRIED, *Sämmtliche Werke*, ed. Bernhard Suphan, 33 vols. (Berlin: Weidmann, 1877–1913).

HUMBOLDT, WILHELM VON, Letter to A. W. Schlegel of 23 July 1796, in: Anton Klette, *Verzeichniss der von A. W. v. Schlegel nachgelassenen Briefsammlung* (Bonn: Cohen, 1868), v–vi.

—— *Wilhelm von Humboldts Gesammelte Schriften*, ed. Albert Leitzmann, 17 vols. (Berlin: Behr, 1903–36).

JUNCKHERROTT, JOHANN JACOB (trans.), *Das Neue Testament des HERREN Unserer JESU Christi, eigentlich aus dem Griechischen Grund-Text gedollmetschet und in das Teutsche übersetzt, durch weyland Johann Jacob Junckherrott* (Offenbach: Schaeffer, 1732).

LESSING, GOTTHOLD EPHRAIM, *Werke*, ed. H. G. Göpfert, 8 vols. (Munich: Hanser, 1970–9).

LUTHER, MARTIN, *Drei Schriften*, ed. Arnold E. Berger (Hanover: Wissenschaftliche Verlagsanstalt, 1948).

NOVALIS, *Schriften*, ed. Paul Kluckhohn and Richard Samuel, 3rd edn., 5 vols. (Stuttgart: Kohlhammer, 1977–88).

OPITZ, MARTIN, *Buch von der Deutschen Poeterey*, ed. Richard Alewyn (Tübingen: Niemeyer, 1966).

Pindars Olympische Siegshymnen, verdeutscht von Friedrich Gedike (Berlin: Decker, 1777).

QUINTILIAN, *Institutio Oratoria*, with an Eng. tr. by H. E. Butler, 4 vols. (London: Heinemann, 1968).

SCHLEGEL, AUGUST WILHELM, *Sämmtliche Werke*, ed. Eduard Böcking, 12 vols. (Leipzig: Weidmann, 1846–7).

—— *Kritische Schriften und Briefe*, ed. Edgar Lohner, 7 vols. (Stuttgart: Kohlhammer, 1962–74).

SCHLEGEL, FRIEDRICH, *Kritische Ausgabe*, ed. Hans Eichner et al., 35 vols. (Paderborn: Schöningh, 1958–).

SCHLEIERMACHER, FRIEDRICH, 'Ueber die verschiedenen Methoden des Uebersezens', in Störig, 38–70.

SCHNEIDER, J. G., *Versuch über Pindars Leben und Schriften* (Strasburg: Stein, 1774).

SCHOTTEL, JUSTUS GEORG, *Ausführliche Arbeit von der Teutschen Haubt-Sprache* (Braunschweig: Zilligern, 1663).

STAËL, MADAME DE, *De l'Allemagne*, 2 vols. (Paris: Garnier, 1932).

TYTLER, ALEXANDER FRASER (LORD WOODHOUSELEE), *Essay on the Principles of Translation*, 2nd edn. (London: Cadell & Davies; Edinburgh: Creech, 1797).

VENZKY, GEORG, 'Das Bild eines geschickten Übersetzers', *Beyträge zur Critische Historie der Deutschen Sprache, Poesie und Beredsamkeit, herausgegeben von einigen Mitgliedern der Deutschen Gesellschaft in Leipzig*, pt. 9 (Leipzig, 1734), 59–114.

VOSS, JOHANN HEINRICH, 'Pindaros erster püthischer Chor; nebst einem Briefe an Herrn Hofrath Heyne', *Deutsches Museum* 1 (Leipzig, 1777), 78–93.

—— *Homers Werke von Johann Heinrich Voss*, 2nd edn., 4 vols. (Königsberg: Nicolovius, 1802).

—— *Homer: Ilias/Odyssee in der Übertragung von Johann Heinrich Voß* (Munich: Winkler, 1967). [This contains the 1793 *Iliad* and the 1781 *Odyssey* with modernized spelling and punctuation.]

Other works

BENJAMIN, WALTER, *Gesammelte Schriften*, ed. Rolf Tiedemann and Hermann Schweppenhäuser, 7 vols. (Frankfurt a. M.: Suhrkamp, 1972–89).

BLAKE, WILLIAM, *Poetry and Prose*, ed. Geoffrey Keynes (London: Nonesuch, 1941).

BONNEFOY, YVES, 'L'Acte et le lieu de la poésie', in: id., *L'Improbable et autres essais* (Paris: Gallimard, 1983), 107–33.

CATULLUS, *(Gai Valeri Catulli Veronensis Liber)*, tr. Celia and Louis Zukofsky (London: Cape Golliard, 1969).

CELAN, PAUL, *Gesammelte Werke*, ed. Beda Allemann, Stefan Reichert and Rolf Bücher, 5 vols. (Frankfurt am Main: Suhrkamp, 1983).

COLERIDGE, S. T., *Select Poetry and Prose*, ed. Stephen Potter (London: Nonesuch, 1971).

—— *Biographia Literaria*, ed. J. Shawcross, 2 vols. (Oxford: Oxford University Press, 1979).

COWLEY, ABRAHAM, *Poems* (London: Moseley, 1656).

ELIOT, T. S., 'Tradition and the Individual Talent', in: id., *The Sacred Wood*, 4th edn. (London: Methuen, 1934), 47–59.

HEANEY, SEAMUS, *The Redress of Poetry: An Inaugural Lecture Delivered before the University of Oxford on 24 October 1989* (Oxford: Clarendon Press, 1990).

KIRK, G. S., RAVEN, J. E. and SCHOFIELD, M., *The Presocratic Philosophers*, 2nd edn. (Cambridge: Cambridge University Press, 1990).

MALLARMÉ, STÉPHANE, *Oeuvres*, ed. Yves-Alain Favre (Paris: Garnier, 1985).

PINDAR, *The Odes*, tr. C. M. Bowra (Harmondsworth: Penguin, 1969).

SISSON, C. H., *In the Trojan Ditch: Collected Poems and Selected Translations* (Cheadle: Carcanet, 1974).

On Hölderlin

ADLER, JEREMY, 'Friedrich Hölderlin on Tragedy: "Notes on the Oedipus" and "Notes on the Antigone"', *Comparative Criticism* 5 (1983), 205–44.

—— 'Philosophical Archaeology: Hölderlin's "Pindar Fragments". A Translation with an Interpretation', *Comparative Criticism* 6 (1984), 23–46.

—— 'Friedrich Hölderlin on Tragedy: Part II: "The Ground of Empedocles" and "On the Process of Becoming in Passing Away"', *Comparative Criticism* 7 (1985), 147–73.

ADORNO, THEODOR W., 'Parataxis: Zur späten Lyrik Hölderlins', in: id., *Noten zur Literatur* (Frankfurt a. M.: Suhrkamp, 1981), 447–91.

ALMHOFER, WERNER, '"Wildniß" und Vergnügen: Hölderlins mythologische Bildersprache in den späten Korrekturen von "Brod und Wein"', *HJb* 26 (1988–9), 162–74.

BAUM, MANFRED, 'Hölderlins Pindar-Fragment "Das Höchste"', *HJb* 13 (1963–4), 65–76.

BEAUFRET, JEAN, *Hölderlin et Sophocle*, rev. edn. (Saint-Pierre-de-Salerne: Monfort, 1983).

BEISSNER, FRIEDRICH, *Hölderlins Übersetzungen aus dem Griechischen* (Stuttgart: Metzler, 1933; repr. 1961).

BENN, M. B., *Hölderlin and Pindar* (Anglica Germanica, 4; The Hague: Mouton, 1962).

BERMAN, ANTOINE, 'Hölderlin, ou la traduction comme manifestation', in: *Hölderlin vu de France*, ed. Bernhard Böschenstein and Jacques Le Rider (Tübingen: Narr, 1987), 129–42.

BERTAUX, PIERRE, *Hölderlin: Essai de biographie intérieure* (Paris: Hachette, 1936).

—— *Hölderlin und die Französische Revolution* (Frankfurt a. M.: Suhrkamp, 1969).

—— *Friedrich Hölderlin* (Frankfurt a. M.: Suhrkamp, 1981).

—— '"Sterbliche Gedanken"—S. G.', in: *Hölderlin-Variationen* (Frankfurt a. M.: Suhrkamp, 1984), 89–93.

BEYER, UWE, (ed.), *Neue Wege zu Hölderlin* (Würzburg: Königshausen & Neumann, 1994).

BINDER, WOLFGANG, 'Hölderlins Dichtung Homburg 1799', in: *Friedrich Hölderlin: Studien von Wolfgang Binder*, ed. Elisabeth Binder and Klaus Weimar (Frankfurt a. M.: Suhrkamp, 1987), 157–77.

—— 'Hölderlin und Sophokles', in: id., *Friedrich Hölderlin*, 178–200.

BÖSCHENSTEIN, BERNHARD, '"Die Nacht des Meers": Zu Hölderlins Übersetzungen des ersten Stasimons der *Antigone*', in: *'Frucht des Gewitters': Hölderlins Dionysos als Gott der Revolution* (Frankfurt a. M.: Insel, 1989), 37–53.

—— 'Die *Bakchen* des Euripides in der Umgestaltung Hölderlins und

Kleists', in: id., 'Frucht des Gewitters', 72–90.

—— '"Brod and Wein": Von der "klassischen" Reinschrift zur späten Überarbeitung', in: Valérie Lawitschka (ed.), *Turm-Vorträge 1989/90/91: Hölderlin: Christentum und Antike* (Tübingen: Hölderlin-Gesellschaft, 1991), 173–200.

—— 'Göttliche Instanz und irdische Antwort in Hölderlins drei Übersetzungsmodellen: Pindar: Hymnen–Sophokles–Pindar: Fragmente', *HJb* 29 (1994–5), 47–63.

—— 'Le Renversement du texte: Hölderlin interprète de Pindare', *Littérature* 99 (Oct. 1995), 53–61.

BREMER, DIETER, and LEHLE, CHRISTIANE, 'Zu Hölderlins Pindar-Übersetzung: Kritischer Rückblick und mögliche Perspektiven', in: Beyer, 71–111.

BURDORF, DIETER, 'Der Text als Landschaft: Eine topographische Lektüre der Seiten 73 bis 76 des Homburger Folioheftes', in: Beyer, 113–41.

BUTLER, E. M., *The Tyranny of Greece over Germany* (Cambridge: Cambridge University Press, 1935).

CONSTANTINE, DAVID, 'The Meaning of a Hölderlin Poem', *Oxford German Studies* (1978), 45–67.

—— 'Hölderlin's Pindar: The Language of Translation', *MLR* 73 (1978), 825–34.

—— *The Significance of Locality in the Poetry of Friedrich Hölderlin* (Texts and Dissertations, 12; London: Modern Humanities Research Association, 1979).

—— 'Translation and Exegesis in Hölderlin', *MLR* 81 (1986), 388–97.

—— *Hölderlin* (Oxford: Oxford University Press, 1988).

—— *Friedrich Hölderlin* (Beck'sche Reihe, 624; Munich: Beck, 1992).

—— 'Saying and Not-Saying in Hölderlin's Work', in: David Jackson (ed.), *Taboos in German Literature* (Oxford: Berg, 1996), 43–58.

CORSSEN, META, 'Die Tragödie als Begegnung zwischen Gott und Mensch: Hölderlins Sophokles Deutung', *HJb* (1948–9), 139–87.

FINK, MARKUS, *Pindarfragmente: Neun Hölderlin-Deutungen* (Untersuchungen zur deutschen Literaturgeschichte, 32; Tübingen: Niemeyer, 1982).

FRANZ, MICHAEL, 'Die Schule und die Welt: Studien zu Hölderlins Pindarfragment "Untreue der Weisheit"', in: Jamme and Pöggeler, 139–55.

—— and JAKOBSON, ROMAN, 'Die Anwesenheit Diotimas: Ein Briefwechsel', *LpH* 4/5 (1980), 15–18.

—— and KNAUPP, MICHAEL, 'Zum Delphin: Eine hermenautische Expedition', *LpH* 8 (1988), 27–38.

FREY, HANS-JOST, 'Ändern: Textrevision bei Hölderlin', in: id., *Der unendliche Text* (Frankfurt a. M.: Suhrkamp, 1990), 76–123.

GASKILL, HOWARD, 'Hölderlin's Contact with Pietism', *MLR* 69 (1974), 805–20.

—— 'Hölderlin and Revolution', *Forum for Modern Language Studies* 12/2 (April 1976), 118–36.

GRODDECK, WOLFRAM, 'Die Nacht. Überlegungen zur Lektüre der späten Gestalt von "Brod und Wein"', *HJb* 21 (1978–9), 206–24.

—— 'Die Revision der "Heimkunft": Hölderlins späte Eingriffe in den Text der ersten Elegie im Homburger Folioheft', *HJb* 28 (1992–3), 239–63.

GRUNERT, MARK, *Die Poesie des Übergangs: Hölderlins späte Dichtung im Horizont von Friedrich Schlegels Konzept der 'Transzendentalpoesie'* (Studien zur deutschen Literatur, 135; Tübingen: Niemeyer, 1995).

HAMBURGER, MICHAEL, *Friedrich Hölderlin: Poems and Fragments*, tr. M. H., 3rd edn. (London: Anvil, 1994), Introduction.

HARRISON, R. B., *Hölderlin and Greek Literature* (Oxford: Oxford University Press, 1975).

HELLINGRATH, NORBERT VON, *Hölderlins Pindar-Übertragungen*, ed. N. von H. (Berlin: Blatter fur die Kunst, 1910), Introduction.

—— *Pindarübertragungen von Hölderlin: Prolegomena zu einer Erstausgabe* (Jena: Diederich, 1911).

JACCOTTET, PHILIPPE, 'La seconde naissance de Hölderlin', in: id., *Une transaction secrète: Lectures de poésie* (Paris: Gallimard, 1987), 42–72.

JAMME, CHRISTOPH, and PÖGGELER, OTTO (eds.), *Jenseits des Idealismus: Hölderlins letzte Homburger Jahre (1804–1806)* (Neuzeit und Gegenwart, 5; Bonn: Bouvier, 1988).

KILLY, WALTHER, 'Welt in der Welt. Friedrich Hölderlin', in: id., *Wandlungen des lyrischen Bildes* (Kleine Vandenhoeck-Reihe, 22/3; Göttingen: Vandenhoeck & Ruprecht, 1956), 30–51.

KOCZISZKY, ÉVA, 'Die Empedokles-Fragmente als Übersetzung', *HJb* 26 (1988–9), 134–61.

—— 'Warum ist der Kentaur ein Stromgeist?', *Jahrbuch der ungarischen Germanistik* (1992), 67–79.

KOPPENFELS, MARTIN VON, 'Der Moment der Übersetzung: Hölderlins Antigonä und die Tragik zwischen den Sprachen', *Zeitschrift für Germanistik*, n. s. VI, 2 (1996), 349–67.

KUZNIAR, ALICE A., *Delayed Endings: Nonclosure in Novalis and Hölderlin* (Athens: University of Georgia Press, 1987).

LACOUE-LABARTHE, PHILIPPE, 'La Césure du spéculatif', in: Hölderlin, *L'Antigone de Sophocle*, tr. P. L.-L. (Paris: Bourgois, 1978), 183–223.

LEFEBVRE, JEAN-PIERRE, 'Der Fährmann und die Hebamme: Ein Vergleich der Oden "Der gefesselte Strom" und "Ganymed" auf Grund der komparativen Übersetzung', *HJb* 29 (1994–5), 134–49.

LÖNKER, FRED, *Welt in der Welt: Eine Untersuchung zu Hölderlins 'Verfahrungsweise des poëtischen Geistes'* (Palaestra, 288; Göttingen:

Vandenhoeck & Ruprecht, 1989).

—— NICKAU, KLAUS and TURK, HORST, 'Hölderlins Sophokles-übersetzung', *HJb* 26 (1988–9), 248–303.

LÜTZELER, HEINRICH, 'Hölderlin als Übersetzer', *Neue Jahrbücher für Wissenschaft und Jugendbildung*, 2 (1926), 687–700.

MENZE, CLEMENS, 'Weisheit und Bildung: Eine Interpretation von Hölderlins Pindarfragment "Untreue der Weisheit"', in: Jamme and Pöggeler, 157–71.

MÖGEL, ERNST, *Natur als Revolution: Hölderlins Empedokles-Tragödie* (Stuttgart: Metzler, 1994).

NÄGELE, RAINER, 'Friedrich Hölderlin: Die F(V)erse des Achilles', in: Lucien Dällenbach and Christiaan L. Hart Nibbrig (eds.), *Fragment und Totalität* (Frankfurt a. M.: Suhrkamp, 1984), 200–11.

—— 'Vatertext und Muttersprache: Pindar und das lyrische Subjekt in Hölderlins späterer Dichtung', *LpH* 8 (1988), 39–52.

OGDEN, MARK, *The Problem of Christ in the Work of Friedrich Hölderlin* (Texts and Dissertations, 33; London: Modern Humanities Research Association, 1991).

REINHARDT, KARL, 'Hölderlin und Sophokles', in: Alfred Kelletat (ed.), *Hölderlin: Beiträge zu seinem Verständnis in unserm Jahrhundert* (Tübingen: Mohr, 1961), 286–303.

ROMAIN, ALFRED, 'Ganymed', *HJb* (1952), 51–84.

RYAN, LAWRENCE, *Hölderlins Lehre vom Wechsel der Töne* (Stuttgart: Kohlhammer, 1960).

SCHADEWALDT, WOLFGANG, 'Hölderlins Übersetzung des Sophokles', in: id., *Hellas und Hesperien*, 2 vols. (Zürich: Artemis, 1970), ii 275–332.

SCHÄFER, GERHARD, 'Der spekulative württembergische Pietismus als Hintergrund für Hölderlins Dichten und Denken', in: Valérie Lawitschka (ed.), *Turm-Vorträge 1989/90/91: Hölderlin: Christentum und Antike* (Tübingen: Hölderlin-Gesellschaft, 1991), 46–78.

SCHMIDT, JOCHEN, *Hölderlins Elegie 'Brod und Wein': Die Entwicklung des hymnischen Stils in der elegischen Dichtung* (Quellen und Forschungen zur Sprach- und Kulturgeschichte der germanischen Völker, n. s. 26; Berlin: de Gruyter, 1968).

—— *Hölderlins später Widerruf in den Oden 'Chiron', 'Blödigkeit' und 'Ganymed'* (Studien zur deutschen Literatur, 57; Tübingen: Niemeyer, 1978).

SEIFERT, ALBRECHT, *Untersuchungen zu Hölderlins Pindar-Rezeption* (Münchner Germanistische Beiträge, 32; Munich: Fink, 1982).

—— 'Die Rheinhymne und ihr pindarisches Modell', *HJb* 23 (1982–3), 79–133.

—— '"Die Asyle": Überlegungen zu einer Interpretation des Hölderlinschen Pindarfragments', in: Jamme and Pöggeler, 173–8.

STEINER, GEORGE, *Antigones* (Oxford: Oxford University Press, 1984).

SZONDI, PETER, *Hölderlin-Studien* (Frankfurt a. M.: Suhrkamp, 1970).

—— *Poetik und Geschichtsphilosophie II*, ed. Wolfgang Fietkau (Studienausgabe der Vorlesungen, 3; Frankfurt a. M.: Suhrkamp, 1974).

WACKWITZ, STEPHAN, *Friedrich Hölderlin* (Sammlung Metzler, 215; Stuttgart: Metzler, 1985).

WALSER, MARTIN, *Hölderlin zu entsprechen* (Biberach an der Riss: Thomae, 1970).

Wörterbuch zu Friedrich Hölderlin, 1. Teil: Die Gedichte, compiled by Heinz-Martin Dannhauer, Hans Otto Horch and Klaus Schuffels (Indices zur deutschen Literatur, 10/11; Tübingen: Niemeyer, 1983).

ZUBERBÜHLER, ROLF, *Hölderlins Erneuerung der Sprache aus ihren etymologischen Ursprüngen* (Philologische Studien und Quellen, 46; Berlin: Schmidt, 1969).

ZUNTZ, GÜNTHER, *Über Hölderlins Pindar-Übersetzung* (Kassel: Thiele & Schwarz, 1928).

Modern critical works not related to Hölderlin

ABRAMS, M. H., *The Mirror and the Lamp: Romantic Theory and the Critical Tradition* (Oxford: Oxford University Press, 1953; repr. 1979).

ALEWYN, RICHARD, *Vorbarocker Klassizismus und griechische Tragödie: Analyse der 'Antigone'-Übersetzung des Martin Opitz* (Reihe Libelli, 79; Darmstadt: Wissenschaftliche Buchgesellschaft, 1962).

BEIERWALTES, WERNER, *Proklos: Grundzüge seiner Metaphysik*, 2nd edn. (Philosophische Abhandlungen, 24; Frankfurt a. M.: Klostermann, 1979).

BENJAMIN, WALTER, 'Die Aufgabe des Übersetzers', in: id., *Gesammelte Schriften*, iv 9–21.

BERMAN, ANTOINE, *L'Epreuve de l'étranger: Culture et traduction dans l'Allemagne romantique* (Paris: Gallimard, 1984).

BLOOM, HAROLD, *The Anxiety of Influence*, 2nd edn. (New York: Oxford University Press, 1997).

DAVIE, DONALD, *Articulate Energy: An Inquiry into the Syntax of English Poetry*, 2nd edn. (London: Routledge, 1976).

HÄNTZSCHEL, GÜNTER, *Johann Heinrich Voß: Seine Homer-Übersetzung als sprachschöpferische Leistung* (Zetemata, 68; Munich: Beck, 1977).

HUBER, THOMAS, *Studien zur Theorie des Übersetzens im Zeitalter der deutschen Aufklärung 1730–1770* (Deutsche Studien, 7; Meisenheim am Glan: Hain, 1968).

HUYSSEN, ANDREAS, *Die frühromantische Konzeption von Übersetzung und Aneignung: Studien zur frühromantischen Utopie einer deutschen Weltliteratur* (Zürcher Beiträge zur deutschen Literatur- und Geistesgeschichte, 33; Zürich: Atlantis, 1969).

OESTERLE, INGRID, 'Paris—das moderne Rom?', in: Conrad Wiedemann (ed.), *Rom—Paris—London: Erfahrung und Selbsterfahrung deutscher Schriftsteller und Künstler in den fremden Metropolen* (Germanistische Symposien der Deutschen Forschungsgemeinschaft, 8; Stuttgart: Metzler, 1988), 375–419.

PAULIN, ROGER, 'Die romantische Übersetzung: Theorie und Praxis', in: Nicholas Saul (ed.), *Die deutsche literarische Romantik und die Wissenschaften* (Munich: iudicium, 1991), 250–64.

SENGER, ANNELIESE, *Deutsche Übersetzungstheorie im 18. Jahrhundert (1734–1746)* (Abhandlungen zur Kunst-, Musik- und Literaturwissenschaft, 97; Bonn: Bouvier, 1971).

STEINER, GEORGE (ed.), *The Penguin Book of Modern Verse Translation* (Harmondsworth: Penguin, 1966).

—— *After Babel* (Oxford: Oxford University Press, 1975).

STÖRIG, HANS JOACHIM (ed.), *Das Problem des Übersetzens* (Wege der Forschung, 8; Darmstadt: Wissenschaftliche Buchgesellschaft, 1969). [This contains important texts on translation by Goethe, A. W. Schlegel, Schleiermacher and Rosenzweig among others.]

TOMLINSON, CHARLES (ed.), *The Oxford Book of Verse in English Translation* (Oxford: Oxford University Press, 1980).

VALÉRY, PAUL, 'Variations sur les *Bucoliques*', in: Jean Hytier (ed.), *Oeuvres*, 2 vols. (Paris: Gallimard, 1957), i 207–22.

INDEX OF HÖLDERLIN'S WORKS

Translations

GENERAL INDEX